The
MANY FACES
of
EROS

Books by Joyce McDougall

Dialogue With Sammy (with S. Lebovici)
A Plea for a Measure of Abnormality
Theaters of the Mind
Theaters of the Body

A NORTON PROFESSIONAL BOOK

The
MANY FACES
of
EROS

**A PSYCHOANALYTIC EXPLORATION
OF HUMAN SEXUALITY**

Joyce McDougall

W. W. Norton & Company • *New York* • *London*

Composition by Bytheway Typesetting Services, Inc. Manufacturing by
Haddon Craftsmen Inc.

Library of Congress Cataloging-in-Publication Data

McDougall, Joyce.
    The many faces of Eros : a psychoanalytic exploration of human
sexuality / Joyce McDougall.
            p.   cm.
    "A Norton professional book."
    Includes bibliographical references and index.
    ISBN 0-393-70215-4
    1. Sex (Psychology)   2. Psychoanalysis   I. Title.
BF175.5.S48M33   1995   95-36340
155.3--dc20   CIP

W.W. Norton & Company, Inc., 500 Fifth Avenue, New York, NY 10110
W.W. Norton & Company, Ltd., 10 Coptic Street, London WC1A 1PU

1 2 3 4 5 6 7 8 9 0

To the memory of Robert Stoller, eminent writer and researcher into the mysteries of human sexuality, with continuing gratitude for his stimulating thoughts and his valued friendship over many long years.

Contents

PROLOGUE

Sexuality in Search of Solutions: An Eternal Quest?

There is the other universe, of the heart of man
that we know nothing of, that we dare not explore.
A strange grey distance separates
our pale mind still from the pulsing continent
of the heart of man.
Fore-runners have barely landed on the shore
and no man knows, no woman knows
the mystery of the interior
when darker still than Congo or Amazon
flow the heart's rivers of fullness, desire and
distress.

— D. H. Lawrence

HUMAN SEXUALITY is inherently traumatic. The many psychic conflicts encountered in the search for love and satisfaction, arising as a result of the clash between the inner world of primitive instinctual drives and the constraining forces of the external world, begin with our first sensuous relationship. When the baby encounters the "breast-universe," the period of "cannibal love," in which erotic and sadistic strivings are conflated, is inaugurated. The slowly acquired notion of an "other" — of an object separate from the self — is born out of frustration, rage, and a primitive form of depression that every baby experiences in relation to the primordial object of love and desire. Felicity lies in the abolition of the difference between self and other.

It is not surprising, therefore, that in the course of the analytic voyage we discover traces of what might well be termed "archaic sexuality," bearing the fused imprints of libido and mortido, in which love is indistinguishable from hate. The tension that emanates from this dichotomy, with its depressive potential, impels an eternal quest for resolution and, indeed, provides a vital, ever-present substratum to all forms of adult love and sexuality.

The recognition of otherness is followed by the equally traumatic discovery of the difference between the sexes. Today we
know that this discovery is not primarily linked to oedipal conflicts, as Freud had concluded, but occurs well before this so-
called classical phase. Roiphe and Galenson's (1981) many years
of research are enlightening in this respect. Their observational
studies have demonstrated that, long before children struggle with
the anxious conflicts surrounding the oedipal crisis, the fact of
difference in itself is anxiety-arousing. However, the discovery of
sexual difference is found to have a maturational effect (different
for the two sexes), once the anxiety has been somewhat alleviated.

In both its homosexual and heterosexual dimensions, the oedipal crisis obliges children to come to terms with the impossible
wish to incarnate both sexes and to possess both parents. Concom-
itantly, in accepting their ineluctable monosexuality, humankind's
young must compensate in other ways for the renunciation of
their bisexual longings. (These "other ways" are explored in the
chapters dealing with creativity and sexual deviations.) The discovery of sexual difference contributes to the slowly acquired representation of a "core gender," in the sense in which Stoller (1968)
defines this term. Upon this foundation the child will form a
self-identity as "masculine" or "feminine" through mental representations that arise not from biological givens, but from the dictates of the biparental unconscious and the concepts transmitted
by the cultural and social milieu to which the parents belong.

To the extent that sexual orientations are shaped by the experiences of early childhood, psychoanalysis has a specific contribution to make to the study of aberrations in core gender identity as
well as psychic conflicts relating to sexual role identity. Although
it is beyond question that a baby boy has different anatomical
sensations from a baby girl, this "given" does not imply that a
psychic representation of core gender identity is inborn. Freud
emphasized that the objects of sexual desire are not innate but
have to be "found" (1905); he also proposed that the sense of self
and of sexual orientation, although established in early childhood,
are "rediscovered" in their full force shortly after puberty.

As Lichtenstein (1961) remarked, the development of our sense
of personal identity is Janus-like in its construction: on the one
hand, our identity is comprised of "that which resembles me" and,
on the other, "that which is different from me." In Lichtenstein's

words, "the identity of the animal is 'fixed' [whereas] the man has forever to struggle with the need to define himself, to create an identity not basically inherent in him by dint of inborn automatisms."

It is evident that the acquisition of a secure feeling of both personal and sexual identity requires a series of mourning processes in order to relinquish the desire to possess "that which is different from me." These steps in maturation are not achieved without pain and sacrifice. Some children receive more parental help than others in accomplishing the work of mourning that is imperative at this early stage of psychic development.

Two central concepts concerning the origins of the sexual self form a continuing background to the chapters that follow: the far-reaching significance of *psychic bisexuality*, and the profound importance of *primal-scene fantasies* in the psychosexual structure of humankind.

PSYCHIC BISEXUALITY

Although undecided about the role of genetic factors in bisexuality, Freud gave considerable importance to the concept as a *psychological* structure and contended that bisexual wishes were universally present in childhood (Freud, 1905, 1919, 1930). Since most infants have two parents, it is to be expected that children will feel libidinally attracted to both parents, giving rise to the wish to obtain the exclusive love of each parent for themselves. In point of fact, every child wants to possess the mysterious sexual organs and fantasized power of both father and mother, man and woman. The obligation to come to terms with one's monosexual destiny constitutes one of childhood's most severe narcissistic wounds.

By what means do we integrate these bisexual demands into our psychic structure, while at the same time assuming our predestined anatomical identity? After some 30 years of reflection and clinical observation, I am convinced that *the confusion to which bisexual wishes give rise in the early organization of the psychosexual structure considerably affect many areas of adult life.* Although the integration of these wishes is a source of psychic enrichment, their *non-integration* is a frequent cause of symptoms and inhibitions in adults. Thus the multiple ways in which we attempt to deal with the impossible wish *to be* and *to have* both sexes merits clinical and theoretical consideration.

Libido: Homosexual or Heterosexual?

Concepts such as "homosexual libido" or "heterosexual libido" need to be defined. *Libido* was the word selected by Freud to describe all aspects of instinctual sexual energy in human beings. He also emphasized that libidinal energy could be directed toward different people, to both sexes, and toward one's own self. Consequently, the term "homosexual libido" would designate that part of the libidinal impulses which, in childhood, is directed toward the same-sex parent.

Little recognized is the fact that in children of both sexes, homosexual desires always have a double aim. First there is the wish *to possess sexually the same-sex parent* for oneself; then there is the equally strong wish *to be the parent of the opposite sex* and thereby incarnate all the privileges and prerogatives with which that parent is felt to be endowed. It is important to differentiate between these two complementary and somewhat contradictory homosexual aims, since they coexist in every small child — and are ever-present in the unconscious of every adult! Moreover, taking these primary wishes into account may further our understanding of the different ways in which the two homosexual currents may find expression in both homosexual and heterosexual adults.

PRIMARY HOMOSEXUALITY

The primary homosexuality of the little girl impels her to want to possess her mother sexually, penetrate her vagina, "climb right inside her," and "eat her up" as a way of incorporating her mother totally, along with all her magical powers. The girl-child also wants to be penetrated by her mother, create children with her, and thereby become the unique object of her mother's love, excluding the father. At the same time, she desires just as ardently to be a man like her father — to have his genitals as well as the power and other qualities her mother attributes to him — and, in this way, to play as important a role in the life of her mother as does her father. (This constellation is explored in the chapters on female sexuality in Part I.)

The boy-child, in turn, develops his own form of primary homosexuality in which he imagines himself as his father's love-partner, incorporating his father's penis orally or anally, and thus "becoming" his father by taking possession of his genitals and masculine privileges.* Additional fantasies common to boy-children include penetrating Father as the son imagines his Mother is penetrated—a daydream that implies destroying the father's penis—which coexists with the desire to take Mother's place in the hope that Father will give him a baby to grow inside his own imagined inner space.

This last point brings back the memory of a lively discussion that occurred between my four-year-old grandson Daniel and his mother who, at that time, was six months' pregnant. Daniel was stroking his mother's abdomen and asking her, for the hundredth time, how the baby had gotten inside her. She explained patiently that Daddy had put the seed of the new baby in her tummy and that Daniel would soon have a little brother or a little sister. That evening when his father came home, Daniel shouted impatiently, "Daddy, I've got something special to ask you. Would you please put a baby in *my* tummy too?" His father explained that a daddy only puts babies into a mummy's tummy, but added that, one day, Daniel would have a wife, and then he could put a baby in *her* tummy. With an expression of determination in his eyes, Daniel ran to his mother and, patting her on the abdomen, said, "Mummy, when you've finished with it, would you *please* pass it to me?"

The following day there was an amusing aftermath to this incident. Accompanying Daniel and his friend John to their kindergarten, I heard Daniel say, "Hey, John, you know what my mummy's got in her tummy?" "No, what's she got?" "A baby!" A look of disgust came over John's face and he replied, "Ugh, did she eat it?" "No, stupid! My dad put it there." John, whose parents had

---

*These fantasies of incorporation in little children of both sexes recall the beliefs of primitive tribes that eating the heart of the lion (or lioness), for example, would endow one with the animal's strength, power, and invincibility.

separated before his birth, went on to proclaim that Daniel was talking nonsense. His mother had told him that only God puts babies into mothers' bodies. "Well, he didn't put *this* one in my mum, anyway!" replied Daniel firmly. (I thought to myself how true it is that "reality" does not exist in any absolute way and, indeed, is constructed almost entirely from parental communications about it.)

The Ambivalence of Unfulfilled Longings

These childhood bisexual longings are destined to remain unfulfilled, for the little girl will not become a man, will never possess her mother sexually, will never make babies with her, and will never receive a baby from her father. Likewise the little boy will not become a woman and will never make babies with his father or become his father's sexual partner, as he had once imagined. Because this phantasmic form of possession, common to all children, implies the destruction of the "other," it brings in its wake confused feelings of guilt and depression. Inevitably, complex emotions are grafted onto these early unfulfilled longings, as the lack of success in satisfying primary homosexual wishes becomes associated with feelings of narcissistic injury, aggression, and envy. Thus *profound ambivalence complicates the attachment and attraction to both parents*. The homosexual components of human sexuality are infiltrated by affects of both a highly positive and a strongly negative nature.

Although the identical statement might be said to apply to the heterosexual components, primary heterosexual wishes, while in no way devoid of envy and hatred, are destined to encounter less scornful response and irreconcilable impediments to their subsequent fulfillment than those attached to the early homosexual drives. (One of my patients, a 60-year-old professor of psychiatry, still vividly remembers the humiliation he suffered in front of his entire family when, at the age of three, he had begged for a "doll baby" for Christmas.) It is probable that primary heterosexual wishes contain a somewhat lesser potential for generating a conflicted or envious form of sexual desire.

Eventually, all children must accept the fact that they will never possess both genders and will forever be only half of the sexual constellation. This scandalous affront to infantile megalomania is further complicated by the need to come to terms with the oedipal crisis in both its homosexual and heterosexual dimensions, and with the impossibility of sexually possessing either parent.

A study of the manifold processes by which little children achieve these monumental psychological tasks could further our understanding of the manifest homosexualities as well as the unconscious homosexual strivings of the heterosexuals. It should also be emphasized that homosexual orientation in adult life cannot be adequately apprehended as a mere fixation to the universal bisexual wishes of infancy. Innumerable elements contribute to the complex development of both homosexual and heterosexual identity and object choice.

It is important to study the different ways in which the dual versions of primary homosexual longings are transformed and integrated into the life of adult individuals as a way of securing some measure of harmony in sex and love. The conflicts around bisexual strivings, while they may create neurotic suffering, may just as readily enrich the personality. There are many channels available for investing this essential libidinal current in adult endeavors. For example, the bisexual substratum may serve as a fundamental element in stimulating creative capacities. In the event of unconscious conflict in this area, however, severe inhibition can also arise. Moreover, although the conflictive aspects of bisexual wishes may appear to have been successfully dealt with through repression or sublimatory activity, breakdown is always liable to recur, giving rise to symptoms or creative blockage. (These aspects will be illustrated in the chapters of Parts I and II.)

The child's discovery of the difference between the sexes is matched in traumatic quality by the earlier discovery of otherness and the later revelation of the inevitability of death. Some individuals never resolve any of these universal traumas, and all of us deny them to some degree in the deeper recesses of our minds — where we are blessedly free to be omnipotent, bisexual, and immortal!

Primal Scenes and
Primitive Sexualities

The concept of "primal scene" encompasses the child's total storehouse of unconscious knowledge and personal mythology concerning human sexual relations, particularly that of the parents. Apart from the genital aspects of the primal scene and the phallic-oedipal conflicts associated with it (described by Freud as typical of the neuroses when these inhibit any or all forms of libidinal expression), this scene can also be depicted in pregenital terms, such as oral-erotic and oral-devouring fantasies, anal-erotic and anal-sadistic exchanges, bisexual confusions, archaic fantasies of vampire-like exchanges, or the fear of losing one's sense of identity or the representation of one's body-limits. When such fantasies play a predominant role in the individual's psychic reality, sexual and love relations readily become equated with castration, annihilation, or death.

Deepening insight into the unconscious significance of primal-scene fantasies also led me to the discovery of their profound influence in borderline states, and even more strikingly, as a contributory factor to psychosomatic eruptions. In striving to hear the somatic "communications" of my polysomatizing analysands, I learned that the terrors of dissolving, of losing one's bodily limits or sense of self, of exploding into another or of being invaded and imploded by another, were both frequent and revealing of the buried links to archaic sexual and love feelings originating in earliest infancy. These baby-like fears, which were linked to the first transactions between mother and nursling and had no verbal representations, had been stored in the *body's* memory.

Frequently these analysands come to understand that beneath their inexplicable tendency to attack their own somatic functioning, and coupled with their fear of bodily or mental destruction in the sexual relationship, they are equally afraid of their own disavowed, destructive tendencies toward their sexual partners. Such anxieties recapitulate the baby's rage as well as the vampirizing and lethal wishes formerly projected upon the parental figures. In the psychic world of infancy, where hate and love coincide in a dynamic stream of libidinal investment, these fantasized exchanges with the parental objects contribute to the formation of fascinating, if fearful, primal-scene imagery.

The verbalization of these primitive desires and the archaic terror they arouse play a cardinal role in the psychic change that occurs as the analysis of the retrieved fantasies proceeds. Some analysands find that their relationships to significant others are infused with a new depth and, in particular, that their love-life and sexual relations become considerably richer. Some achieve the resolution of lifelong psychosomatic symptoms, such as allergies, gastric ulcers, essential hypertension, and respiratory and cardiac dysfunctioning. Others are able to overcome severe creative inhibitions or to develop artistic and intellectual skills that, previously, were only dimly perceived or perhaps totally unrecognized. From a vast amount of clinical material I have selected a few examples to illustrate primal-scene fantasy in relation to primitive sexuality.

CLINICAL ILLUSTRATIONS

The Love That Strangles

Jean-Paul is speaking: "Once I put a spider and an earwig together in a spider's web. They fought to their deaths. It was atrocious! I also loved watching spiders strangle flies with their silken threads. They're so frightfully aggressive and poisonous."

My patient went on to recount other entomological dramas of which he was the theatrical director: Hours of childhood play in which wasps, bees, ants, snails, and worms were thrown into endlessly repeated primal scenes of insect dimensions. The deadly sting, the crushing and strangling encounter, were invariably present and recalled with relish. Beneath Jean-Paul's associations I could sense an excited and anguished little boy trying to contain and master, through the medium of play, terrorizing fantasies of his parents' sexual relationship in which each strangles the other to death. In his adolescent masturbation practices, Jean-Paul recalled that he used to strangle his penis with tightly-bound cords; however, the profoundly disturbing sexual fantasies that were discharged through this practice had disappeared from his adult consciousness.

As Jean-Paul grew into adulthood, the horror of the "strangling vagina" gave way, among other defensive maneuvers, to a phobia of spiders. Meanwhile his lovemaking presented no inhibitory expressions. Instead, as his analytic adventure advanced, we discovered that his apparently symptom-free sexual life was closely linked to the outbreak of psychosomatic symptomatology. His childhood sexual desire for his mother had remained conscious, but the fantasy-wish of strangling and devouring his mother in erotic and deathlike ecstasy had been totally obliterated from consciousness, along with similar, equally primitive, daydreams. At the same time, these buried fantasies protected Jean-Paul from recognizing an even more regressive wish: to completely merge with his mother—in fact, to *become her*. Meanwhile, the unconscious fantasy of the primal scene in its most archaic form—that of an erotically fused but deathlike struggle—found expression in allergic skin reactions and severe gastric ulcers. (A further dimension of Jean-Paul's analysis is used to illustrate the theme of Chapter 9.)

Cannibal Love

Georgette had suffered all her life from allergic reactions to fish, shellfish, and fruits (such as strawberries and raspberries), all of which she found enticing and longed to eat. Any transgression of these somatic taboos resulted in massive edema or startling dermatological outbreaks. Georgette's dreams, free associations, and transference feelings all revealed, among other elements, a hidden connection between certain odors (in particular, that of shellfish and seafood) and her fantasies concerning her parents' love-life. In one session she reported a dream in which she was an infant seeking the breast, but the nipple was replaced by a raspberry. In another dream a woman's body was strewn with strawberries, which turned to glue when she reached out to grasp one. In the dream she realized that she had to tear off her skin in order to escape death, and then awoke in terror. On another occasion she recalled that, when she was about four years old, her father had offered her a clam. "I still see him opening the two little lips and placing some drops of lemon juice into it. I swallowed it avidly. It was delicious." Her severe allergic reactions to all forms of seafood developed around this time. With the recovery of this memory, 35 years later, Georgette was able to reconstruct the erotic significance of the odorous and gustatory "primal scene" in which Father had dropped his "juice" into Mother's "clam"; as we worked through this material, her numerous allergies to these "forbidden fruits" gradually disappeared. (This part of Georgette's analysis is recounted more fully in Chapter 8.)

Other anxieties linked to primal-scene fantasy had caused Georgette, as a little girl, to be constantly afraid of "falling through space or breaking into fragments." During childhood she had taught herself to hold her breath "in magical ways" to prevent these fantasized catastrophes. We came to understand that, among other aims, this activity would also suspend the parents' sexual relationship and give her unconditional rights as mother's sole sexual partner. As our work continued, Georgette discovered through a transference fantasy that the wish to swallow up her mother in a relationship of passionate fusion would also enable her to replace her mother in her father's eyes, thus becoming *his* sole sexual partner as well.

Another analysand, quoted in an earlier book (McDougall, 1982), recalled similar oral fantasies, in which sexual wishes as well as the anxiety they aroused, found their place. "Isaac" feared he would be "swallowed" or "mangled" by inanimate objects; this phobia eventually led to the uncovering of a fantasy in which he was in danger of being "eaten" by his mother. His father, also in Isaac's fantasy, was in imminent danger of suffering the same fate. "Perhaps my mother, with her devouring ways, was the cause of my father's cardiac attacks," Isaac mused. As our analytic voyage continued, the revelation of Isaac's childhood belief that his parents devoured each other in their sexual union was a dramatic moment, as was the discovery that he himself harbored a profound *longing to be eaten by* his mother.

Respiratory Love

At the outset of her analysis, Louise (whom we meet again in Chapter 7) described a "problem" with her mother. "Mother lives in Strasbourg where I was born. I often go to visit her, but no sooner do I start to prepare my voyage than my breathing becomes asthmatic — and gets steadily worse the nearer I draw to my birthplace." As the analysis progressed, we were able to piece together a deep unsuspected attachment to her mother, whom she consciously hated.

We came to understand that, in Louise's adult attempts to maintain a relationship with her (ironically described) "smother-mother-lover," she would feel "crushed" by close contact with anyone who reminded her of her mother. This later led to the recovery of a childhood belief that the parents "crushed" and evacuated toxic substances into each other, in the course of their sexual encounters. With the continuation of her analytic voyage, Louise's respiratory pathology became linked to other forms of pregenital erotic excitement, which generated an entirely new version of her parents' sexual life. As a consequence, important changes took place in Louise's relationship with her husband, and her psychosomatic pathology diminished markedly.

Urophiliac Love

When Nancy was 18 months old, her father was recruited to fight in World War II, whereupon Nancy took her father's place in her mother's bed. She reported that she "inundated" her mother nightly with streams of urine, to which "Mother did not seem to object." It required some years of analysis to discover that this was Nancy's vision of the parental relationship and of the way in which babies were made. A baby brother was born nine years later, and with her urinary love thus betrayed, Nancy's bedwetting ceased abruptly. (Nancy's story is discussed in Part III.)

A Union of Vampires

Marion, who suffered from severe asthmatic attacks throughout childhood and contracted tuberculosis in adolescence, relived in analysis the terror she felt as a child whenever she heard water running in the bathroom or kitchen. She believed she had to struggle against the danger of being sucked down the drain. Following these revelations came dreams and fantasies permeated with sexual scenes in which both partners were in imminent danger of being sucked into an endless void, losing all bodily limits, if not life itself. Over the course of the analysis this frightening fantasy was transformed into an arousing one in which the mutual merging gave rise to boundless excitement and ineffable pleasure.

OVERVIEW

These clinical fragments predominantly illustrate psychosomatic expressions of primal-scene fantasy. It took me many years to understand the deep, protosymbolic meaning underlying psychosomatic phenomena and to discern the early forms of sexuality that lay behind the corporeal facade. The chapters that comprise Part III of this book were written as a result of difficulties encountered in trying to conceptualize my clinical observations regarding my analysands' psychosomatic problems. These chapters continue the research begun in *Theaters of the Body* (McDougall, 1989). The incestuous child's desire to possess both parents and incarnate the imagined power that each parent is felt to possess, and the primal-scene fantasies that accompany these wishes, may also be expressed in many non-somatic ways, such as sublimatory activities, neurotic symptomatology, and deviant sexualities.

Part II explores the inspiration and inhibition associated with the creative process. Part IV examines the complex knot of problems surrounding the development of oneself as an individual and the extent to which deviant and addictive forms of sexuality may be used to strengthen a fragile sense of personal or sexual identity.

In this book I explore bisexual and primal-scene fantasies in their pregenital and archaic forms as well as the dynamic reverberations of these fantasies in sexual deviations, psychosomatic symptoms, and character disorders, and their sublimated expressions in all fields of creativity. In the course of the psychoanalytic voyage, when primal-scene fantasies are recognized in their multifarious disguises and then voiced, for the first time in the patient's memory the internalized parental objects are freed from the pregenital and archaic projections of the child of yesteryear. The infantile vision of the primal scene can now be elaborated psychically, envisaged as a mutually gratifying experience, and, finally, be accepted by both the child and adult parts of the personality. The dread of violent destruction of oneself or one's partner disappears, along with the anguish that one might lose one's bodily limits or personal identity in sexual and love relationships. As the erotic imagination moves out from under its death-like shadow, sexual relations of whichever orientation are once more joined with the forces of the life drive.

When love is no longer equated with catastrophe, castration, or death; when parents can be recognized in their individuality, their separate sexual identities, and their genital complementarity; then the internalized primal scene in its transformed version becomes a psychic acquisition that gives adult-children the right to *their* place in the family constellation, to *their* bodies, to *their* sexuality.

The
MANY FACES
of
EROS

PART I

Femininity and Sexuality

CHAPTER 1

The Homosexual Components of Female Sexuality

> *. . . the need for the conciliation of the two parts of woman's nature is an age-old problem. . . . It is rather a matter of how she may adapt to the masculine and feminine principles which rule her being from within.*
>
> — Esther Harding

BEFORE CONSIDERING THE QUESTION of the integration of primary homosexual wishes in the heterosexual woman, let us first review Freud's concepts concerning the little girl's accession to womanhood and motherhood.

Freud's revolutionary discoveries regarding the dynamic importance of human sexuality in child and adult life are now almost a century old. They are so much an established part of Western thought that we take them for granted. Yet modern analysts remain highly critical of Freud's conceptual limitations — above all, his theories on female sexuality. This is, admittedly, an area in which Freud was particularly vulnerable. It is interesting to recall, however, that Freud owed to women the initial insights that led him to the concept of the unconscious. Anna O, Lucy R, Irma, Emmy von N, Dora, Katarina, and many others were the fountainhead of his inspiration. It is equally remarkable that, in his day and age, he actually *listened* to them and regarded everything they told him as significant and important. In Freud's dominantly phallocratic epoch, this receptivity in itself was revolutionary. Of all explorers into the functioning of the human mind, he was the first to take a serious and scientific interest in women's sexuality. Obviously he was fascinated by the mystery of femininity and by the female sex itself (a characteristic, he claimed, that he shared with men of all centuries).

But Freud was also a little afraid of the objects of his fascination. His metaphors repeatedly revealed a representation of the female genital as a threatening void, a lack, a dark and disquieting continent wherein one could not see what was going on. He also insisted that, in this line of research, he was obliged to proceed from his knowledge of male sexuality. With this refracting telescope in hand, it is no surprise that he "deduced" what he was convinced would be a little girl's response: extreme envy of the boy's visible and interesting organ and her desire to possess a penis of her own. The notion that boys would also be envious of a girl's vagina, her capacity for bearing children, and her potential attraction for the male precisely because she did *not* have a penis, did not occur to Freud insofar as we know.

But it was also Freud himself, with his typical honesty, who first expressed feelings of deep dissatisfaction and uncertainty concerning his theories about women and the nature of their psychosexual development. In fact, he waited until 1931 to publish "Female Sexuality," his first paper on the subject. He was 75 years old. Perhaps he felt that, at this phase of his life, there was less cause for fear of the female, her sexual mysteries, and the revelation of his theories about her.

In his second renowned and much criticized paper, "Femininity," published two years later, Freud wrote: " . . . psychology . . . is unable to solve the riddle of femininity," noting further that " . . . the development of a little girl into a normal woman is more difficult and more complicated, since it includes two extra tasks, to which there is nothing corresponding in the development of a man." The "tasks" refer to Freud's two major concepts concerning the difficulties in growing to womanhood: The little girl must first come to terms with her anatomical configuration and effect a change in the organ of excitement, from clitoris to vagina; second, she must effect a change of object. "When and why does she give up her fixation to her mother in favor of her father?" Freud asked himself.

Although I agree that these two dimensions do present genuine

challenges to the attainment of adult femininity and sexual pleasure, they are nevertheless far from exhaustive as explanatory
concepts. Let us examine them more closely.

ANATOMY AS DESTINY?

Today most analysts, male or female, would agree that the envy
of her father's penis is but a partial explanation of the difficulties
encountered by the little girl on her path to mature womanhood.
Indeed, many would concede that "penis envy" is not specific to
the young female. Boys, too, suffer from their own characteristic
form of penis envy, invariably finding their penises too small in
comparison with their fathers'. If the belief persists into adult
life that one's penis is smaller than it should be, founded on the
unconscious fantasy that the only adequate sex is the paternal one,
neurotic symptoms and anxieties are precipitated as frequently as
those arising in the sexual life of the young woman who clings
unconsciously to the fearful fantasy that she is a castrated boy.
Clinical experience also confirms that the boy's envy and admiration of his mother's body and sexuality is similar to the girl's envy
and admiration of her father's penis and sexual prowess. Children
of both sexes are aware that Mother embodies the magical power
to attract Father's penis and make the babies whom the two parents desire.

In this context it is pertinent to recall that the *phallus* (which
invariably refers to the erect penis in the ithyphallic Greek rites) is
not, etymologically speaking, the symbol of the male sex organ
but of fertility, narcissistic completion, and sexual desire. From
this point of view the phallus could be considered the fundamental
signifier of human desire for both sexes. (We owe much to Lacan's
precision in this terminology, even though many analysts take
issue with some of his views concerning female sexuality.) The
word *symbol* comes from the Greek word *symbolon*, an object
which, when cut in two, was intended to serve as a sign of recognition between people, who each possessed half of the symbolon.
We might say that each sex possesses half of what is required to
complete the symbol. In terms of the sexual relationship, the erect
penis is intimately linked to the receptive vagina, and from the

point of view of the feminine partner (provided her attraction to a male partner is free of conflict and anxiety), is responded to by vaginal excitement and interpreted as a sign of mutual desire.

This digression is necessary because the word *phallus* is often used indiscriminately in English to mean *penis*. Feminist writers engaged in detecting and denouncing denigratory attitudes toward women fulminate against the use of the word *phallus*. That they equate *penis* and *phallus* suggests, paradoxically, a hidden phallocentric attitude on their part! To confound the symbol (phallus) with the part-object (penis) may obfuscate research into cardinal questions pertaining to sexual identity, masculinity, and femininity.

As already noted, for both males and females monosexuality remains one of humankind's major narcissistic wounds. Internalizing a symbolic representation of the complementarity of the two sexes requires a renouncement of the childlike wish to *be* and to *have* both. The ensuing complications, arising from our psychic bisexuality and primary homosexual longings, are discussed later.

Let us return to the question of the girl's biological "destiny." Many analysts would concede that the little girl's anatomical configuration presents her with specific vicissitudes in her psychosexual development, and that envy of the boy's visible organ is but one aspect of her preoccupations. Psychoanalytic theory had to await the work of women analysts — in particular, the seminal research of Karen Horney (1924, 1926) and Melanie Klein (1945) — to highlight additional complications that fell to the lot of the young female. As early as 1926 Karen Horney pointed out that, in view of the female child's vaginal sensations, " . . . she must from the outset have a lively sense of this specific character of her own sexual role; a primary penis envy of the strength postulated by Freud would be hard to account for."

Years later, Klein (1945) formulated the notion that the possession of a penis is narcissistically reassuring to the little boy because of its visibility and facility for mental representation. In contrast, the little girl cannot see her vagina and has difficulty visualizing her clitoris. As a result, although she is intimately aware of clitoral and vaginal sensations, she experiences her genital as lacking when compared to the boy's — and the father's — visible organs. She must wait until puberty to gain visual confirmation of her own unique sexual identity through the growth of her breasts and the beginning of her periods. With these external changes comes the narcissistic reassurance that her feminine body and genitals are designed to awaken desire as well as to carry the promise of creating babies.

Another landmark in psychoanalytic research concerning female sexuality is Judith Kestenberg's (1968) original paper on the important distinction between "inner" and "outer" anatomical configurations and the different fears and fantasies to which these give rise. This viewpoint, explored in detail in her paper, draws attention to the importance of the girl's representation of her genital as an inner space which affects her total experience of her femininity and her sexual relations.

Other difficulties inherent in the girl-child's development of her sense of gender identity also have their roots in her anatomical destiny. Since her sex is, in essence, a portal into her body, the vagina is destined to be equated in the unconscious with *anus*, *mouth*, and *urethra*, and therefore liable to share both the masochistic and sadistic libidinal investments and fantasies carried by these zones. The little girl (and frequently the woman-to-be) is more likely than her male counterpart to fear that her body will be regarded as dirty or dangerous because of these zonal confusions, in addition to the anatomical fact that there is no visible organ that can be controlled and verified.

Even the adult woman frequently experiences her body as a dark continent in which anal and oral monsters lurk. Of course, much of her unconscious representation of her body and her genitals will reflect the libidinal and narcissistic significance that the mother gave to her daughter's physical and psychological self, as well the extent to which the mother transmitted unconscious fears concerning her own bodily and sexual functions. The nonverbal sensuous (and, later, verbal) communications between mother and daughter determine, in large part, whether oral eroticism triumphs over oral aggression and whether anal erotic impulses become more important than, or combine harmoniously with, anal sadistic ones.

A third aspect of feminine anatomical destiny involves autoerotic experience. Since the little girl cannot visually verify her genitals, and therefore tends to create an imprecise or zonally condensed psychic representation of them, she has difficulty locating the sexual sensations of which she has been aware since early infancy. Clitoral, vaginal, urethral, and other internal sensations tend to be confused. This blurring of internal sensations has important repercussions on female fantasies concerning masturbation.

MASTURBATION AND FEMININITY

Although masturbation is a normal expression of children's sexuality, it is eventually inhibited by parental constraints. All children learn that it is not permissible to defecate, urinate, or masturbate in public. Even when these restrictions are imposed with kindness and understanding, they leave an imprint on unconscious fantasy life. When they are imposed harshly, because of the parents' own internal disquietudes and subsequent need to diminish their anxieties through controlling their *children's* bodies, the risk of later neurotic problems is notably increased.

When told to give up masturbating publicly, the little boy is apt to imagine, if he fails to do as he is told, that his father will attack his penis because he has guessed his son's sexual desire for Mother, as well as his ambivalent feelings toward his father. In the same phase of oedipal reorganization, the little girl is more likely to fantasize that her mother will attack and destroy *the whole inside of her body* as a punishment for her wish to take her mother's place, to share erotic games with her father, and to make a baby with him. Thus the boy's feared punishment for his masturbatory fantasies is castration, whereas the girl frequently equates the retribution for masturbation and erotic daydreams with death.

Death by Masturbation

A young woman psychiatrist, highly intelligent and thoroughly informed on psychoanalytic theory, claimed that she had never masturbated as a child—or even as an adult. She also expressed an emphatic doubt that masturbation could be an inevitable part of infantile experience. The thought of autoerotic activity was so dirty and denigrating to her, it took two years of analytic work before she could even allow herself to pronounce the word *masturbation*. Although she had no apparent difficulties in her sexual relationships, she suffered from an array of somatic manifestations that seemed to be linked to states of sexual tension and anxiety. (She was in no way alexithymic or dominated by operatory ways of thinking.) A slim and attractive young woman, she experienced her body as shapeless, large, and dirty. When she had her periods, she would cry in distress, fearing that I would find her presence distasteful.

In the fourth year of her analysis, she brought the following dream: "I was picking flowers in the garden outside the house where I lived as a child. I was dancing with delight, when suddenly my cousin Pierre appeared in the doorway and I woke up with a scream."

Since this was the first time cousin Pierre had appeared on the psychoanalytic stage, I asked her to tell me more about him. She sighed and said, "I suppose I've never wanted to think about him. He was many years older than I, and he once played with me sexually when I was little. Then, when he was 21 and I was about 12, he was electrocuted in his bath. At least, that's what we were told."

Because she seemed to question this version of the facts, I asked, "What did *you* think about the manner of his death?" With great difficulty, she admitted that she believed he had been electrocuted because he was playing with his penis in the bath. After all, she had known since childhood that he was a bad "sexual" boy. She then began to cry. I asked her to tell me what she was feeling at that moment and she said, "You are well aware that my husband has been away for three weeks, and I'm so afraid you might think I've been masturbating. But I swear it isn't so . . . I'm sure you don't believe me!" I replied, "Of course, I believe you—otherwise you'd be dead!"

For the first time in our analytic voyage, my patient was able to laugh about her sexual fears and fantasies, but it still required many months for us to reconstruct—beyond signifying elements such as "electricity," "picking flowers," and "dancing"—all the long-repressed memories of a little girl's spontaneous sexual sensations and masturbation fantasies. As was to be expected, my patient's love-life with her husband became erotically fuller and considerably more satisfying following this phase of her analysis. However, another interesting fact for which I can offer no conclusive theoretical explanation is that two somatic symptoms also disappeared. For many years she had suffered from recurring arthritic pain and bronchial asthma. Neither of these returned in the remaining three years of her analysis with me.

HOW TO EAT YOUR MOTHER
AND HAVE HER TOO

The second area of difficulty specific to female sexuality is the integration of the profound homoerotic tie to one's mother. From birth, babies of both sexes begin to weave strong libidinal and sensuous ties to both parents, provided the parents are tender, sensual, and loving with them. In its mother's arms every infant experiences the earliest psychic blueprint (and perhaps a corporeal imprint?) of sexual and love relationships to come. The father's attitude is equally vital in this transmission of early libidinal investment. A father who is absent or uninterested in his tiny offspring, and who regards the mother as being solely responsible for the welfare of their baby—or who accepts his wife's view of him as a nonentity in relation to their baby—runs the risk of leaving his children vulnerable to fulfilling a role that arises solely from the mother's libidinal needs and unconscious problems. A mother who considers her baby to be a narcissistic extension of herself, or who takes her children as her love objects in place of her husband, may be laying the foundation for future conflictive relationships. It should be noted that a mother who brings her children up single-handedly does not necessarily incur these risks, if she does not regard her relationship with them as a substitute for an adult love relationship.

From infancy on, if children see their parents behave as a loving couple who respect and sexually desire each other, and if they also observe that even fierce quarreling between parents does no lasting harm (that is, they learn that aggression is not dangerous when love is stronger than hate), the children will tend to follow the parental model in their adult lives. The little girl will want to identify with her mother, not only in her motherhood, but also in her sexual and love relations, often daydreaming about the man (typically modeled after the image of the father) who will one day be her lover, her husband, and the father of her children.

In its primordial beginnings, libidinal seeking is deeply intertwined with the desire to live, and it is the mother's task to incite her child to want to live. (The life force is not as strong as we are apt to imagine; an unwanted infant is liable to fall ill or even die.) This essential relationship, which infants normally share with the mother in the first months of life, provides the baby girl, in contrast to the boy, with a double identification. The somatopsychic images that are destined to become mental representations of her feminine body and its erogenous zones are already being formed. It is at this early stage that mouth and vagina become linked in their erogenous significance and, along with other erogenic organs and internal sensations, are integrated into the somatopsychic representations.

To these must be added the clitoral sensations stimulated by the mother's physical handling and cleaning of her baby. These specific sensations were the only erogenous body links to which Freud gave much attention in his theory of the development of feminine eroticism. For reasons of his own, Freud assimilated the female clitoris into the male penis. He was unaware of the fact that the clitoris is an extremely complex organ, and in view of its considerable extensions into the female body, a relatively large structure. It is interesting to note that the complete clitoral organ with its internal appendices was neither charted, nor even named, until relatively recently (see the remarkable book, *A New View of a Woman's Body*, 1981, compiled by the Federation of Feminist Women's Health Centers).

The psychosexual structure described above provides the primitive foundation of the little girl's future love-life. In the best of circumstances, upon it will be grafted the elements of the heterosexual model mentioned earlier: A relationship with each parent that is physically and psychically loving and sensual; and a model of a parental couple who love each other, enjoy their sexual relationship, and do not make the child their chosen object for erotic or narcissistic completion.

In addition, the little girl needs to hear her father express appreciation and value for her femininity *and* for her mother's—his wife's—femininity. Similarly, the little girl needs to hear her mother express value and respect for the father as well as for her little daughter's sexual identity, even as she accords value to her own sexual and social life as a woman. A girl who is told that men are selfish pigs, only out to seduce, profit from, or dominate women, will have difficulty liking or trusting anyone male; she will also find it difficult to separate from her mother. Should she "learn" from her father that girls are weak, incapable, unintelligent, and less entitled to esteem and consideration than boys, she may create a narcissistically damaged image of herself and her sex, and feel fear, suspicion, or hatred of the male world.

Freud's question (1931) regarding the little girl's strong libidinal tie to the mother remains, nevertheless, pertinent: How does she detach herself from her mother and integrate the profound erotic tie they have shared? Where is this vital homosexual component invested in her adult life?

Freud's theory in this respect (1931, 1933) can be summarized as follows: The little girl's first desire is to possess her mother sexually; she then replaces this focus with the desire to possess a penis; then to have a child from her father; and finally to have a male child of her own. Within the seemingly implacable logic of this chain of signifiers is the implication that the girl's desire for a baby is merely a substitute for the penis she does not possess and that her love for her father is a mere consequence of penis envy! Although the fantasies on which Freud based his theory are frequently present in a woman's psychic universe, they are far from being the only factors, or even the dominant ones, among the complexities that contribute to each woman's image of femininity and motherhood. Furthermore, Freud's concept of these object substitutions implies that the little girl's homosexual ties are simply eliminated through penis envy. Yet Freud (1905) also articulated the theory of universal bisexual wishes in infancy — a concept which is important to consider from the female point of view.

PRIMARY HOMOSEXUALITY

The little girl wants to possess her mother sexually, create children with her, and be singularly loved by her in a world from which all men are excluded. She also wants to be a man like her father and possess his genitals as well as the idealized qualities she attributes to him. Through lack of fulfillment, these drives tend to become associated with narcissistic injury.

Although the double polarity of homosexually-oriented libido in infancy is equally strong in both sexes, the girl's problem is more intricate than her brother's in relation to the wish to possess her mother sexually, in that the girl and her mother are not sexually complementary. Unlike her little brother, the girl is not able to believe that she has a uniquely different sexual configuration — and therefore a specific value for this reason — in her mother's eyes. How does the young female extricate herself from this doubly complex situation with her mother? Further complicating this developmental task is her strong erotic attraction to her father, which impels the little girl to introject many aspects of the mother's image. These, in turn, will coalesce to form a fundamental figure of identification affecting all future feminine development.

At this point there are a number of different "internal mothers" in the feminine psychic world. One maternal introject is *adored*, another *desired*, another *resented*, another deeply *feared*. The young girl needs to wrest from her mother the right to *be* her by identifying with her mother in her own internal psychic world, but she also needs her mother externally as a guide, comforter, and helper for some years to come. After the turmoil of adolescence, during which time the daughter typically rejects the mother in almost every way, she will often turn toward her mother with renewed attachment when she herself becomes a mother. It is at this point that many young women finally forgive their mothers for all the infantile resentments they have harbored against them, and the two may then become close adult friends. Just as every child an adult daughter bears represents, in unconscious fantasy, a baby she has made with her father, so too her babies are often felt to be a gift to the mother — and, indeed, in the deeper layers of the unconscious, a baby she has made in magical fashion with her mother. While any one of these factors can cause psychic pain and conflict, they can also add to the immense joy of each new birth.

Some women may identify with the mother as a sexual adult but do not themselves desire children. In this case, they are liable to experience their professional, intellectual, or artistic activities as the birthing of symbolic children. Nothing prohibits adult women from enjoying motherhood as well as experiencing the pleasure in personal creativity, but here again specific feminine problems arise. Many women in analysis reveal a fear that they must *choose* between motherhood and professional activities; others express a similar feeling of dichotomy between their lives as lovers and their lives as mothers. Accomplishing these three dis-

tinct feminine desires — the sexual, the maternal, and the professional — requires a delicate balance, if women are to avoid the
conviction that they are impelled to sacrifice their own narcissistic
and libidinal needs in any one of these areas.

THE INVESTMENT OF
HOMOSEXUAL STRIVINGS

These considerations concerning women's love-life, social life,
work life, and motherhood bring us back to the question of bisexual wishes and homosexual libido in the adult woman. How and
where are they invested? How are the complementary desires to
have the mother and to *be* the father transformed and integrated
into the life of the woman, whether her orientation be heterosexual or homosexual? To what extent does failure to integrate this
vitally important libidinal energy create neurotic problems when
unacknowledged homosexual wishes give rise to psychic conflict?

My reflections upon my own process, as well as my analytic
work with women patients for over 35 years, have led me to identify five potential paths for integrating the homosexual oedipal
constellation. Despite the profound differences between the genders, the paths of integrating homosexual wishes described below
apply to males as well as females.

1. *Stabilization of Self-Image.* Female homosexual libido serves
to enrich and stabilize the narcissistic self-image. Every little girl
needs to be able to give to herself some of the early love and
appreciation that she experienced toward her mother and her
mother's body, in order to have affection and esteem for her own
feminine self and sex organs. In other words, the young girl gives
up wanting to *have* the woman in order to *be* the woman. Through
the same psychic movement, her envy of the penis is transmuted
into desire for it.

2. *Intensification of Erotic Pleasure.* The profound wish to be
the other sex, if and when it is relinquished, finds an important
investment in a woman's love-live, particularly in the sexual relationship itself, in which identification with her partner's pleasure
and desire enhances her own erotic pleasure. It is in lovemaking

that we can recreate the illusion of being both sexes and losing, even if momentarily, the narcissistic limits that monosexuality imposes upon humankind.

3. *Enhancement of Maternal Feelings.* Women's relationship to their children is also a treasure trove of homosexual riches. I can still remember my overwhelming pleasure in giving birth to my son and the feeling of pride in his penis, as though it were also mine. After the birth of my little daughter, I also well remember my pride in her exquisitely female body, my appreciation of what seemed already to be essentially feminine gestures, and my narcissistic wish for her to achieve in her lifetime all that I considered as failures in my own accomplishments. These memories leave me with little doubt about the contribution of the homosexual dimension to my maternal feelings.

4. *The Creative Use of Homosexual Identifications.* It has always seemed to me that the pleasure experienced in intellectual and artistic achievements is impregnated with considerable narcissistic and homosexual fantasy. In such productions, everyone is both male and female at the same time. In this sense, our artistic and intellectual products are parthenogenetically-created offspring. Clinical observation has convinced me that conflicts over either of the two poles of feminine homosexual goals—that is, the unconscious wish to possess the mother's creative power as well as possessing the potency of the father's penis—may create serious inhibition, or even total sterility, in the capacity to put forth "symbolic children."

5. *Enrichment of Same-Sex Friendships.* Finally, the homosexual investment, usually divested of its conscious sexual aim, gives warmth and richness to the affectionate and essential friendships women maintain with other women. Although the lesbian woman has experienced a different elaboration of her primary homosexual drives, she, too, may have warm desexualized relationships with women.

These five pathways represent a somewhat idealistic description of the way in which narcissistic and homosexual wishes may be harmoniously invested in sexual life, family life, social, and professional activities. In analytic work with women who identify themselves as heterosexual, innumerable signs of profoundly *un-*

conscious homosexual conflict can be found, potentially leading to a sudden breakdown in any of the fields of investment mentioned above and giving rise to symptoms and inhibitions associated with the investments in question. An endless array of domestic disputes, sexual problems, difficulties with children, colleagues, co-workers, and friends, as well as with creative pursuits, are all liable to reveal their conflictive homosexual counterpart in the course of the analytic process.

What about the therapeutic relationship itself? How often are homosexual fears, wishes, and projections overlooked in this critical arena? When there is a stalemate in elaborating any of the above dimensions of the psychosexual structure, *whose* unconscious homosexuality is obstructing the analytic process? The unrecognized homosexuality of the analysand? Or of the analyst? With the aid of a clinical illustration, we shall pursue this question further in the following chapter.

CHAPTER 2

The Female Analyst and the Female Analysand

> *. . . everyone possesses in his own unconscious an instrument with which he can interpret the utterances of the unconscious in other people.*
> —Sigmund Freud

IN ORDER TO EXPLORE the dimension of unconscious homosexuality in the analytic situation, I will briefly recount the analysis of one of my women patients. An important turning point in her analytic adventure was catalyzed by a dream she reported in the second year of our work together. On the night following this session, I had a dream whose theme was related to the fact that certain unconscious fantasies of my own had been activated by my patient's dream and her associations to it.

THE FIRST ENCOUNTER

Marie-Josée, 35 years of age, came to see me because of a number of crippling phobias—most notably, she was claustrophobic as well as agoraphobic. She was unable to take a plane (particularly if the flight path crossed over water) without taking heavy medication some hours in advance. A lover of opera and theater, she suffered several days prior to each performance she was to attend, for fear she might be unable to escape should an anxiety attack suddenly overtake her. An impending appointment with an unknown person filled her with anticipatory panic. In all these threatening circumstances she regularly had recourse to psychiatric medication. She had no children and felt too disturbed within herself to contemplate motherhood. I gathered that much of her time was spent in cultural pursuits and that she was a talented hostess to her husband's many business acquaintances and their wives.

During our first meeting Marie-Josée also told me that the phobia which caused her the greatest suffering occurred when she was forced to stay alone at night because of her husband's frequent absences due to his professional obligations. At these times she would become overwhelmed by feelings of terror in response to a compelling conviction of impending danger. Once in bed, she was either unable to sleep or would wake up throughout the night. To combat her insomnia, she would drug herself with sleeping pills or, as a last resort, go to her parents' house until her husband returned. She had no difficulty sleeping when her husband, to whom she was deeply attached, was at home.

An only child, Marie-Josée spoke of her father with love and admiration. But he, like her husband, had been absent more often than present. She described her mother as "a classical example of smother love" and expressed irritation about her over-protectiveness. She claimed that she returned home during her husband's lengthy absences largely at the insistence of her mother. Marie-Josée hinted that she thought her mother was somehow benefiting from her daughter's phobic fragility.

THE EMERGENCE OF A NEW THEME

At our second exploratory interview Marie-Josée spoke, in passing, of another symptom, but was emphatic that this was the least of her problems: She had to urinate many times a day. Two eminent urologists had confirmed that there was no physiological cause for her urinary frequency. She was constantly concerned that she might have a sudden urge to urinate at inappropriate moments, such as at a dinner party or during an opera performance. I asked her what she thought might be the cause and she replied, "Oh, it's not a psychological problem; it's just that my bladder is smaller than other women's bladders."

In my notes following this interview I had written that this symptom, which she appeared to minimize, might well be an indication of a central psychological conflict, one that was perhaps difficult for her to accept. Thinking of her assertion that "her bladder was smaller than other women's," I had written: "Does she think she has a little girl's bladder, not a grown woman's one?"

At this point in my career I was a young and relatively inexperienced analyst, and was very pleased to have received this referral. Marie-Josée appeared to suffer from classical neurotic symptomatology (whereas most of my other patients were considerably more disturbed). In addition, we were the same age and I found her charming and intelligent. So our psychoanalytic adventure was inaugurated under auspicious circumstances. The work began, with little delay, on a four-times-weekly basis.

Marie-Josée's phobia of being alone at night and her symptom of urinary frequency were essential elements in her analytic voyage with regard to discovering her infantile longings and primitive erotic fantasies related to the theme of unconscious homosexuality.

THE VOYAGE BEGINS

In the first year of our work together, my analysand spent many sessions describing her nocturnal dread when alone in her home. As time went on we learned that her anxiety became uncontrollable only at the moment she was preparing to go to bed. With my encouragement she tried to identify the thoughts that might be capable of arousing such strong emotion.

MARIE-JOSÉE Well, as I think about it, I *do* know what I'm afraid of — somebody will try to gain entry through my bedroom window.

J. MCDOUGALL Can you tell me more about this person?

MARIE-JOSÉE It's a man, of course.

JM What's he doing there?

MARIE-JOSÉE Oh, it's obvious! He's going to try to rape me. Of course, I won't allow that, so it's quite likely that he will kill me.

It took quite some time for Marie-Josée to accept an intervention to the effect that she was the *author* of this nightmarish script and that the character of the rapist-killer was also a *personal creation*. To try to prove her point to me, she would scan the daily newspapers for evidence that women were constantly in danger of sexual assault from unknown men and bring the results of her research work into her sessions. However, she never managed to find an incident in which the assaulting male climbed through a woman's window. Nevertheless, she continued to assert that her fear was perfectly rational. Her insistence was such that I decided to tell her the joke about a woman who dreamed that a handsome man with a strange light in his eyes was approaching her bed. The woman cries: "What are you going to do to me?" whereupon the handsome fellow replies, "I'm sorry, lady, I don't know what happens next — you see, it's *your* dream."

For the first time, Marie-Josée was able to laugh about her rapist-killer and to accept that he was truly a creation from her own inner theater. As time went on, we even discovered that the fantasy was no longer frightening — it was exciting! Erotic elements were added to the fantasy, which Marie-Josée appeared unwilling to divulge until she was ready to do so on her own initiative. Her terror of nocturnal solitude slowly disappeared, but she finally revealed that she now had an irrepressible urge to masturbate whenever she was alone at night. On this condition alone, she could sleep peacefully and without medication. Her newly discovered autoerotic activity had become as addictive as the sleeping tablets had been; indeed, she admitted she felt "compelled to masturbate," whether she wanted to or not.

Around this same period in her analysis, other important associations centered on her feeling of being persecuted by her mother's overwhelming solicitude. I began to dislike Marie-Josée's mother. I thought to myself, *She's a real cannibal mother, and perverse as well! She complains to all her friends that her daughter has been neurotically crippled for more than 30 years, yet she does everything in her power to keep her in this state!* Although I kept reminding myself that this portrayal was merely one version of Marie-Josée's internal representations of her mother, and that she *needed* to present her in this light, I still saw her as a threatening external object who was preventing her daughter — my patient — from getting well!

A REVEALING DREAM

The following session fragment occurred towards the end of our second year of work.

MARIE-JOSÉE I had a frightening dream last night. I was swimming around in a tumultuous sea and I feared I might drown, although I noticed that the water and the scenery were rather pretty. I had a feeling I'd been there before. The waves got larger and I said to myself, *I'll have to find something to cling to or I shall die in this water*. At that moment I noticed one of those—I forget what they're called—sort of hitching posts that are used to attach boats. I reached out to grasp it. It was made of stone. Anyway, I woke up in a state of panic.

As I listened to her account, my free-floating associations led me initially to ask myself whether the dream was connected to her feelings about being smothered or drowned by her mother's attentions (in French the words for *mother* and *sea* sound identical). But I wondered about the "hitching post" whose name she couldn't remember. The detail that it was "made of stone," which in French is *pierre*, led me to remember that her father's name was Pierre-José and also that a part of her name derived from his. Marie-Josée was silent a moment.

MARIE-JOSÉE I don't think there's anything new in this dream. It's just the panic I always feel when I have to go outside, and it's all got to do with my mother. She's everywhere, threatening to possess me.
JM What about the hitching post, whose real name escapes you?
MARIE-JOSÉE Oh, I remember! It's *une bitte d'amarrage*—or is it *une bitte de mouillage*? I can never remember the difference.

These vertical posts are called *bollards* in English. The first French phrase refers to the bollard placed on a boat and the second phrase to that on the wharf. There is also an implicit play on words in these phrases. *Bite* (although the spelling is different) is the popular slang word for the male sex organ, and *mouiller* is a slang term referring to a woman's genital when she is experiencing sexual desire. The word *amarrer* means "to tie something up safely" or "to moor a boat." The term *hitching post*, on the other hand, refers to a post used only on land for tethering horses. It would seem that Marie-Josée wished to repress the underlying significance of these words by confusing or forgetting them. However, she herself saw the connection between *bitte* and *bite* ("mooring post" and "cock").

MARIE-JOSÉE Oh, this has something to do with my father and my memory of seeing his penis that day in the bathroom, when I was about four. I was afraid my mother would be angry with me for having spied on him with such excitement. Perhaps that's why I woke up with a feeling of panic?

She then insisted once again that the dream held no real interest, that it was the same old problem. In the face of her resistance, I hesitated to push her to associate to the *bitte de mouillage,* or to seek some link between her continuing urinary problem and the angry dream-sea (*la mère*) that had threatened to engulf her. While listening to her dream, it had occurred to me that one underlying meaning behind her symptom of urinary frequency might be the wish to drown her mother in her urine, but I had no associative material from Marie-Josée that would have allowed a constructive interpretation of this kind.

In line with my hypothesis I also thought it possible that Marie-Josée might reverse the situation in the dream-scene and fear that her mother would drown *her* in a vengeful sea of urine. Her only recourse would be to turn to her father, the *bitte d'ammarage,* the "stone phallus," with potentially lifesaving capacities. This paternal symbol would secure her against being wrecked at sea— that is, being wrecked by her overwhelming mother and also by her wish to maintain angry infantile ties to her mother.

In her flight from the dream, Marie-Josée turned her attention to what she saw as lack of progress in our work. Clearly I had now become the bad mother who was neither helping her to find her way out of this maze of frightening fantasy, nor teaching her to swim in tumultuous seas, nor indicating the means by which she might turn to her father in a protective and erotic fantasy wish.

MARIE-JOSÉE It's all very well that my panic about being alone at night has gone, but my daytime terrors are as strong as ever, and I feel more and more ashamed of them. I'm not getting anywhere in this analysis. Let me just tell you what happened yesterday.

I had promised to have tea with old Suzanne, who's a good friend of my mother's and whom I love dearly. But as usual, I couldn't find a parking place anywhere near her house. She lives on a one-way street and the only possible parking spot was on the other side of the *Boulevard Haussmann*. There wasn't a soul in sight, and the thought of crossing that empty boulevard almost made my heart stop beating. I just couldn't do it. I thought, there *must* be some way around the problem. Suddenly I had the brilliant idea of driving *backwards* into the one-way street, though I was really scared of getting caught by a cop. When I arrived, about half an hour later than the agreed time, Suzanne said, "Oh, dear, I thought you weren't coming. You're rather late, you know."

Marie-Josée then proceeded to give numerous associations to her daytime panic, drawing on everything we had discovered together during the past year. Her expressed transference feelings, as well as certain personal relationships, had led us to the conclusion that her multiple phobias were a way of projecting onto the world's stage an inner drama in which she was constantly trying to escape any situation or relationship that was apt to represent an archaic image of her mother as an omnipotent and omnipresent being seeking to devour her. In particular, she was compelled to avoid empty spaces, heights, balconies, and open windows. (I felt certain that, in her unconscious fantasy and in childlike fashion, she was still awaiting an amorous encounter with her father, disguised as the rapist-killer of her past fantasy.) This nexus of infantile sexual wishes seemed to me to be one possible dynamic behind her fiercely phobic anxieties. On this occasion Marie-Josée herself proposed that her unconscious wishes for her father's exclusive love, as well as his protection from her engulfing mother, had once again pushed her to enact a scene of agoraphobic terror.

Drawing on what we had already constructed, Marie-Josée reiterated that she continued to endow her mother with environmental omnipotence, which she interpreted as her mother's wish "to possess me, body and soul," and perhaps also "to prevent me from having a closer relationship with my father." In response to a question on my part, she conceded that since she herself was the scriptwriter of her dream, no doubt she had some hidden need to keep this infernal drama alive.

At the end of the session I had a feeling of dissatisfaction. We were treading familiar ground; similar content had dominated

many sessions. I was convinced there was a link between her terrifying night-dream and her daytime "nightmare" (as expressed
through the return of the agoraphobic symptom on the way to
visit her friend). However, I could not discern particular details of
this connection, although I suspected that both experiences were
connected with frightening images of her mother. Meanwhile, I
had completely overlooked the fact that Suzanne was a mother-
figure for whom Marie-Josée expressed feelings of love rather
than resentment, and that in her predicament over parking her
car, she was only able to reach her friend by taking a *forbidden
one-way street*. I had also set aside my previous notion that some
part of Marie-Josée *wished* to be engulfed by the tumultuous maternal sea. In reflecting on the play on words in the dream, in
which Marie-Josée was grasping at a stone object that recalled her
father's name as well as the masculine part of her own name, I
again questioned the conflicts that might motivate her to place a
symbolic image of her father on the dream-stage, to prevent her
from drowning in a sea which she herself had created.

These, then, were the day residues that contributed to a dream
of my own, which surprised me by a manifest content so intense
that it awakened me in the middle of the night and created a
strange impression that I have not forgotten to this day. One
further significant detail is that I, too, was sleeping alone that
night, since my life-partner was temporarily absent. Moreover we
had quarreled the previous day over my insistence that I needed to
discuss a paper with a woman colleague, whereas he had wanted
me to save the evening for him.

A COUNTERTRANSFERENCE DREAM

I am supposed to meet someone in a *quartier* of Paris (which is little
known to me) that has the reputation of being dangerous at night, particularly the underground railway in that area. I am permeated with a sense
of something uncanny yet vaguely familiar at the same time. Several
people get in my way and I hurry on, pushing them aside. Suddenly I am
inside a house and find myself in the presence of an attractive Asian
woman, dressed in a provocative, sexy manner. She looks at her watch
and then remarks, *You're rather late, you know*. I stammer out some
sort of excuse and reach forward to caress the silken fabric of her dress,

as though to seek forgiveness by being seductive. At that moment it becomes evident that I am supposed to have some erotic contact with this mysterious stranger. I feel embarrassed because I am not sure what is expected of me. I decide that I have no choice: I must renounce all will-power and passively submit to whatever this exotic creature wants. The anxiety, probably mingled with excitement aroused by the disquieting erotic scene, woke me up with the jolting conviction that my life was in danger.

Unable to return to sleep, I had plenty of time to ponder the potential significance of this manifestly homosexual dream. As far as I could remember, I had never had such a dream. This led me to reflect that my two analysts, both men, had never interpreted any genuinely homosexual material throughout my years of analysis (probably because I had not furnished the necessary associations to allow it!). So here I was, in the dead of night, left to fathom this complicated problem on my own.

The first association that came to mind, through the verbal link of "being late" for an appointment, was my session with Marie-Josée. Why had I followed in my patient's footsteps? Yet my appointment was not with an elderly mother-substitute but a langorous and erotic Asian! What was she doing in my dream? Slowly I recalled the memory of a Chinese patient who had come to consult with me some years earlier. I must have seen her a total of five or six times, and the nature of her therapeutic demand had completely disappeared from my mind. What I did remember was that her father had three legal wives, her mother being the third. I then recalled that she had said of her mother, "She wasn't important in the family and was more of a big sister than a mother to me. We would play games together and shared secrets about the other members of the household." I also recalled my feeling of empathy with her disappointment at having had a "mother-sister" rather than a "real mother." The only real mother, she had explained, was the first wife who ruled over the household.

I wondered now why it had not occurred to me that, even if the little girl were jealous of her father's first wife and wished she had been her child or had taken her place, could it not also be highly agreeable to have a mother-sister, an ever-ready accomplice to play games and share secrets? For some obscure reason I then felt that I must remember the *name* of this patient. After groping around in my memory her first name came back to me in a flash: it was *Lili*. I could no longer deny the unconscious representation of the glamorous creature of my dream. My mother, who in no way resembles an exotic Oriental, is called *Lillian*! But perhaps to my childhood eyes she *was* glamorous and beautiful? And had we not shared complicity over Mater, my paternal grandmother, who, according to my mother, "ruled the roost and expected all her sons to 'kowtow' to her." Was not Mater the equivalent of the "real" mother in my patient's discourse, and were not my mother and I also "sisters" in revolt against her?

From there I began to search for clues of evidence that I had *denied* my childhood erotic feelings for my mother. I recalled an evening when I was eight or nine years of age. She had come in to say goodnight to my sister and me because she and my father were going to a party. She was wearing a dress of shimmering apricot material that seemed to change color as she walked. I asked her what kind of material the dress was made of and she said, "It's shot-silk." I thought I had never seen anything so beautiful!

My first response to this memory was that I must have been jealous because my father was taking *her* out instead of me. But that supposition did not necessarily exclude the other possible wish: that *my mother would choose me*, rather than my father, to go to the party, and that I, too, would be dressed in apricot shot-silk. Was this the mother-sister I had never known? For whom perhaps I had yearned? I continued to explore, gradually understanding other obscure references in the dream theme which, in turn, led to latent thoughts embedded in its manifest content. I began to feel a nostalgic longing for a barely remembered past, redolent with primitive and erotically-toned feelings of love and hate. Long-forgotten fantasies of the fear of death—my own or my mother's—also returned. As for my father, the little girl in me believed him to be immortal. Only he could save my mother and me from some kind of erotic, fusional death!

Next I began to wonder in what way my dream might be connected with Marie-Josée's analysis. For the first time I allowed myself to recognize that in many ways, my mother was quite opposite in character to the mother described by Marie-Josée. My mother's days were occupied with social activities. She worked devotedly for the church to which we belonged; she was an enthusiastic player of croquet and golf; she took singing lessons and practiced playing her violin in spare moments when she was not cooking for the family or making elegant little dresses for my sister and me. In fact, my sister and I had congratulated ourselves on our freedom from maternal constraint in comparison to some of our school friends. In short, my mother bore no resemblance to the portrait of the hovering, demanding mother whom Marie-Josée described.

In attempting to uncover the links between my patient's session and my dream, I came to the astonishing conclusion that I was *envious* of Marie-Josée's possessive mother—always phoning, always proposing that they share cultural and other activities, forever inviting her to come home as soon as her daughter's husband was away. (Surely her mother would have suggested that Marie-Josée try on her apricot silk dress and that they go to the opera together!) Why did I not have a mother like that? I had analyzed so carefully the hostile feelings attached to the internal mother-image, in both myself and Marie-Josée, but had I not, at the same time, overlooked the importance of my patient's positive feelings and a *disavowed homoerotic tie* to her mother? If I had done so, this oversight had been clearly influenced by my need to maintain the repression of *my own infantile wish to be the chosen object of my mother's love-life*! To have waited so many years for a dream to reveal the wish-fulfillment of a totally unconscious desire confirmed that I was "rather late" in recognizing the importance of the homosexual longings of the past. Even more disquieting was the suspicion that I may have overlooked Marie-Josée's disavowed pleasure in having a homosexually desirous mother. I had failed to realize that she never tired of demonstrating the negative aspects of the mother-daughter relationship. In other words, I had taken her complaints at face value!

At our next session Marie-Josée's continuing negative remarks about her mother provided the occasion to ask her if, beneath all her expressed dissatisfaction with her demanding mother, might there also be a wish to prove to me and to herself just how much she was *loved* by her mother? Perhaps she had even felt a secret pleasure in complying with these maternal demands? My intervention was received in tense silence, followed by an embarrassed confession.

MARIE-JOSÉE Well, it could be that *I* am more demanding than I've realized. The other day, when I rang asking if I could spend the weekend with my parents, my mother made it clear that she and my father were a little tired of "baby-sitting" me every time my husband went abroad. I just couldn't believe my ears!

[*She began to cry quietly and, after a short while, continued through her tears.*] She . . . well . . . she even said that they were planning to go away alone again for a few days and they didn't want to be constantly worried about how I was doing back in Paris!

Tears again interrupted Marie-Josée's sentence, but she managed to stammer, " . . . *and Mother actually said that they dreaded my phone calls at such times.*"

I was struck silent by this revelation. Although I was not in doubt about her mother's complicity in their interdependent relationship, above all it was *my own* unconscious complicity that had hindered Marie-Josée from recognizing her desire to be the exclusive object of her mother's love and to put her mother in the place of her husband, whenever the opportunity arose. As a consequence of working through my countertransference, I was now able to turn to another "late" area in my understanding of Marie-Josée's conflict with her mother: her nightly autoerotic activity and its accompanying fantasies. According to her account, masturbation had now become the prime condition for falling asleep. In a sense, it had taken the place of her fantasy of the rapist-killer. Would the hidden erotic tie to her mother be revealed in her autoerotic fantasies, I wondered?

My newly acquired receptivity bore immediate fruit and uncovered a fundamental element that lay behind Marie-Josée's symptom of urinary frequency. In a session a few weeks later, in which my patient once again referred to her past nocturnal anguish, I pointed out that she seemed to avoid talking about what had taken its place: the compulsive masturbation.

MARIE-JOSÉE Yes, it's very difficult for me to talk about that.
JM Do you remember, when you were so afraid of being alone at night, we discovered that your fear was linked to violent sexual images and a buried fantasy of your father as an intruder and a rapist-killer?

I recalled the difficulty she had experienced in recognizing feelings of attachment for her mother and asked whether it might be

difficult for her to explore autoerotic fantasies if they were linked
in any way to childhood fantasies about both her parents.

MARIE-JOSÉE Not at all! It isn't difficult for me to tell you what I imagine. There are both men and women in my sexual daydream. But
what is truly painful for me to tell you is . . . er . . . the way in
which I do this sexual thing. Okay, I must say it. I stimulate myself
with a water-jet apparatus for cleaning teeth!
JM Can you tell me more about this apparatus?
MARIE-JOSÉE It was a present given to me by my mother, but I haven't
used it in the way she intended!
JM So maybe it's a way of making love with your mother?
MARIE-JOSÉE [Laughing, and visibly more relaxed] Yes, I'm sure that's
right. It's that little girl who's still longing to be her mother's erotic
treasure. And, perhaps, as you said the other day, it's my need to be
able to identify with her as a sexual woman so that the small girl in
me can grow into womanhood, too.

Following this session we were able to bring to light multiple
fantasies associated with the "apparatus" and its erotic jet of water. We turned back to the dream of the tumultuous sea, which
elicited common childhood sexual fantasies, particularly urinary
fantasies of parental coitus. These could now be explored in both
their erotic and sadistic aspects. We were able to uncover that the
window intruder of the past was a thoroughly *bisexual* figure.
Marie-Josée recalled that she had experienced her mother as an
implosive intruder because of her concern over her daughter's
toilet training. Also recalled were other eroticized traumatic incidents from the past—foremost among these anxious memories,
her childhood terror of bed-wetting.
My countertransference deafness, together with my repressed
fantasies, had functioned like an opaque screen, preventing the
analytic "light" from clarifying not only Marie-Josée's unsatisfac-
tory adult sex life, but also a dominant fantasy element in her
partial frigidity: namely, her unacknowledged homosexual wishes.
These could now be verbalized and thus allow insight into Marie-
Josée's previously unrecognized envy of her mother and her mother's sex and her childhood longing to take possession of her
mother in order to be a woman and a mother in her own right.
These new insights eventually gave access to the significance of
her rejection of the wish for a child of her own. She was still the

child, with a little girl's genital and a little girl's bladder. Finally, Marie-Josée was able to tell me about her feeling of hatred for her body, which she experienced not only as incomplete and unclean, but also as dangerous — should it become sexually alive in relation to a man. Through the medium of the dental apparatus she was able to maintain a certain distance from her own genitals and, at the same time, act out the infantile wish to have imaginary erotic contact with her mother in order to absorb some of the idealized qualities Marie-Josée attributed to her. This insight constituted an important step toward fuller feminine identification. But much analytic work still lay ahead before this "transitional" erotic object gave way to a genuine identification with the genital woman and mother, whom Marie-Josée believed her mother to be. With these new insights the urinary frequency diminished and, apart from its occasional recurrence during certain stressful situations, finally disappeared.

Toward the end of her analysis Marie-Josée began to travel more often with her husband; her love for him had deepened as she grew to value her status as an adult woman. The desire to become a mother and to bear her husband's child also began to emerge. It appears that the tumultuous sea of her dream was slowly becoming an ocean of internal wisdom and peace.

As can be seen from this fragment of Marie-Josée's (and my own) analytic voyage, the path from girlhood to adult femininity is tortuous and full of pitfalls. The roots of feminine eroticism are germinated in early infancy, potentially giving rise to a multiplicity of zonal confusions. There is a continual struggle to integrate conflicts concerning the earliest love relations, even when the orientation to heterosexuality appears to have been successfully achieved. This fragment of analysis also illustrates the extent to which dreams, both of the analyst and the analysand, continually search for solutions to long-buried problems. By revealing the deeply submerged erotic wishes of childhood, dreams permit their conscious verbalization and open the way to their integration into a more harmonious adult self.

CHAPTER 3

Female Sexualities: Themes and Variations

> *Considering the rose as the universal symbol of love, we can also look at what precedes and prepares for the flower—not only the stem and the leaves but the roots, enmeshed in the soil of mother earth, rich with nutrients, yet crawling with worms and snails and abounding with possibilities. We must look at the whole rosebush.*
> —H. Wrye and J. Welles

IT IS ESSENTIAL to define the word *femininity* because the models of what is referred to as *feminine* or *masculine* are in no way absolute but change from one culture to another, as well as from one epoch to another within any given culture. I will restrict my remarks to Western civilization; in certain other cultures the place of woman and what is regarded as appropriate feminine behavior vary considerably from that which is familiar to the Occidental world.

When the family environment has played a facilitating role in the daughter's acquisition of, and pleasure in, a feminine sexual identity, the mourning processes involved in the integration of bisexual and oedipal wishes have probably been accomplished. Most analytic theoreticians contend that this integration strengthens the narcissistic as well as the libidinal investment in one's body and feminine self and fosters a profound attraction to the other sex. Social discourse adds that this orientation tends to be coupled with the desire to find gratifying love relationships and, eventually, have children with the man of one's choice. The integration of homosexual oedipal longings* as well as heterosexual wishes gives rise to the desire for a lover of the opposite sex and for motherhood, and these desires are in accord with the accepted definition of what is considered feminine in Occidental society. Three variations of female sexuality that are not in accord with societal notions include *homosexuality in women, female transsexualism*, and *female "perversions."*

THE LESBIAN ANALYSAND

Does the lesbian woman find a different resolution of her early homosexual longings toward both parents from that of the woman who has maintained the conviction of her heterosexual identity from childhood onward? Clinical observation leads me to suggest that the impression of having "taken possession" of the mother's feminine prerogatives in childhood, as outlined above, is sometimes still awaited by the lesbian analysand. Although usually repressed into the unconscious layers of the mind, the desire for sexual possession of the mother, and/or the wish to become the father, have never been relinquished for reasons difficult to determine. Sometimes the lesbian analysand appears to reenact these wishes in the attempt to *give to* another woman what she longed for as a child; sometimes she seeks to *receive from* her lover (who may embody the role of mother *or* father) the narcissistic confirmation that she as a person, as well as her body and its erotic pleasure, are both esteemed and appreciated by her lover.

As a way of discussing specific clinical findings with lesbian analysands, I will answer a question that is frequently asked by audience members attending my lectures in different countries: How do homosexual and heterosexual women differ in the context of the analytic process?

Clinical issues with lesbian analysands are not significantly different from those that arise in analytic work with heterosexual patients. To the extent that the homosexual woman who wants an analysis is not in conflict with her sexual orientation, her quest for

---

*In particular, these include the wish to incorporate the mother's psychic contents, frequently fantasized as containing the father's penis, the potential babies, as well as the secrets of femininity.

help usually revolves around the same issues that attract other women to the analytic adventure. Many women, whether heterosexual or homosexual, seek psychoanalytic help in response to an inhibition of or breakdown in their professional work, which is usually intellectual or artistic in nature.

Classical neurotic suffering arising from severe phobias or obsessional symptoms are no different, whether the patient is homosexual or heterosexual. These symptoms also frequently contribute to the inhibitions mentioned above.

Sexual difficulties within a love relationship are next in importance in both heterosexual and homosexual women. Difficulty in achieving or providing sexual gratification is a prominent cause for seeking therapeutic help. However, in addition to this general similarity, here there is a difference between the two sexual orientations. Heterosexual women complain of failure to achieve orgasm with their partners and frequently add that their main source of satisfaction comes through masturbation. In contrast, lesbian women often complain of *lack of interest* in obtaining sexual pleasure for themselves. Several analysands claimed that their main source of sexual satisfaction came from providing erotic pleasure for their lovers and they feared or resented the demand of the lover that they, too, should enjoy the experience of orgasm. Three of my patients said that they did not want to be touched, and one was afraid that an old vomiting phobia might return if she permitted sexual stimulation from her partner. For each of these women, the conscious motivating factor in seeking help could be summarized as follows: "Why am I not able to receive sexual pleasure? And why do I have to, anyway? My lover says she can no longer support my refusal. If I don't solve this problem, I'm afraid our relationship will break up." Two other analysands complained of the counterpart to this difficulty: their disappointment in the lack of sexual response from their lovers.

The loss or the threat of breakdown in a lengthy love relationship is a common cause of psychic suffering that may, or may not, be connected with sexual inhibition. Here again there are no marked differences between heterosexual and lesbian women.

Ubiquitously negative attitudes of many people toward individuals who are part of a minority are an additional motivating factor for seeking analysis, and one that is specific to homosexual women. (More often than not, the men and women who express virulent criticism or speak mockingly of female homosexuals are discharging their own fear of unacknowledged homosexual tendencies.) The patient's own family may also be a source of these same negative attitudes, which only intensifies the person's psychological suffering and breeds ego-dystonic homosexuality.

My findings generally concur with those of Hooker (1972), who concluded that the only obvious difference between homosexuals and heterosexuals is their psychosexual object choice. Most experienced clinicians and research workers report that the personality differences among individual homosexuals are more apparent than the similarities (Simon & Gagnon, 1967; Richardson, 1984). Since the most striking feature of human beings is their *singularity*, it is not surprising that this quality applies to homosexual and heterosexual individuals alike. Furthermore, from the clinical viewpoint we stand to gain more insight into the understanding of human sexuality through its deviations from the so-called norm than by intensive study of supposedly problem-free heterosexuality.

Defining Homosexuality

At this point it is important to define what is understood by the term *homosexuality*. I agree with Isay (1989) that homosexual orientation should not only be defined by active homosexual practice, but should also take into account desires, fantasies, and investments from earliest childhood to adulthood, whether or not these are acted upon.

Burch's (1989) research, in a book devoted to the subject of complementarity in lesbian relationship and the development of lesbian identity, suggests that lesbians fall into two distinct categories: Those who have been acutely aware of their sexual orientation since childhood and those who have had considerable heterosexual experience and only self-define as lesbians, years later, in their adult lives. Burch offers the terms "primary lesbianism" and "elective or bisexual lesbianism" to describe these two carefully defined categories, but cautions that they cannot be considered as exhaustive.

Let us remind ourselves that it is essential to refer to "homosexualities" in the plural, since there are as many variations in act, object, and personality structure as are found in the heterosexualities. With regard to specific clinical aspects of the analyses of lesbian women, it is important (as with any patient) to listen carefully to each analysand's "theory" of herself, her problems, and her past history. Many attempts have been made to delineate the etiological factors that may be presumed to "explain" homosexual identity feeling and object choice. Apart from the complexities involved, such research frequently overlooks the fact that, in the clinical setting, we are listening to a patient's personal theory of her history and her particular representation of her parental imagos. While it is important to grasp the traumatizing effects of reported actual events, these may tell us little about the "real" parents, because the historical account of dramatic events, "remembered" from childhood onwards, changes with the passage of time (as does history in general). Moreover, factors that are recounted in the lesbian's childhood history are revealed just as often in patients with different orientations and sexual identity feeling.

As mentioned, my clinical observations indicate that there are no specific differences between lesbian and heterosexual women in respect to professional and social conflicts and the suffering caused by symptoms or inhibitions in these areas. However, certain differences between homosexual and heterosexual orientations do appear when comparing and contrasting the sources of sexual inhibition and the underlying causes of fractured love relations in a hitherto stable couple.

The Lesbian Couple

Distress in a lesbian couple often occurs when one partner wants sexual relations and the other does not meet this demand with equal interest. I noted that three of my homosexual women patients expressed their lack of interest in receiving sexual pleasure as a major reason for seeking therapy. Here we cannot fail to recognize a common problem presented by a number of heterosexual women patients when their husbands or lovers complain about *their* lack of interest or satisfaction in sexual relations. In both cases we may find a similar set of unconscious fantasies that proclaim sexual pleasure to be forbidden or threatening. The fantasies attached to classical injunctions and warnings conveyed by the parents to the growing child, and any transgression of these, carry the risk of losing the love of the internalized parents.

But beyond this shared parental-oedipal aspect, the homosexual frequently experiences profound fears arising from fantasies of bodily damage, of the loss of bodily or psychic boundaries, and disintegration of the sense of self. In my experience, such dread is more frequently encountered in the unconscious (or sometimes conscious) fantasies of lesbian patients than in those of heterosexual analysands.

Conflicts stemming from parents' unconscious fears and wishes may give rise to a damaged or fragile image of the child's body as a whole. If this should be corroborated later by a denigrating or threatening parental discourse concerning sexuality, then the child's narcissistic image and existence as an individual may readily be transposed onto the sexual self and to the significance attached to "femininity." In turn, this leaves a lasting imprint on core gender and sexual role identity that every child constructs from infancy onwards.

Disparagement of female sexuality in the family or the social discourse is often exacerbated by a mother's excessive concern over her child's health and her sleeping, eating, and eliminatory functions, which may then be internalized by the child as a depreciative image of the bodily and sexual self. Several lesbian analysands particularly recalled their mother's anxiety over bowel functioning and fecal matters in general. My patient Karen (McDougall, 1978b) claimed to have truly believed as a child that she was the only female member of her family who defecated—it was her "dirty secret," for which she felt total humiliation. Benedicte (discussed in Chapter 5) recalled with horror her mother's activity with the enema, and at times would equate her own literary creations to a shameful fecal production. As a little girl, Olivia (McDougall, 1964) was not allowed to mention eliminatory functions and was instructed to cough politely to indicate her need to defecate. These analysands all had somewhat distorted or disquieting images of their bodies and their somatic functioning. Many heterosexual women recount similar childhood histories but do not necessarily transpose this maternal problem onto their psychic representations of their sex or their femininity.

Other lesbian patients convey the conviction that all that is feminine belongs solely to the mother. For the daughter to presume to possess these inner treasures would be tantamount to destroying the mother, as though there could not be two women in this particular family or in this mother-daughter relationship.

In some cases, perceiving the impression of being unacceptable in the mother's eyes is interpreted by the little girl as a demand that she should psychically acquire "masculine" attributes in order to merit her mother's love and attention.

Destiny sometimes appears to play a role as well. Two of my lesbian analysands were born following the death of a baby boy. During the course of the analysis, one of them asked her aunt, who was living with the family when she was born, what the aunt remembered about the reaction of her parents to her arrival some 30 years earlier. Without hesitation the aunt replied, "Your father said, 'I have some very sad news — it's a girl,' and then he burst into tears." A third example was furnished by my patient Sophie (McDougall, 1978a), who was born after the premature death of male twins. Sophie had the distinct impression that her parents were disappointed by her biological sex from the day of her birth. The family discourse was felt to confirm this and led to a guilty need to compensate in some way for the two dead sons.

Other traumatizing antecedents recounted by lesbian patients give rise to thematically similar fantasies of an equally persecutory nature. They may take various forms:

1. "I should have been the boy they were longing for."
2. "I'm supposed to be a girl, but I'm the wrong sort of girl."
3. "My mother is the only true, real woman in this family and will not allow me to take from her what I need in order to become a woman with a woman's rights and privileges."
4. "My mother is confused and defensive in her attitude toward femininity — my only wish is to be totally different from her."
5. "My father despises me, or is rarely at home, so I must be at fault."
6. "My father loves me but as a son."

Similar fantasies may also be revealed in the analyses of many heterosexual women, but their resolution of the painful self-image has taken a different road.

Let us also bear in mind that generalities pertaining to sexual identity or particular sexual practices cannot be made solely on the basis of those who seek psychotherapeutic help for *psychological* problems (whether these problems derive from their sexual lives or from any other aspect of living). Psychoanalytic patients represent a relatively small proportion of the population and are self-selected to demonstrate more psychological suffering linked to their sexual orientation than many gay and lesbian individuals who feel no need of psychotherapeutic help or, perhaps, deny their mental pain. Therefore, I wish to emphasize that I am basing my observations and conclusions only on my work with lesbian women who sought the help of psychoanalysis in relation to their psychic suffering.

Thirty years ago I wrote a paper on "Homosexuality in Women" (McDougall, 1964) based on a very limited sample of patients. My inexperience as an analyst compounded the fact that my understanding of the dynamics of lesbian love relations was based on a meager sample of cases. These deficiencies led me to a number of formulations which, while pertinent to the analysands in question, were less applicable to other lesbian patients with whom I worked analytically in the years that followed my early research in this area. Likewise I do not wish to give the impression that my findings today are generalizable to and applicable for all homosexual women.

FEMALE TRANSSEXUALISM*

The American psychiatrist Harry Benjamin (1953) was the first writer to clearly define transsexualism and to differentiate it clearly from sexual perversions or psychosis. Other writers have also emphasized that transsexual individuals are also unambiguously different from those who self-define as homosexual. However, some research analysts (Limentani, 1989; Stoller, 1975) have regarded women seeking sexual reassignment as demonstrating a specific form of female homosexuality.

The central cause of suffering in transsexuals of both sexes derives from the profound conviction of an antinomy between anatomical and psychological gender. In other words, transsexuals experience their sexual identity as totally incongruent with their anatomical genitalia. This pervasive sense of incongruence, of biological dysharmony, is often accompanied by the impression of being disfigured, impaired, even monstrous. It should be emphasized that the transsexual does not suffer from a *delusion* regard-

---

*I am indebted to Paulo Seccarelli for permission to use his research material pertaining to female transsexualism (Seccarelli, 1994).

ing his or her anatomical gender; it is recognized for what it is but *experienced as* a deformity. In general, the transsexual should not be categorized as psychotic.

A distinction made by Ovesey and Person (1973, 1974) is relevant here. These authors differentiate between primary and secondary transsexualism in a manner similar to the distinctions made by Burch (1989) regarding lesbianism. The primary transsexual has always been aware of feeling like an anomaly and has dreamed of the surgical solution usually from late adolescence onward. The secondary transsexual seeks this solution much later, sometimes after 40 years of age or more.

The demand for sexual reassignment raises radical questions about the identificatory processes that contribute to the acquisition of the sense of sexual identity. A central query concerns the effects of the biparental unconscious in creating this kind of gender discomfort. Stoller (1975) observed that mothers of transsexuals consistently displayed a depressive emptiness, as though devoid of any desire. He hypothesized that, in the case of male transsexuals, their "transsexual destiny" was established in infancy, perhaps in the first year of life, and that the tendency to behave like a little girl often manifested itself before the age of three. However, Stoller's observations with regard to the little girl led him to postulate that the wish for, and assumption of, masculinity gender identity appeared between the third and fourth years of life. In these cases the mother seemed incapable of investing her girl-child's femininity with value, and sometimes it was the father who took care of his daughter. More typically, the fathers appeared equally disinterested in the child's femininity and even encouraged masculine activities and attributes. According to Stoller, the daughter receiving this kind of distorted reinforcement eventually assumed the role of "husband" to her own mother. The same role was subsequently sought in later homosexual relations, in which case the girl wished to be recognized by her partner not as a woman but as a man.

This dynamic again brings to mind my patient Sophie, who was born after the death of twin boys. She was sometimes told by her lesbian lovers that she was not "a true lesbian." One lover asked her directly if she felt confused about her identity; another said, "You're basically a transsexual, not a lesbian." These remarks puzzled Sophie, although she admitted that she sometimes believed she had a "phantom limb" where her penis should have been. Her parents appeared to reinforce the impression that Sophie possessed a masculine rather than a feminine identity. She frequently recalled her father saying, as he left on business trips, "Now look after your mother while I'm away. Remember, you're the man of the house." On one occasion Sophie felt the need to discuss her homosexual relationships with her mother in order to explain why she was often unhappy in her love-life. Her dearest wish, she told her mother, was to play the role of husband to her lovers. But they failed to appreciate this impulse and she regretted she hadn't been born a boy. Her mother replied, "Well, you know, I've heard that people can have an operation done to fix that. Why don't you inquire about getting 'something' grafted on?"

Patients like Sophie confirm Seccarelli's thesis (1989) that, in a sense, the transsexual choice is made by the parents, often before the child is born. Seccarelli (1994) states:

If [the future transsexual] has come into existence to complete a mourning process, whether real or imaginary, to fill a gap, to "heal" a wound that dates from the child's prehistory, it is possible that the transsexual "choice" presents itself, faced with the threat to individual and sexual identity, as the only possible path to escaping more catastrophic solutions . . . and thus avoiding the danger of psychosis.

Limentani (1989) emphasizes the overwhelming anxiety associated with separation and individuation on the part of those destined for transsexual reassignment in adulthood. He adds that the need to be a separate individual may take precedence over the preservation of the corporeal self. He notes an even more serious perturbation with regard to the girl, in that the mother cannot tolerate her own feminine body. Thus the daughter is unable to identify with her mother as a woman and comes to accept that she is a boy in a girl's body. Later she will seek a sex change, with the hope of being recognized as a person of worth by the mother. Limentani questions whether the postulate of an identification with the father is a necessary element. He emphasizes the role of the absent father (apparently in both a real and a symbolic sense).

Seccarelli, in contrast, has observed that the father frequently plays a predominant role in the childhood of the woman who later seeks sexual reassignment. He describes the case of "Mark" who, as long as she could remember, felt ill at ease in her feminine body and always regarded girls as being "the opposite sex." She was accepted as a boy by all the boys of her age; they played football together and shared other masculine activities requiring physical force. Her father was her constant "pal" and treated her as a son from early childhood. The mother did nothing to discourage her husband or daughter in pursuing this masculine identity.

Seccarelli (1994) emphasizes that a central point of research into the origins of the transsexual wish is to determine the way in which the mother invests her baby's genitals from birth. With regard to the girl he states that

. . . her wish to acquire a penis is not related to penis envy as conceptualized by Freud, but to the fact that this is felt to be required by either or both parents. Thus the acquisition of a penis, since it is symbolic of masculinity, will bring her bodily appearance in accordance with her profound conviction of male sexual identity.

Sexual Deviations in Women

The value of Freud's legacy to the topic of female sexuality and its relation to sexual perversion can be debated for several reasons. One obvious factor is his phallocentrism: His reasoning was based entirely on a male standpoint, from which came his overemphasis on penis envy. In addition, his idealization of motherhood (in accordance with the social discourse of his era) has played a role in impeding research into the question of perverse motherhood. Mothers are not universally good or even always "good enough"; the challenge to the psychoanalyst is to understand what lies beneath the behavior of mothers who abuse their children either physically or sexually. Almost invariably the pattern of abuse goes back three generations or more. The nature of the mother's relationship to the child who is destined to be treated perversely can frequently be traced to factors that gave rise to traumatic events in the parents' own childhoods—factors often affecting the place or destiny that this child, even before his or her birth, is expected to fulfill. Sometimes the parents implicitly impose demands that the child "pay" for what the parents have suffered or that the child embody certain aspects of the parents, for which they themselves do not assume responsibility. (These may be either negative or positive qualities and attributes.)

Much of the pioneering work into the question of perverse motherhood has been initiated by Estela Welldon, a psychiatrist and analyst at the Portman Clinic in London, who worked with women with sexual problems (Welldon, 1989). It is obvious that mothers occupy a unique place in the lives of their nurslings and therefore possess unique power over them. Welldon points out that the misuse of this power can manifest itself through battering children or through committing incest with them. Verbal abuse, which is frequently more damaging than physical abuse, is another misuse of maternal power. Similarly, giving false or frightening information about gender and sexual realities can have effects as destructive as incest on sexual identity and gender role.

One of the conceptual difficulties in discussing and exploring perverse behavior in women stems from the fact that, since Freud's time, perversion has been closely identified with male sexuality and the penis. Perverse constructions were understood as defenses against castration fears and the conflicts of the male oedipus complex. Thus the literature suggests that women do not create sexual deviations (Welldon, 1989). Freud believed that the oedipus complex of the little girl was resolved once she accepted the fact that she could have a child from her father in lieu of a penis. This view implies that women had no need of perverse sexual creations — they simply had babies instead!

In contrast to Freud's formulation, it could be hypothesized that female castration anxiety is more intense and more pervasive than that of male fears, since the woman's fears encompass the whole body, with particularly intense focus on the "inner space" where genital sensations are experienced. In both sexes, there is marked anxiety at the phase of oedipal genital wishes and fantasies, but beyond this, we also find deep insecurity regarding subjective identity. This insecurity is invariably accompanied by rage and violence that also has to be contained in the sexual invention. Stoller (1976) defined perversions as "the erotic form of hatred." In both sexes the original hate-objects (or part-objects) are relatively unconscious. Welldon (1989) states that, whereas in men the perverse act is aimed at an external part-object, in women it is usually carried out "against their own bodies or against objects they see as their own creation: their babies. In both cases, babies and bodies are treated as part-objects."

Some little girls who develop deviant forms of sexual acts or relationships in adulthood (such as exhibitionism or sadomasochism) often felt unwanted, ignored, or smothered by the mother. Others experienced themselves as a part-object belonging to the mother and therefore treated as a narcissistic prolongation of her. Each of these scenarios creates raging hatred. From being victims these women may sometimes become victimizers, in which case the "other" (child or lover) is treated as a part-object. This behavior often serves as a manic screen against the unconscious fear of losing the mother and, consequently, the loss of all sense of identity.

Eroticization may be used as a defense against shocking childhood experiences. Beneath many forms of compulsive and deviant sexual practice we find a common theme: that childhood trauma was rendered bearable by turning it into an erotic game. In his book *Pain and Passion* (1991), Stoller explored the reasons some people associate pain or humiliation with violent erotic desire. After extensive research in "S and M" and "B and D" private clubs, he discovered that many of the participants (for example, those who indulged in piercing or being pierced as a form of sexual gratification) had been hospitalized for medical reasons as children and had endured intense pain. It is conceivable that the capacity to transform pain into a source of sexual ecstasy served to preclude a more psychotic outcome.

A case might be made for extending the concept of deviant sexuality in women to deviations of normal bodily functions, as Kaplan does in her book *Female Perversions* (1989). As examples of "perversion" she cites anorexia and bulimia, also including other behaviors such as self-mutilation and kleptomania. However, I believe this extension clouds the issue. I prefer to limit the significance of the term, as Freud did, to sexual behavior *per se*. Although recognizing the existence of non-sexual drives (the self-conservative instincts), Freud did not consider alcoholism to be a perversion of the need to drink, for example, or anorexia and bulimia to be a perversion of the nutritive instincts. At most, it might be claimed that early libidinization of these self-conservative functions plays a role in their later perturbation.

DEVIANT MASTURBATION

In the course of their analyses, many women recount what might be considered to be perverse forms of masturbation — that is, autoerotic activity in which use of the hand appears to be forbidden and is replaced by the use of hurtful objects that are inserted into the vagina or anus. Analysands often reveal that their hands had been experienced as forbidden; either the hands were associated with severe chastisement for masturbating or had been tied in such a way that the girls were unable to reach their genitals and therefore had to discover other means of generating erotic stimulation. Still others, like Kate and Louise (discussed in Chapter 7), felt compelled to use their urine or feces in order to achieve orgasm.

As with research into the construction of masculine and feminine gender identities, analytic exploration of these pregenital and archaic modes of sexual excitement teaches us a great deal about the unconscious fantasies of analysands who suffer from severe sexual inhibitions but have not invented deviant masturbatory acts. More often than not, these patients have problems in achieving sexual satisfaction precisely because erotic scenarios of this kind have been repressed. It is only in the course of the analytic voyage that they discover the extent to which they are resisting such erotic dreams in relation to their partners.

Case Example: The Exhibitionist

Dr. C, a professional woman whose official role was to protect women's rights, asked if she might discuss a specific problem that had arisen in the course of her work. Among other tasks, she had to deal with problems of sexual harassment in industrial, educational, and commercial enterprises employing women. This led to newspaper reports of her lectures to the managing directors in places where a number of complaints had been registered. One day she received a call from the Mother Superior of a girl's convent, asking if she could help them, since they believed they were the object of sexual harassment. Every Thursday, the Mother Superior explained, three of the nuns took a number of young girls to the swimming pool. On each occasion, standing at a street corner (where it was known that the teachers and the girls passed) was a man who would open his long black raincoat and, clad in nothing but his sneakers, "flash" his genitals at the line of children.

Dr. C informed the police of this menacing exhibitionist. The police requested that she inform the nuns that they were not to telephone the police but to phone her when he appeared, and Dr. C would be given a hotline to the vice brigade. The following Thursday an anguished call was transmitted immediately to the vice brigade, who appeared on the scene within four minutes. The exhibitionist was collared. To everyone's astonishment, the flasher was a woman! The nuns and the girls had apparently *not noticed* that the flasher had no penis but did have breasts!*

A discussion then ensued as to whether the female flasher should be arrested for breaking the law or held for psychiatric examination to determine whether she was psychotic. When Dr. C consulted me in Paris about this unusual case, I was even more astonished that the flasher's responsibility for her exhibitionism should be in doubt. Apparently the specialists already consulted held the classical Freudian view that in order to indulge in a sexual perversion, you must have a penis. (The argument is probably based on the belief that a woman has nothing to exhibit – or that it would be psychotic for a woman to reveal herself publicly in her penis-less state!)

I discussed the question of female exhibitionism with my good friend and colleague, Dr. Estela Welldon. She agreed that it was generally believed that there was no such thing as female exhibitionism but that, nevertheless, she had been consulted by a number of female exhibitionists who were troubled by their compulsion. She added the significant observation that in her experience, they, like the male exhibitionists, almost always exhibited to *women*, but more particularly, to women who appeared to embody authority. Dr. Welldon agreed with my supposition that the female exhibitionist was waiting for a mother-figure to take notice of her daughter, to recognize her biological sex, and to order her authoritively to get dressed and go home.

Since then I have been informed of other cases of female exhibitionists who follow the same pattern as well as some who exposed themselves to men rather than women. It is evident that we cannot generalize from symptom to structure. There are probably as many varieties of female and male exhibitionism as there are of any other category of sexual deviation. As always, the outstanding

---

*This example illustrates an important perceptual principle: We can only observe that which falls within the parameters of our theories. The result is that we see what we expect to see! If what comes into sight is not in accordance with our theories, as usual, psychic reality wins out over external reality.

characteristic is the unique quality of every individual's inner world, his or her own psychic theater.

COUPLES AND SHARED DEVIANCY

I have observed that female analysands who engaged in sexual practices dominated by pregenital, fetishistic, or sadomasochistic acts frequently did so at the insistence of their lovers or husbands. Although each woman complained about this, in most cases we were able to reconstruct the woman's infantile past in such a way as to understand why she had chosen this particular mate and how she had gained secret satisfaction in their sexual rituals.

Two clinical examples illustrate this form of erotic expression. In each case the husband was in analysis with a colleague and I was fortunate enough to be able to discuss our mutual analytic work in a study group with the analysts in question. Marie-Madeleine was referred to me by the colleague who had her husband in treatment. In the second case, Kate and her husband had independently obtained referrals from a psychiatrist in their hometown.

Case Example: Urinary Sex

Marie-Madeleine came to analysis because of crippling social phobias; at cocktail or dinner parties she would find herself unable to utter a word, sometimes for hours on end. In addition, she complained that her husband talked constantly when they were out socially, which she attributed to his heavy drinking. At that time they had a two-year-old boy; the three of them were living in a maid's room because the husband's alcoholism had severely reduced his earning capacity. Marie-Madeleine claimed that her husband drank in order to control his ever-present fear of having a heart attack. (In contrast, Marie-Madeleine refused alcohol as a solution to her phobic anxiety.) Despite his erratic work performance, he was nevertheless regarded as a promising, and even brilliant, member of his chosen profession.

It was not until we had worked together for over a year, four times weekly, that my patient spoke with trepidation about her sexual relationship with her husband. She said that the only sexual activity he found erotically arousing was to have her urinate upon him. She claimed she hated this behavior; not only did it render her extremely anxious, but "it was particularly embarrassing when he insisted on doing this during vacations in a hotel bedroom." Her husband asserted that the transgression involved only added to his excitement. Shortly after the birth of their child, Marie-Madeleine decided to refuse to comply with her husband's demands.

My attempts to understand the nature of *her* participation in this pregenital form of lovemaking unexpectedly evoked a memory from Marie-Madeleine's childhood. She lived in the country and was often left in the charge of a nanny. On one occasion, when she was between three and four years old, three playmates, all boys, persuaded her to take off her panties and climb up a tree so that they could look at her sex. This she did with alacrity. Once in the tree, the boys asked her to "please show us how you do pee." She remembers being delighted at having something important to show the boys, which was also a source of excitement for them, so she began to urinate. At this very moment, her nanny surged forth into the garden and angrily ordered Marie-Madeleine to climb down and put on her panties. She was then soundly spanked. But the most humiliating part of the whole recovered episode was her parents' shocked anger and disapproval of her "bad" behavior.

Although many boys pursued Marie-Madeleine amorously as she grew into adulthood, she refused any sexual encounters until she met her husband at the age of 20. To her he seemed to be a most intelligent and engaging companion, different from the others and free in his erotic advances. For the first time in her life she fell in love and longed for sexual fulfillment. Thus, still virginal, she married Mr. B. She complained about the "urinary game" from the beginning of their marriage, and although she had complied with his requests for several years, she still felt guilty about her recent refusal because of "how exciting and important" the deviation was for her husband. It was not until she recovered the forgotten memory of her humiliation at the age of three that her feelings about her husband's demands began to make sense.

It was quite some time before Mr. B's analyst spoke to me of his patient. He was puzzled by his patient's perversion and wondered if the wife had ever mentioned it. He said, "For the past two years or so he has paid prostitutes large sums of money to urinate on him while he masturbates them." Although this was crippling the family financially, the analyst felt that there must be some conscious or unconscious complicity on the wife's part. He added that Mr. B urgently sought this deviant sexual practice whenever he was overcome with phobic anxiety on the street. His phobias took various forms, among which was the fear of a sudden heart attack. In driving to work he could only use streets in which a known cardiologist was in practice. The "urinary couple" was suddenly clearly delineated.

Case Example: Fecal Complicity

The second case of unconscious erotic complicity came to my notice through a patient whom I called Mrs. O. I have cited fragments of her analysis in former writings, but did not mention her specifically perverse form of masturbation. In order to achieve orgasm, she had to urinate on her own hands. Mr. O was also in analysis and in our small study group, Mr. O's analyst and myself managed to talk briefly about the Os. Kate lost her mother when she was less than three, at which time her father took over her upbringing. She recalled that he would leave her at school and collect her in the afternoons. Throughout her childhood he was particularly strict about bowel training, and little Kate had to answer truthfully whether she had, or had not, had a bowel movement during the day. If she said she had not, or she couldn't remember, he administered an enema to the little girl. It seems that this incestuous and pregenital relationship induced constipation, for in Kate's memory, rare were the days when she didn't receive the enema. In any case, this daily treatment was administered until she reached the age of 11, at which time her father remarried. The new wife insisted that the practice be stopped.

Kate also related another daily practice from her adult life, which seemed to be close to a perverse sexual activity. Constantly concerned that she might have bowel cancer, she would regularly finger her fecal matter, looking for traces of blood in her stool. She also admitted that even though she had received medical reassurance that she was free of cancer, she still felt the urge to play with her fecal matter. We were able to reconstruct her juvenile excitement over the daily enemas administrated by her father throughout childhood and her fear of bowel cancer as a possible punishment for forbidden sexual wishes toward him. She also complained a great deal about her husband's desire for intercourse, claiming that "everyone knows that only men enjoy sex."

Some two years later Mr. O began to tell his analyst about his sexual secrets. The only truly exciting sexual act he experienced was to self-administer a boiling hot enema while masturbating, at the same time imagining that he was giving an enema to a woman. The origin of this fetishistic act was in part traced to Mr. O's memories of hearing his mother give herself an enema every week and imagining how exciting this must be for her. Neither wife nor husband recognized how carefully their unconscious fantasies had led them to one another. With Kate, as with Marie-Madeleine, it seems that the men had chosen women who were destined to *resist* their husbands' sexual demands. Meanwhile the women had themselves chosen men whose perversions, of which they had no conscious knowledge, were directly linked to pregenital excitement in their own early lives.

PART II

Sexuality and Creativity

CHAPTER 4

Sexuality and the Creative Process

The spontaneous gesture is the True Self in action. Only the True Self can be creative and only the True Self can feel real . . . The True Self comes from the aliveness of the body tissues and the working of body functions, including the heart's action and breathing . . . the summation of sensori-motor aliveness.

— D. W. Winnicott

THE MYSTERIES OF the creative mind have fascinated psychoanalysts since the beginning of psychoanalytic reflection. In 1908 Freud, in his essay on "Creative Writers and Daydreaming," asked two major questions: "From what sources does that strange being (the creative writer) draw his material?" And "How does he manage to arouse in us emotions of which perhaps we had not even thought ourselves capable?"

In attempting to answer his first query, Freud states that children at play behave like a creative writer in that they create a world of their own. He points out that children "take . . . play very seriously and expend large amounts of emotion on it." However, in the same paper Freud goes on to say that "as people grow up they cease to play" and that the adult "knows that he is expected not to go on playing or phantasying any longer." This somewhat critical attitude toward fantasy and play in adulthood appears throughout Freud's writings, as though fantasies — and even the enjoyment of contemplating creative works — were, for him, a guilty preoccupation. Further in his paper Freud states: "We may lay it down that a happy person never phantasises, only an unsatisfied one." If we were to follow Freud's logic, "dissatis-faction" and "unhappiness" would appear to befall not only to the creative artist but anyone who uses imaginative resources to make life a more creative adventure.

The analytic world had to wait for D. W. Winnicott to bring a more optimistic view of fantasy, play, and creativity to the field. Winnicott begins his research into this area of human experience with the postulate of what he terms "primary creativity": the nurs-ling's experience of a first inkling into the loss of the caretaking object—a realization, though fleeting, that he and this source of life are not one. The baby then seeks to *recreate*, in hallucinatory fashion, the lost fusion with the maternal universe.

Winnicott's designation of "the intermediate area of experienc-ing"—a potential space to which both inner reality and the exter-nal environment contribute—is a basic concept that can facilitate a more profound exploration of the mysteries of the creative pro-cess. As Winnicott expressed it: "The subject [of transitional space] widens out into that of play, of artistic creativity and ap-preciation, and of religious feeling and of dreaming . . . " In a chapter entitled "Playing: A Theoretical Statement" (1971), Win-nicott writes that what he has to say about children playing applies to adults as well—a statement similar to that of Freud in 1908, but with a more positive slant. Among the many attributes that contribute to the creative process, it could be said that the creative individual (in whatever field) is also *playing*.

MYTHS AND FACTS OF THE CREATIVE LIFE

For many years I have been interested in trying to catch a glimpse into the role of "play" among the many mysterious origins of innovative expression in whatever form this may take in my analysands: writing, painting, sculpture, music, the performing arts, scientific and intellectual creativity, as well as creativity in the world of politics, business, and industrial invention.

Although both Freud and Winnicott advanced the notion that creativity involves playing, this must not be taken to mean that creative activity is *carefree*. On the contrary, creative or innova-tive activity of any kind is invariably associated with considerable violence and frequently arouses intense experiences of anguish and guilt. The resistance to continuing to work is a common experience of the creative artist, and my analysands have shown me that this resistance is often acutely experienced when they feel particularly inspired by a pristine vision, invention, or idea that is clamoring for expression.

It was not until Melanie Klein (1957) proposed that creativity derives from the tumultuous relationship between infant and mother that new light was thrown upon the inner world of the creative being and the inhibitions to which its conflicting emotions may give rise. Perhaps more incisively than any other psychoanalytic writer, Klein emphasized the dimension of violent emotion in the primal substratum of the human psyche. Although she tended to attribute blockage in creative acts to a lack of integration of infant destructiveness in relation to the breast universe, her perspective has interested me in that observation and reflection have led me to conclude that *violence is an essential element* in all creative production. Apart from the force and intensity of the creative urge in itself, innovative individuals are necessarily violent to the extent that they exercise their power to impose their thought, image, dream, or nightmare on the external world.

It is not surprising that a measure of anxiety and psychic conflict so often accompanies the act of creating. Creative people tend to seek psychoanalytic help at times when their productivity is endangered or even totally inhibited. Thus analysts are presented with a privileged insight into the factors that contribute to creative activity as well as those that are the force behind the sudden failure to create. Nevertheless, I would emphasize that psychoanalysts lay no claim to holding the key to artistic creativity; on the contrary, we hope that creative individuals, through their inspired works, will provide us with further keys to unlock the mysteries of human nature.

At this point I would like to dispel the common myth of the creative individual as a starving artist or writer who is probably emotionally unstable and/or sexually deviant. In point of fact, the lives of famous creative people are as varied in historical content and psychological structure as are those of the average banker, butcher, plumber, or politician. Many of them have led rather ordinary bourgeois existences. Many have been devoted parents. Some have combined their active creative lives with successful activities in other fields: Rubens was named ambassador; Matisse began his professional life as a lawyer; Chekhov was a doctor; Claudel was a diplomat; Moussorsky was a military man who rose to the rank of lieutenant, and so on.

Certainly creative individuals have also manifested recognizably psychotic, perverse, or psychopathic behavior, but perhaps *the part of the personality that allowed them to create — and impelled them to keep on creating — was the healthy part*!

It is also significant to note that the majority of creative people, in whatever field, are astonishingly productive. It took musicians of later generations many years to compile a catalog of Mozart's compositions; Rubens painted thousands of pictures; by the age of 16 Toulouse-Lautrec had completed 50 paintings and 300 drawings; van Gogh's productions, even during the years when he was the most ill, would fill a small museum; Euripides wrote 92 plays; Donizetti composed 63 operas; Thomas Edison patented over a thousand inventions. In this context it is pertinent to quote a statement often attributed to Picasso, to the effect that "the only work that counts is the work that has not yet been created."

We might envisage the internal universe of the creative person as something like a volcano. Within its depths, the volcano conceals ever-present heat and churning energy, sending out sparks, rocks, and flames at appropriate moments. If prolonged blockage were to occur, however, an explosion would soon follow. An aspect of this relentless drive in the creator's inner world is explored in Kavaler-Adler's (1993) work, *The Compulsion to Create*, in relation to famous women writers.

A colleague, who is also a prominent Parisian painter, wrote the following lines for a psychoanalytic journal, summing up what she had learned from her own analysis with regard to the creative urge:

The profound primordial drives that surge up in me can become powerful enough to cause discomfort; the constant build up of tension has to be put outside me into the outer world in order to restore some feeling of harmony inside. It is creation, but it is fired by feelings of destruction. When I cannot paint, I become the target of my own violent aggression.

I understand so well the frustration of my dear friend A, who says he hates his paintings because "they never depict the painting he has in his mind." Then there is B, who periodically destroys every painting he still has in his studio. Is this what Freud called the "death instinct"? (Kahnert, 1992).

It is possible that the drive toward self-destruction is always in action during any creative process, and even becomes part of the movement that brings fragmentation and structure together. My experience over the last 30 years with creative and innovative analysands has led me to appreciate this fact. Feelings of depression, self-hatred, anger, and frustration, leading to a wish to destroy the work in progress, are often encountered.

EROGENIC ORIGINS OF THE CREATIVE ACT

Clinical considerations have led me to the overall impression that creativity originates in the erogenic body; its course of development is influenced by the way in which its drives are represented and its somatic functions structured by the caretakers of the infant. In attempting to follow the complex links between the creator, the created work, and the public, I have identified four fundamental factors which, to my mind, form part of the background for any creative thought or act. Each of these factors is intimately linked with the body and its libidinal drives in both their object-related and narcissistic orientations. These highly charged representations give rise to a multitude of fantasies about the body-image and its somatic functioning; all are a frequent source of creative inspiration — and its inhibition.

Two of these important dimensions concern the creator's interaction in the external world with (1) the *medium of expression* itself, and (2) the *imagined public* for whom the creative production is intended. The other two cardinal aspects are located within the psychic world of the creative personality in the form of (3) the role that *pregenital sexual drives* play in his or her psychic economy (including oral, anal, and phallic impulses), and (4) the integration — or non-integration — of the *bisexual wishes of infancy* into the psychic structure of the creator.

Work with creative and innovative analysands has shown me that the unconscious repercussions of any one of the above four factors can give rise to the emotional experience of indulging in a form of *transgression*. Such a fantasy is apt to arouse mental pain and psychic conflict, which in turn inhibits productivity. Sometimes the creative productions will continue, but at tremendous cost to the creator in terms of panic-anxiety, profound depression, psychosomatic manifestations, or other forms of decompensation. Creative individuals are often dealing with fragmented parts of themselves and, at the same time, fervently seeking a sense of individuality and cohesion through their created works or inventions.

The External World

1. *The Medium of Expression*. Underlying the struggle of every creative person with his or her chosen medium of creative expression is always a fantasy of fusion (or *confusion*) with the medium itself. This experience may give rise to contradictory feelings in the course of analysis: At one and the same time, the creator wishes to caress his or her medium of expression *and* to attack it in an effort to master it. This is clearly observable in the fields of painting and sculpture, where artists often destroy the piece of work they are trying to create. Musicians frequently complain that they love their music but hate, as much as they love, their instruments. Creative people in the field of industry and scientific research also show remarkable ambivalence toward their instruments, computers, tools.

I am reminded of a talented promotor who achieved world fame with his industrial innovation, only to destroy the empire he had created when his financial success outstripped that of any member of his family for generations. It was at that point that he sought analysis. This type of ambivalence is common in many innovative and "self-made" men and women, who are often liable to be "killed by success."

Thus the medium—whether it be paint, marble, words, the voice, the body, a musical instrument, or a social or political institution—will always present itself as both an ally and an enemy. The medium of creative expression has to be "tamed" so that the creator can impose his or her will upon it; it must translate the creator's inner vision, sometimes evoking a transcendent feeling of union with it. At the same time, the creator must regard the medium with objectivity and feel convinced that it has the power to transmit to the outer world the message or vision or new concept.

2. *The Imaginal and the Public*. The public to whom the creative product is directed is, first of all, an internal public, com-

posed of the significant objects from the past who may be experienced as either hostile or supportive. Once some form of truce has been formed in the individual's mind with these inner object-representations, the creator is then able to release the created work for external "publication." Creators and innovators frequently feel they must struggle with the outside world in order to obtain the right to display the most intimate expressions of their inner universe. The relation between the creative personality and the anonymous public is a love affair that bristles with hazards and anguish for many an individual. The creator seeks to share with the public a personal inner vision, but first must be convinced that the product has value and will be desired and appreciated by the public for whom it is intended.

The analyst's first area of exploration concerns the nature of what is *projected* upon this external public: Is it seen as welcoming, appreciative, desirous of receiving the creative offer — or, on the contrary, as persecutory, critical, rejecting? Such projections are common and decisive factors in the creator's choice either to allow or refuse the "publication" of the creative work.

The Internal World

3. *Pregenital Sexuality.* The libidinal foundation of all creative expression is invariably infiltrated with pregenital drives as well as archaic aspects of sexuality, in which eroticism and aggression, love and hate, are indistinguishable from one another. Although oral, anal, and phallic drives all contribute to creative production, the anal component holds a place of pre-eminence, since it is the source of the first "interchanges" between the infant and the external world. The initial "creation" the infant offers to the first caretaker is the fecal object, with all the erotic and aggressive meanings invariably associated with anal activity and fecal fantasy. Thus this unconscious libidinal origin plays a vital role for the creative person in every domain. But the repressed fantasies involved add an element of uncertainty, because fecal production is invariably experienced in two distinct ways: On one hand, it is something of great value, a gift offered to an "other" (usually the mother) with love; on the other hand, it is experienced as a weapon, to be used to attack and dominate this other. It is also noteworthy that, while the pleasure experienced in satisfying oral and genital impulses may arouse conflict, they are scarcely capable

of being sublimated. The spontaneous expression of anal impulses and their fecal productions, on the other hand, are subjected to rigid control and therefore impel a sublimated solution. The unconscious nature of anal-erotic and anal-sadistic investments in the act of creation is thus one important determinant of the creator's capacity—or incapacity—to continue producing.

4. *Bisexual Wishes of Infancy*. As discussed in the Introduction, an infant normally identifies with both parents and desires the privileges and magic powers of each for itself. These attributes are usually symbolized by the parents' sexual organs. To the extent that the masculine and the feminine parts of every individual are well integrated and accepted, we all have the potential to be creative—to sublimate, so to speak, the impossible wish to be both sexes and to create children with both parents. This resolution may then permit us to produce parthenogenetic "infants" in the form of creative productions.

THE INHIBITORY POTENTIAL OF PRIMAL-SCENE FANTASIES

The four factors identified above—the creator's struggle with the medium of expression, with his or her projections upon the public, the force of pregenital drives, and the importance of psychic bisexuality—might actually be considered as *four versions of the primal scene*, any or all of which can become a source of fertility or sterility. Thus in addition to the instinctual force that nourishes the four situations, each is also represented psychically as being forbidden or fraught with danger for the self or for an anonymous other. There is probably no creative act that is not unconsciously experienced as an act of violence and transgression: One has dared to play alone, through one's chosen medium of expression, in order to fulfill secret libidinal, sadistic, and narcissistic aims; one has dared to display the resulting product to the whole world; in one's production, one has dared to exploit pregenital sexuality, with all the attendant ambivalence; finally, one has dared, in unconscious fantasy, to "steal" the parents' generative organs and powers and, with these, proceed to make one's own creative offspring.

These notions will be elaborated with brief clinical vignettes to illustrate the ways in which pregenital and bisexual wishes can play a cardinal role in either stimulating or paralyzing the creative process. These unconscious wishes are important areas for psychoanalytic research into the causes of creative inhibition.

PREGENITAL EROTICISM

Pregenital sexuality draws its importance and richness from the fact that it involves the five senses as well as all bodily functions. Certain senses, erogenous zones, and bodily functions are often unconsciously experienced as forbidden sources of pleasure or as being potentially dangerous and violent. For example, to take into one's body and mind impressions received through any of the five senses is a creative act in itself. The artist (in any field) is inevitably inspired by something in the external world, and once these impressions, perceptions, and thoughts are mentally incorporated, they fertilize the inner psychic reality of the creative mind. However, this perpetual movement between the two worlds—inner and outer—can be experienced *and feared* as an orally devouring or destructive act.

I recall a portrait painter who, in spite of a strange abstract technique that had earned him a certain reputation, usually succeeded in capturing a likeness. Nevertheless, he frequently ruined portraits that were highly important to him. Through our analytic work we came to realize that, in a megalomanic and childlike manner, he held himself responsible for his mother's partially paralyzed face, which, in unconscious fantasy, he had orally attacked and devoured with his mouth and eyes. In a sense he had spent his life trying to repair the catastrophic damage "caused" by his infantile oral projections. His portraits were explosive attacks upon the visual world, and yet, at the same time, reparative, in that they restored a striking likeness to the individual portrayed.

A similar unconscious drama was revealed during the analysis of a plastic surgeon who claimed that his mother was an unusually ugly woman. On the few occasions when his work was not impeccably successful, his self-denigration enabled us to uncover unconscious fantasies that *he* had rendered his mother ugly. Any patient who reminded him of his mother made him unduly anxious. Yet, by means of a highly original surgical invention, he was able to invest his operations with the same violence he had experienced in his early relationship to his mother. "I cut to cure," he announced one day, when faced with what he considered to be unfair criticism from other medical specialists. In deconstructing this phrase we learned that, through cutting, he satisfied different pregenital drives, while at the same time making reparation for the fantasized destruction of which he believed himself to be the author. From there on, he accepted criticism without suffering.

In the same manner in which *taking in* perceptions from the environment can be both enjoyed and feared as an orally destructive act, the activity of *giving out* something of oneself to the external world may also be experienced unconsciously as an act of defecation and therefore of potential humiliation. In a similar vein, the pleasure and excitement felt in the act of displaying and rendering public one's creative production is frequently equated with exhibiting one's body or masturbating in public. Hanna Segal's paper, "Symbolic Equivalents" (1957), comes to mind here: In it she described the case of a musician who responded aggressively when she attempted to analyze his total refusal to play in public. He told her that she was encouraging him "to masturbate" in front of the whole world. In her discussion Segal points out that to confuse playing a musical instrument with a masturbatory act indicates that the instrument was not a true symbol but, rather, a "symbolic equivalent" in which internal and external reality are confused — a mechanism that is tinged with psychotic overtones.

PRIMITIVE SEXUALITY AND
THE CREATOR'S PROJECTIONS

The former reflections emphasize the extent to which the creator is capable of projecting onto an anonymous public an image that is either welcoming or rejecting of his or her personal self or created product. Although hostile projections are certainly a major source of creative inhibition, paradoxically, overwhelming pleasure at being well-received may also lead to episodes of depression or profound feelings of failure. The complex nature of these projections is of considerable concern to the analyst.

Clinical observation leads me to believe that the creative process, as well as its blockage, is intimately allied with the maternal image, whereas the "public" for whom the creation or performance is intended frequently embodies the image of the father. However, overwhelmingly critical maternal images may also predominate when the fantasized public is felt to be hostile or condemnatory. These different projections vary in level of distortion from the purely neurotic to the frankly psychotic. (The latter is exemplified by the patient of Segal's cited above, who failed to distinguish between inner and outer realities.) In the case example below, a violinist projected upon her public an angry and critical maternal image as well as a paternal image endowed with destructive potential. The two cases that follow illustrate some of the above notions in relation to the inhibiting effects of fecal and urinary fantasies.

Case Illustration: The Libidinized Violin

Tamara, a talented violinist who was highly esteemed by the Conservatoire de Paris where she had been a prize-winning pupil, suffered such paralyzing anxiety before a performance that she sometimes had to cancel her engagements at the last minute. After many months of mutual research, in which we attempted to reconstruct the unconscious scenario that was being enacted before every anticipated concert, she was able to capture the following fantasy: "I fool the whole world. Everybody will see that all I produce is excrement and that I myself am as valueless as a pile of shit." In addition, she felt that she both hated and loved her musical instrument. Some months later she experienced her violin as an extension of her own body, which she could now permit herself, for the first time, to love and caress.

As the analysis proceeded she began to feel freer to contemplate allowing others to see this libidinized extension of her bodily self into her musical instrument and even to imagine that, one day, she might give a performance with unequivocal affection. With the new investment of her corporeal being came a reevaluation of her body's natural functions. At one session she announced, "You know, I have learned from you that there is 'good shit' and 'bad shit.' Why can't I accept the fact that I want to offer *good* things to the public?"

Shortly after this period of analysis, to my surprise my patient arrived one day with her violin. Throughout the whole session, without saying a word, she played a beautiful sonata. When she had finished, she simply said, "Thank you"; I replied, "Thank *you*." In that moment I had become the incarnation of her two inner parents, whom she had formerly endowed with destructive intentions but who were now felt to accept the little Tamara with all the bodily fantasy and emotional significance that sparked her wish to play in public. In the sessions that followed we came to understand that, beneath her fear that she would exhibit what she believed to be an ugly and sexless body, there was also a desire to drown the whole world (father and mother) in murderous feces. Slowly she began to believe that she had valuable gifts to offer the outside world.

A year after the termination of her analysis, she sent me two tickets for a concert in which she gave a most moving performance. Once her primitive libidinal fantasies were well integrated in their positive aspects, her severe inhibitions were alleviated.

Case Illustration: Erogenic Sculpting

A further example of the intimate link between the pregenital psychosexual body and creative expression was provided by a young woman sculptor from South America. Cristina sought analytic help many years ago during her art studies in Paris because she had reached a point of complete paralysis in her artistic production. She explained to me that although she dreamed of creating monumental sculptures, she was only able to make very small constructions; and these, it turned out, she invariably sculpted in a fragile medium so that they were frequently chipped or broken, often by Cristina herself. She also spoke of her marital problems and her fear that she was not a good-enough mother to her two small children (as if they, too, were fragile and easily broken). Cristina then mentioned that she was incapable of showing her work publicly, in spite of the encouragement of friends, among whom were a couple of gallery owners. The very thought of such an exhibition induced insomnia and brought her work to a complete halt.

The analysis was conducted on a four times weekly basis and lasted six years. Cristina spent many sessions recalling her anguish over her body and its functions. Intense masturbation guilt, stemming from childhood memories in which she had been severely chastised by her mother, gave rise to lengthy analytic exploration.

Among other recollections she remembered being told that her autoerotic activity would not only lead *her* to damnation but would kill *her mother* to boot! These memories led to an unconscious fantasy that her own hands were imbued with destructive power, and that to exhibit her sculptures publicly would bring about her mother's death.

During the first two years of our work together, Cristina began to sculpt larger pieces and also to experiment with working in metal. She finally plucked up the courage to enter a competition designed to promote young artists in all types of medium. By a curious coincidence, the theme of the competition was, "The Hand." In a dark colored material, Cristina constructed a large effigy of her own hand—a strange and fascinating piece of work, with something of the air of a prehistoric monster about it.

"My sculpture has been chosen for exhibition," she jubilantly announced one day, adding, "The whole world will see it! I'm delighted. I've even sent my parents an invitation! My thing will be displayed and they will be forced to be proud of me for once in their lives." In the days that followed, Cristina was able to put into words her belief that her "thing" brought her a feeling of bodily integrity, as well as affirming the creative aspects of her genital self and her right to her feminine sexuality.

In the long years following the termination of our work together, I frequently received news from Cristina. Many a catalog contained details of public showings of her work in Europe and abroad. Then one day she called to say she was back in France and urgently wanted an appointment. Once again she was suffering from massive anxiety that prevented her from sleeping and also from working. This outbreak of panic-anxiety had occurred on the opening night of a very important exhibition of her work, which was composed of large sculptures in stone and cement in a new style. We arranged for her to come once a week for the coming year.

Her first session back on the couch led her to associations around the new exhibition. "I worked on the pieces for this important show for over a year, and with a totally unusual feeling of freedom and pleasure—which, as you know, is quite rare for me. There's always an anxious undercurrent just before a major exhibition, but this time I wasn't aware of the slightest trace of panic. After the first night the art reporter for the gallery remarked that my sculptures were unlike my former work. He said they were "less austere" and also that I had used a new technique that "was not what we expected from you." I went home in a state of extreme anguish and collapse such as I haven't known for years. For the last three weeks I've not been able to work or sleep."

The following week I encouraged Cristina to tell me more about the new sculptures. "Well," she said, "there *is* something unusual about this recent work. Not only did I truly enjoy creating the pieces, but after they had been disengaged from their casting molds, I added some decorative detail. This decorative addition would have been unthinkable for me even two years ago. Now I'm filled with panic the moment I enter my Paris *atelier*. I can't even daydream about my work or touch the piece I was working on."

In the week that followed, my interest in Cristina and her painful blockage led me to visit the Museum of Modern Art, where I gazed upon the impressive pieces, overwhelming in their size and shape, and highlighted with intriguing surface detail. I thought to myself how far Cristina's work had progressed from the timid little clay shapes of many years ago, and how they had also far surpassed the dramatic "Hand" that had been her breakthrough to the public.

In the sessions that followed, we recapitulated our discoveries of the past: the threat of death associated with masturbation; the early memory from the age of three when her parents had gone away for a week, leaving her in the care of the maid. During this time she had collected her feces and put them in a cardboard box in a cupboard in her bedroom, which was discovered by the maid, who scolded her severely and subsequently informed her parents of her "crime." (In a sense, this collection of feces had been Cristina's very first "sculpture." She had clung to her earliest gift to the outside world, presumably to stave off feelings of abandonment, and thus endowing them with a new value that warranted their preservation.)

Cristina recalled an even earlier childhood incident that had come to mind several times during her first years of analysis. She distinctly remembered being carried by her nanny, naked, in front of a group of visitors. The nanny opened Cristina's legs, and in a voice of disgust, called attention to the fact that Cristina was urinating. This spectacle was greeted with loud laughter. Cristina thought she was between a year and 18 months of age when this occurred. In our earlier work she had recaptured, on many occasions, the experience of urinating with pleasure, to be followed immediately by an intolerable sense of humiliation and public exposure.

During the session that followed this recapitulation, Cristina remarked, "I'm beginning to wonder if the extreme austerity that has always been the hallmark of my work was intended to mask my sexuality and, in fact, to deny all sensuous pleasure. My body's functions have always made me feel anxious and guilty, and any sensuous feelings were obscurely terrifying. Is it pleasure that is forbidden? The orgasm that must be denied, no matter what the cost?"

In the following session Cristina pondered the pleasure she had experienced while preparing her large sculptures for exhibition, adding that the unusual surface detail had been entirely contrived by hand—which was a technique she had never used before. We then understood the unconscious significance of her reaction to the art reporter's critical remark, referring to sculpture details that she had added *by hand*. He had embodied the nanny who "reported" Cristina's "fecal crime" to her parents as well as the mother who threatened that death would result from Cristina's childhood masturbation. Once again, she had indulged in something seriously forbidden—"that was not what we [the parents] expected of you."

For the first time, Cristina was able to express fully her childhood rage at being denied access to her femininity and sexuality. She further realized that her violent reaction to the reporter covered unacknowledged anger and feelings of violence toward the internalized parents (as well as toward the analyst who had not "protected" her creative child from such attacks!). She was finally able to accept that violence was not necessarily destructive—it could also be *creative*. Further elaboration of the traumatic features from the past that had been reactivated in this sensitive and creative artist led to the disappearance of her anguish about the exhibition. Some weeks later she signed a contract for a showing of the same work in another metropolitan city, which she anticipated with delight.

This fragment of analysis illustrates the role of the erogenic body of infancy in artistic creativity; how the art itself derives much of its force, as well as its frailty, from the way in which the creator's body was invested, libidinally and narcissistically, in the early biparental relationship. Although these profound libidinal and narcissistic drives are the primal source of the overwhelming urge to create, it is noteworthy that emotions of anger and rage are of equally vital importance to creative expression.

An interesting example of this violence is contained in the following quotation from the sculptor Noguchi written on the occasion of his 91st birthday:

You might think that when Brancusi took a bronze casting and started filling it, he eventually got to the inside: I go at it in a different way — I actually split it — I break it — I cut — I go for the jugular. Then I come out again and it all becomes one . . . *

Any or all of the factors that mediate the creator's interaction with the external world may contribute to severe inhibition. It is understandable that creative individuals are constantly exposed to sudden disruption — or even complete breakdown — in their productivity when traumatic memories and primitive emotions from the past threaten to resurface. Perhaps the very traumas most closely associated with the psychosexual organization of the body-representation, as it is modulated by the significant objects of the past, are a primal source of neurotic symptoms and inhibitions *and* of creativity itself.

---

*My thanks are due to my colleague from Tucson, Arizona, Dr. Ruth Mayer, who sent me this quotation following a discussion of a paper of mine on the theme of art and violence at the Austen Riggs 75th Anniversary Symposium.

CHAPTER 5

Creativity and Bisexual Identifications

Journalist: What is the best early training for a
writer?
Author: An unhappy childhood.
— Ernest Hemingway

THE PSYCHOANALYTIC CASE illustration below raises both clinical and theoretical questions in regard to identifications or disidentifications with the parental objects in the inner psychic world — and their potential effects on creative activity — particularly when the childhood was pervaded by trauma and tragedy.

THE FIRST ENCOUNTER

Of Russian descent, Bénédicte was born and raised in a northern province of France, where all her close relatives still live. A writer by profession, she sought help in response to an almost total internal blockage in her work. She felt unable to complete a novel she was working on, despite considerable talent and the assurance of having already gained a certain reputation for her writing (though she herself had little esteem for the work she had produced so far).

Bénédicte walked into my consulting room with apparent hesitation. She lowered herself with care into the chair facing mine, all the while looking at me with a tense and grave expression. After a lengthy silence, she began talking in a halting manner — almost stammering — in a voice so soft that I had difficulty hearing her. She would stop abruptly in the middle of a sentence, as though unwilling to allow her words to reach me, or as though each phrase had to be monitored before being spoken aloud. As she stammered on, I noticed that she hesitated before or after pronouncing personal pronouns, as if she feared that to say *you* or *me* were too intimate or too violent a statement.

BÉNÉDICTE Er . . . I . . . er . . . don't . . . er . . . don't know if analysis can help . . . er . . . me. Also er . . . I . . . er . . . don't have . . . er . . . confidence in it. But . . . er . . . I read something written by . . . er . . . you. My . . . er . . . writing, there's something's wrong . . . I can no longer . . . er . . . create . . . I . . . er . . . don't like that word . . . you . . . er . . . might be able to help . . . er . . . me.

J. MCDOUGALL What kind of help do you have in mind?

BÉNÉDICTE Perhaps . . . er . . . you could collaborate with . . . er . . . me . . . That is . . . er . . . I don't think it's a . . . er . . . real analysis that I . . . er . . . need but someone like . . . er . . . you . . . who writes as well.

JM But I'm an analyst, not a writer.

BÉNÉDICTE I'm completely blocked.

JM Perhaps we might discover what is blocking you.

BÉNÉDICTE Er . . . I've accomplished nothing in my life. I . . . er . . . I'm ashamed . . . er . . . to still be alive . . . to have done so little. [*Long pause*] I shall be . . . er . . . 40 years old next week. [*Another long pause*] My . . . er . . . father died . . . at 40.

JM [*In the anguished silence that followed. Bénédicte stared intently at me. Intimidated by her silence and her unwavering gaze, I made a senseless remark — a glimpse of the obvious, so to speak — as a means of gaining time for both of us.*] So you have reached the age at which your father died.

BÉNÉDICTE Yes . . . but . . . I never knew . . . er . . . him. I was only about 15 months old at the time. [*Another long, tense silence*]

JM Perhaps people talked to you about him?

BÉNÉDICTE Er . . . yes . . . and . . . no. No one told me he was dead.

Bénédicte stopped abruptly and appeared to sink into an interminable silence. I continued to feel ill at ease and even began to wonder if she were suffering from some form of thought disorder.

However, her facial expression was most communicative—a desperate expression, as if no words could hope to transmit what she was feeling. To break the anxious silence, I remarked that it must be difficult to talk about a father whom she had never known.

BÉNÉDICTE It's just that my . . . mother hid his death from me. Whenever I asked about him she always said, "He's in the hospital." She made everyone in the family lie to . . . er . . . me also. I was more than five when a neighbor . . . told me the . . . er . . . the . . . the . . . er . . . truth.

Bénédicte went on to say that this discovery had not upset her unduly. Since she had never known her father, she had never given him a thought. I asked myself whether this was the case because she *already knew the truth.* It seemed unlikely that a sensitive child of five would not have suspected some mystery about her supposedly alive but invisible father. As Bénédicte's silence continued, I also wondered whether Bénédicte's mother had invented the fiction of the eternally ill father because she could not deal with her own bereavement. If this were so, the father's death might have become forbidden knowledge for the little girl. Bénédicte said that when she confronted her mother with the news she had gained from the neighbor, her mother burst into tears and she felt upset at having caused her mother such distress. She added that her mother never spoke to the indiscreet neighbor again. Bénédicte's thoughts now turned to a fictitious aspect of her mother's personality.

BÉNÉDICTE My . . . mother is an unreal person. Everything about her is false . . . even her nose that she had remade. Whenever I was worried about anything she would say, "Don't frown! You'll get wrinkles on your forehead." My worries didn't interest her, only my appearance . . . only what the . . . "others" would think if they . . . saw me. [*Bénédicte frowned at me with an inquiring look, as though seeking to reassure herself that I would be more interested in her anxiety than her wrinkles.*] She never understood why I didn't want to be what she called . . . er . . . *feminine.* We have nothing in common, my mother and I. She . . . she can keep it, her . . . femininity! It's totally in authentic. Only what she thinks *others* . . . think you're supposed to be like is what counts. Her infallible system for getting through life! [*Long silence*]

JM So you resisted her system?

BÉNÉDICTE I only like . . . authentic women. [*Another interminable silence ensued before she continued with the thought that preoccupied her.*] To resemble . . . er . . . her would have been . . . er . . . to stop existing . . . to be . . . nothing.

Although Bénédicte spoke slowly and softly, every word and every bodily movement revealed an inexpressible tension. After more stumbling silence, she said she had some difficult life situations to face and resolve in addition to her writing block. She then asked if she could come to see me from time to time. Sensing her extreme anxiety with regard to this new encounter, I proposed a second consultation for the following week, the day of her fortieth birthday. She smiled and replied gravely, "Thank you. I shall stay alive until then."

At our second meeting Bénédicte talked of her love-life, the difficult "life situations" about which she had hinted the previous week.

BÉNÉDICTE Frédérique and I have been lovers for many years, ever since the . . . death of her husband. Her presence was always . . . vitally important to me. But now . . . I've lost interest in the . . . er . . . passionate side of our relationship. We're still very close friends, and see each other every day . . . but I can't bear the pain that I'm causing her. And yet I . . . can't go back either.

Haltingly, Bénédicte then described her relationship of the past three years with Véronique. She had hidden all knowledge of this second relationship from Frédérique, saying that it was the first time she had ever deceived or lied to her dearest friend. Outwardly there appeared to be some similarity between Bénédicte's two lovers: In each case the other woman had initiated the relationship; both women were mothers and both were widowed. Perhaps Bénédicte read in my facial expression an inner reflection that a dead man always appeared on the scene of her life story. In any case, she continued with a statement that appeared like a negation of my unspoken thought. "Neither of these two . . . important women in my life bears the slightest resemblance to my . . . er . . . mother."

Bénédicte stared at me anxiously, as if fearing I might not be in agreement. A few weeks later she believed she had the proof of my "disagreement." Just before a session, she discovered, in a nearby store, a psychoanalytic book dealing with female sexuality; included in this volume was a chapter on female homosexuality that I had written. Bénédicte reported her discovery as soon as she arrived, saying with much stumbling and circumlocution, that she disagreed with what she had read. I replied that I would be most interested to hear her comments.

BÉNÉDICTE Your chapter says that the . . . homosexual girl has an idealized image of her . . . mother as an unattainable model, and so she gives up all hope of rivalry with . . . her. Instead she takes her . . . father as a model. I *loathed* my mother. I had no wish *ever* to be in rivalry with her! As for my . . . er . . . father, since I never knew him, it's improbable that he could have been a model for me, beneficial or otherwise.

Indeed, Bénédicte appeared to be something of a psychic orphan. Her internal world, as she presented it in our initial encounters, was inhabited only by an "unreal" mother depicted as a mannequin and a dead father experienced as never having existed. While she was speaking, I thought to myself that the article in question had been written more than 25 years ago. I recognized that some of my generalizations were unwarranted—the product of insufficient experience combined with overly sufficient exuberance at the time of writing it. With the hope of encouraging Bénédicte to explore further her own critical viewpoints, I limited myself to the statement that there were many hypotheses in that chapter that I would challenge today. Although the chapter emphasized the role of the mother, considerable material also pertained to the father in the homosexual girl's universe. I was struck by the fact that Bénédicte extensively explored her feelings about her mother, but she totally overlooked the possible impact a dead father might have had on a little girl—especially given the strongly negative maternal representation she had presented.

Although reticent about engaging in a "real analysis," Bénédicte asked if she could come to see me more regularly, since she now had a clearer vision of what she was seeking to discover about herself. Eventually the analysis took place on a four-times weekly basis and continued for some eight or nine years.

In my notes following our first sessions, I felt a need to formu-

late the questions aroused by my interaction with her. These que-
ries came under three major headings:

1. *Would this psychoanalytic adventure be dedicated to the search for
   the father?* A 15-month-old child has little capacity to accomplish
   the work of mourning. Where, in this small girl's psyche, might we
   hope to find a buried trace of the dead father?
2. *How would a little girl of this age construct her image of her core
   gender and sexual identity* under the circumstances described by
   Bénédicte?: a father presented to the growing child as alive but
   invisible, and a mother whose behavior was interpreted by the
   daughter as meaning that she was little more than a narcissistic
   extension of her mother.
3. *What might Bénédicte be able to teach me about the creative process and its vicissitudes*? When internal conflicts give rise to inhibitions in creative work, a complicated inner drama invariably un-
   folds.

The first question concerns a situation that has occurred frequently in my own practice as well as that of my colleagues. The
number of analysands whose fathers have disappeared during
childhood due to abandonment or death appears to be greater
than that found in the population at large. Should this potentially
traumatic disappearance occur in the preverbal era of early childhood, it is handled by compensatory defensive structures that
differ from those used by an older child, who relies mainly on
language and verbal thought processes to come to grips with traumatic events. In Bénédicte's case it also appeared that her mother
had not handled her husband's death in such a way as to mitigate
its traumatic potential for her child.

My second question concerns the infantile roots of sexual identity-feeling. What are the central elements that contribute to the
particular way in which an individual structures the representations of his or her gender identity and sexual role? As Freud was
the first to point out, these psychic acquisitions cannot be taken
for granted; they will be constructed by the growing child in relation to information received from the parents. As mentioned in
Chapter 1, there is also the early transmission from mother to
nursling of the basic elements of sexual and love relationships to
come, as well as transmission of the father's libidinal investment
in his wife and his baby.

My third question arose from observations made over a number of years with analysands whose creative work had become sterile. As already noted, much reflection has led me to the conviction that the creative process is founded on the integration of bisexual drives and fantasies among other important factors. A breakdown in the capacity to work creatively often involves an interdiction stemming from unconscious bisexual identifications as well as the nature of the parental imagos in the creator's internal universe.

THE FIRST TWO YEARS OF ANALYSIS

Bénédicte became rapidly and intensely involved in her psychoanalytic adventure, bringing to our sessions dreams, daydreams, thoughts, and feelings, illuminated by an unusual richness of metaphor. At the same time, her way of speaking remained laborious, stumbling, often inaudible, and invariably interspersed with long periods of silence. She gave the impression that every gesture, every word, was retained and carefully monitored before being released. Convinced that Bénédicte could not communicate differently without doing violence to her own way of relating, I did not interpret the possible significance of this hesitancy in the early months of our work together.

There were also glimpses of a fantasy that any rapprochement between us was potentially dangerous. At the beginning of each session, before slowly settling herself on the couch, Bénédicte kept an avid eye on me and my surroundings, as though seeking to drink in information. (Some years later, when I gave her my notes of our work together to obtain permission to use her material for a scientific paper, she wrote, "I felt like a thirsty wanderer warily searching the desert for fear the oasis would become a mirage.") Then she would cease her staring, just as she would abruptly interrupt her phrases. In a painfully halting manner she would comment on the slightest modification in the appearance of my consulting room: the haphazard arrangement of a pile of reviews or the displacement of a lamp or an art object. The same close scrutiny was applied to my general appearance and the exact position of my chair in relation to the couch. These infinitely small changes (of which I was rarely aware) gave rise to timid but insistent questioning on Bénédicte's part. When I invited her to tell me

what she thought the answers might be, she constructed highly
improbable theories to explain the insignificant changes, usually
centered on the same theme: "My presence bothers you, since
you prefer to be with someone else or engaged in some other
occupation." In other words, she constantly sought some sign that
would confirm the contrary, that would dispel her uncertainty
about whether her existence mattered to me.

This incessant search for meaning — which, once found, resembled a child's reasoning — was intimately connected with her childhood attempts to make sense out of her mother's confabulations
and incoherent communications. Bénédicte believed that she must
discover the truth *alone*, not only regarding her father's death
but also about her mother's frequent absences (once widowed,
Bénédicte's mother conducted a feverish search for a new mate).
In their transference version — Was I a widow? Did I have a child?
Did I or did I not have a man in my life? — these preoccupations
added to Bénédicte's struggle with verbal expression, and she continued to stammer, insert lengthy pauses, and muffle the sound of
her voice.

Quite apart from the fantasy of danger attached to communication with others, Bénédicte was frightened of *words in themselves*.
She handled them like concrete objects capable of turning into
dangerous weapons. Her anxious, stumbling way of using language also created confusion, as if the interpenetration of primary
and secondary process thinking that characterizes a free-associ-
ative analytic discourse was, in Bénédicte's associations, closer to
dream work.

THE DEAD FATHER COMES TO LIFE

The following notes, taken from two consecutive sessions in
our third year, provide a glimpse into the internal relationship my
patient maintained with the constraining and implosive representation of her mother. This vignette also illustrates some of the
reasons why all interchange with others, verbal or otherwise, filled
Bénédicte with anxiety.

BÉNÉDICTE I dreamed last night that I was getting on a city bus. I had to
. . . stamp a one-hundred franc note that was for . . . you. But the

machine was blocked. Something was missing on the note. Someone behind me said, "Go on! It'll work," and I . . . woke up.

[*Bénédicte's associations to the dream, announced in a low, stifled voice, led her to think of her friend Frédérique and of the pleasure she experienced in giving money to Frédérique and her family, in spite of the fact that Bénédicte had little money for her own needs. I pointed out that the hundred-franc note of the dream was for me.*]

BÉNÉDICTE I . . . suppose I'd like to be the father of your family, too. Instead, all I can give you is money. But there's something . . . missing. I dare not imagine I could give you anything more valuable.

JM This sounds like a certain image of your mother. You said it was always impossible to know what she really wanted from you.

BÉNÉDICTE Oh! She wanted me not to exist—outside of herself! The machine in my dream . . . it made a crunching noise as though it were chewing off a bit of the note.

JM What does that make you think of?

BÉNÉDICTE The sign that's on the automatic gates of the metro: *Obli-térer votre billet.* [*This notice, which appears in all Parisian metro and bus stations, simply means "cancel your ticket," although the verb* oblitérer *carries the same etymological sense of obliteration as in English.*] That's what you have to do as you get in the bus. I have trouble pronouncing that word because it's so violent. I know *oblitérer* only means that you've got to get your ticket stamped, but it suggests stamping *out*, obliterating, the person. Total destruction. That machine is . . . my mother! The infernal, maternal machine!

JM [*Bénédicte had easy access to her hatred of her mother as a danger-ous and destructive introject, but this highly cathected representation prevented her from recognizing her own primitive, destructive wis-hes. She, too, is the "blocked machine," as am I, for whom the note is intended. I redirected her associations to the transference situation.*] But in the dream the destructive exchange took place be-tween *us*.

BÉNÉDICTE That idea displeases me. *Billet . . . billet-doux . . .* I can recognize tender feelings for you. But violence, even in words, hurts me.

JM Are you afraid that your violence will hurt me? That I do not want to meet this violent one in you who is clamoring to express herself?

Bénédicte was silent for a while but finally continued in a dream-like way to examine other words associated with her dream images, in which both violent and erotic thoughts occurred in rapid succession. I asked Bénédicte if she were afraid that her destructive and erotic wishes might be linked—and perhaps confused—in her mind. Her response was immediate: "My mother made everything seem dirty. That's why I couldn't even pronounce some of the . . . er . . . words that came to mind just now. They . . . er . . . they . . . well . . . er . . . had to do with . . . er . . . excrement."

A phrase from a letter of Ernest Hemingway crossed my mind: "All my life I've looked at words as though I were seeing them for the first time." For a writer, particularly, words, imbued with every form of instinctual excitement, may readily become dangerous objects for the mind.

Bénédicte's chain of anal-erotic and anal-sadistic signifiers revealed some of the classic fantasies that so often underlie infantile sexual theories. However, I did not interpret these, since her dominant anxiety at this point appeared to be centered around symbolic equivalents in which word-presentations and thing-presentations became confused. This contributed to her difficulty in using words to communicate her "excremental" thoughts. At such times, she reminded me of former child patients who had speech defects. Although Bénédicte did not suffer from stammering, a casual meeting with her might have given this impression. I drew attention to her fear of words. "You're right," she acknowledged. *"I'm as terrified of words as children are of ghosts."*

At that moment I felt as though I, too, were encountering a ghost on Bénédicte's psychoanalytic voyage. The strange silence that surrounded her father's fate, his never-mentioned illness and his zombie-like existence—which the mother's confabulations had created in the little girl's mind—continued on the analytic stage. I invited Bénédicte to tell me more about "ghost stories" that children might fear.

BÉNÉDICTE Stories of people returning from the tomb always fascinated me for some reason . . . especially those about ghosts with visible wounds that still continued to bleed.

JM Do you have any particular ghost in mind?

BÉNÉDICTE Oh!! You mean . . . er . . . him? Yes . . . er . . . I think, maybe, I waited for . . . er . . . him to come back.

Bénédicte then talked for the first time about what she knew of her father's sudden disappearance. It had taken three years for her to be able to pronounce the cause of his death. The word, as well as its referent, had seemed literally unspeakable. Bénédicte's father, at the age of 40, had died of *rectal cancer.*

The following day Bénédicte's metaphors from the previous session and the fantasies they evoked in me were still vivid in my mind: an excited yet terrified little girl awaiting the return of her father from beyond the tomb; the father's death in terms of anal implosion; fantasies of the primal scene in oral- and anal-sadistic terms; the conflictual dream images in which traces of an archaic primal scene could be detected in the meeting between the machine (a phallic-anal signifier in Bénédicte's associations) and the hundred-franc note destined to be "obliterated," while at the same time representing a love gift (the *"billet-doux."*) On rereading my session notes I realized that she and I together had somehow created the meaning.

New elements gave rise to further food for thought. Bénédicte began the session with an association concerning her ever-present distrust of verbal communication and "an urgent need to close myself up against invasion from others—especially from my mother, who never took her eyes off me. She believed she had the right to know everything I did and everything I thought."

At this stage of our work together it seemed probable that I, too, would be experienced as an anally implosive and controlling mother, watching Bénédicte's every gesture and seeking the meaning behind every word. But my interpretation of this feeling was apparently untimely. Bénédicte could not yet accept that I might embody this bad mother. Once this aspect of the transference became recognizable and acceptable to Bénédicte, along with the exploration of her fantasies of mutual destruction, she began to speak easily and audibly for the first time, not only in the session, but also with her friends, who commented on the fact that she no longer "mumbled." I learned that Frédérique had always accused Bénédicte of "swallowing her words."

Bénédicte then began to explore the possible reasons for her vocal hesitancy. "As an adolescent I never dared open my mouth . . . as if my mother might fly into it. And I could never close a door. She would surge after me and throw it open. Even now, on my rare visits home, she listens in on all my telephone conversations."

Undercurrent fantasies of oral- as well as anal-sadistic penetration became increasingly transparent. I began to feel as though I, too, were this little girl who believed it was forbidden to close the doors of either her body or her mind to the invasive representation of her mother. Later Bénédicte was able to reconstruct, from forgotten memories, fantasies of her mother killing her father in primitive oral and anal ways.

BÉNÉDICTE My mother constantly cleaned up after me. My papers, my notes, my cigarettes, were all put away the moment my back was turned. I would no sooner get out of a chair than she rushed forward to smooth away the mark of my body on the cushions. I was not to leave the slightest trace of my presence. [*The theme of the "trace," and its "obliteration" was destined to become a richly significant leitmotif.*]

Then I had to look at her, too. She would put on a sort of erotic spectacle for me, dressing and undressing in front of me, asking which of her clothes I found the most seductive. This was part of her ritual for catching a new husband. She would insist that we both get dressed up to impress eventual suitors. "We must look nice for Mr. R, mustn't we?" Violence was the only way out. I closed myself off in stony silence. She complained for years that I wouldn't talk to her.

Bénédicte's words had stirred up feelings of violence in *me*, which perhaps was the reason I asked her at this point if she could tell me more about her fantasies of violence as a protection against her mother's demands. Hesitantly, and to my surprise, she recounted one of her erotic fantasies for the first time. "This is the most exciting scene I can imagine . . . I'm a young man and I'm being violently sodomized by a much older man."

My own associations were as follows: The fantasy of her father killed through anal penetration is transformed into a scene in which her father, the "older man," becomes a lively phallic representation; anal penetration is now erotically exciting and no longer mortally dangerous. The scene implies a fantasy of literally incorporating the father's penis and phallic strength, much as small children imagine taking narcissistic and libidinal possession of their parents.

I then pondered the predicament of a little girl of 15 months, whose father is suddenly missing when she needs him. Most children of this age turn to their fathers in an attempt to detach themselves from their wish for/fear of dependence upon their mothers. With support from the father — his actual presence and the fantasies surrounding him — small children are able to separate from their mothers and, at the same time, strengthen their sense of subjective as well as sexual identity. To whom did Bénédicte turn to accomplish this vital task?

JM You say the only response to your mother's seductive attitude was violence. Could the violent sodomy also be a way of protecting yourself against her by invoking the image of a man?

BÉNÉDICTE I had to hide all my childhood games from her . . . Superman, Batman, and the others were my constant companions. I was always a boy among men. She would never have allowed that!

JM You had to hide your wish to be a boy as well as your wish to have a man as a friend?

BÉNÉDICTE Yes . . . I'm beginning to see . . . this was the only way to have a secret relationship with my father . . . in spite of her!! If she'd found out, she'd have taken him away from me again. I used to spend hours making up stories about these powerful men who were my friends. Oh, I'd forgotten . . . in my adolescence I wrote what I called an "opera." Months of work. Then one day the book disappeared from my room. I never found it again. She destroyed it! It was something that took me away from her.

The theme of Bénédicte's "opera" was revealing. She recounted: "The whole action takes place in the subway. It is an all-male cast. The central characters are a little boy, a gang of bad boys, and a villainous old man. The little boy is betrayed by the old man. At the end of the opera, brokenhearted the little boy throws himself under a train."

In reply to a question Bénédicte linked the intriguing idea of calling her play an *opera* to the word *operation* and fantasies of her father "in the hospital." She surely must have felt betrayed by "villanous old" absent father who, imprisoned in her mother's words, gave Bénédicte no sign of recognition or remembrance. A number of free-floating hypotheses came to mind as I tried to identify with that little girl of the past. Did she have a fantasy that her father, in abandoning her, had castrated her? That he had left her to the mercy of her mother, thus compelling her to keep him alive in daydreams, games, and later, in her written stories? And was she able, in this way, to maintain her own feeling of integrity and identity?

I pondered the role that *words* might play in relation to the

parental imagos in a small child's mind. In reflecting on Bénédicte's opera, it seemed to me that words might well be apprehended as the embodiment of paternal power and presence. There
is little doubt that the *mother* is, as Aulagnier (1975) phrases it,
the *"porte-parole"* for her infant, in that it is she who brings her
child into contact with the external world of language. Through
words, the mother gives meaning to preverbal bodily perceptions
and fantasies—as well as naming her child's emotional states,
bodily zones, and functions. In so doing, she also helps her child
to construct a clear representation of the difference between its
own and its mother's body and self. However, although verbal
communication is transmitted by the mother, it also comes to
represent an external or "third" power that will be used as a protection against the "siren-mother." The mother's *voice* rekindles
fantasies of the wish for fusion, with the consequent loss of both
subjective—and sexual—identity, whereas the *words* learned from
her compel separation and autonomy.

In that words replace a more archaic "language" composed of
preverbal signifiers, they always leave a residue of the thing-
presentation, for which they are the symbol, as well as much of
the meaning (of a somatopsychic order) they are purported to
transmit. In this sense they are doubly symbolic. Over and beyond
the essential importance of language in the structuring of the human psyche, it is obvious that words play a particularly privileged
role for a professional writer. As a synthesis of the "mother"
world and the "father" world, they are inextricably linked with
unconscious bisexual fantasy.

In Bénédicte's case, the paralysis of her creative possibilities
was beginning to reveal itself as an imaginary way of renouncing
her secret link to her father through language and story-building,
since this link was felt to be forbidden by her mother. In destroying her "opera," Bénédicte's mother may well have sensed, in a
confused way, that this work represented a serious rival: Her only
child was escaping her. On the psychoanalytic stage, as the image
of the internal father slowly came alive, mobilizing dynamic
thoughts and fantasies in its wake, Bénédicte began to write again.
The first book she published, two years after the beginning of her
analysis, led to her participation in a national television program
devoted to contemporary authors. During this broadcast a member of the panel asked Bénédicte a question concerning the sophis-

ticated and somewhat impalpable impression conveyed by her novel. Bénédicte replied, "It's because this is a book written by a child."

THE FATHER BECOMES
A PRE-OEDIPAL RIVAL

Bénédicte's search for the lost father did not proceed without a concomitant resistance, however, for there was in her, as in every child, an internal father who must be eliminated as a stumbling-block to the illusory hope of taking full possession of the mother. In addition, the apparent determination of Bénédicte's mother to create in her child's mind an imaginary family where only females counted suggested that oedipal interdictions may have been trans-mitted at an unduly young age, perhaps before a secure sense of sexual identity was established. Thus the mother's unconscious fears and wishes coincided with that part of little Bénédicte who wanted an exclusive relationship with her mother, arising from the primary homosexual longings that are a vital component in acquiring a sense of either masculinity or femininity. It was there-fore not surprising that dreams and daydreams began to surface in which Bénédicte herself was responsible for the death of her father. A dream theme, which had persisted for many years, de-picted Bénédicte being pursued for an unknown crime she had committed.

One day, when Bénédicte was struggling in a confused way with these various internal fathers and mothers, I decided to interpret the different "I's" seeking to express themselves in her associa-tions.

JM There are several Bénédictes talking here at the same time. There's the little boy trying to keep alive an absent father; then the young man who's protecting himself "violently" from his invasive mother; then there's also the woman in you who seeks to repair another woman with her love, as well as trying to be different in every way from her own mother.

BÉNÉDICTE I recognize all of them, but I know some of the Bénédictes better than others.

JM And you seem to be having difficulty in finding the little girl in you who longed to have *both* her parents. You're still struggling with the incoherent images of *your parents* as a couple. [*This phrase aroused a massive negative reaction.*]

BÉNÉDICTE It's absurd to hear you say *your parents*. No child ever wished for *two* parents! In that way, at least, I was lucky. That little girl had no father!

Bénédicte's anger over this interpretation continued for many weeks, during which time she accused me of being the victim of "social bunkum," of using "second-hand ideas," as well as displaying sentimentality over the death of some unknown father.

THE TRACE

An unforeseen incident provided us with the opportunity of crystallizing a "trace" of Bénédicte's father and the catastrophic consequences of his death. One day, the sound of a voice from the small office next to my consulting room alerted me to the fact that I had forgotten to switch off my answering machine. For the first time in some four years of analytic work with Bénédicte, I got up in the middle of the session and left the room to attend to this.

BÉNÉDICTE While you were gone, I dreamed up an amusing scene. I had an impulse to leave the room myself and began to imagine what you would think, on coming back and finding the room empty.

JM What was I going to think?

BÉNÉDICTE Well, first of all you wouldn't be sure if I'd really been there or not before you left the room. But then, just as I imagined myself running away, I remembered that I'd left so quickly, I'd forgotten my jacket on the chair! So the whole scene was ruined.

JM [*Thinking of Bénédicte's mother who "could not tolerate the slightest trace" of Bénédicte's presence, plus the sudden disappearance of her father, I answered without reflecting*], "You would have left a trace behind?"

BÉNÉDICTE Good heavens, yes! The jacket! His jackets!! He must have left his jackets! My cousins told me he had a lightning illness. No one expected him to die. Those jackets—I still remember the smell of them—not my father's but my *uncle*'s. When I was six or seven, after we went back to live with my grandmother, I used to spend hours playing in his wardrobe, smelling and touching his jackets. It was one of my favorite games . . . so exciting . . . But I was very careful to hide it from my mother.

The image of a little girl desperately trying to find her lost father through preverbal — yet identifying — signifiers began to imprint itself on my mind. The jackets and their manly smell appeared to have acquired the significance of transitional objects for the bereaved child.

Later Bénédicte told me how, in early adolescence, she often played a game in which she imagined that it was her job to select and buy men's clothes for an important firm. She would spend hours in clothing stores, examining the cut, the fabric, and the quality of workmanship of the suits and jackets. When her girlfriends played at being adult women picking out the clothes they would buy for themselves, Bénédicte would say that she was a married woman and had to choose her husband's clothes. She was well aware that she did not dream of a future husband, but was totally unaware that, through this game, she sought to keep alive an early sensuous link with her dead father.

Thus we found the first signs of the work of mourning, instituted by an infant who sought some trace of her father through his clothes, in the way that many children create their earliest transitional objects, demanding to sleep with a handkerchief or piece of clothing whose smell and touch recreate the presence of the mother. (This was not the first time I had observed, in children whose relationship with their mothers appeared to have been disturbed, that the highly invested transitional object that made absence bearable was something belonging to the *father*. I began to suspect that Bénédicte's father may well have played a most important role in her early infancy.)

BÉNÉDICTE All my childhood games . . . I've never thought of their meaning before, or why they were different from other children's games. I only knew that my mother would disapprove. I was supposed to play *her* games, not mine!

[*A recurring screen-memory acquired additional poignancy around this time.*] Those twin dolls that someone gave me when I was nearly three, a boy and a girl . . . I only played with the boy, talking to him, dressing and undressing him, I still remember the day my mother said they needed repairing and had to go to the hospital. When they came back, they were both *girls*. The boy . . . my mother assassinated him! I still recognized him by a tiny little trace, but I never *ever* touched either of the dolls again.

Shortly after the session in which Bénédicte recalled the "assassination" of the boy doll, she recounted a new version of the repetitive dream in which she had committed an unknown crime, but this time she was merely a witness to the crime. Bénédicte dreamed that she watched a scene in which a man was killed in a neighbor's kitchen. Her associations led her to think of the film *La Grande Bouffe* (*The Huge Meal*), in which a dead man is laid out amidst the food that has been prepared for the funeral celebration. The main characters were men, but Bénédicte sought to remember the role of the woman in this film. Her various associations to both the dream and the film led me to suggest that, as a little child, she had perhaps believed that her mother had killed her father by devouring him.

This interpretation created a shock effect and triggered a stream of memories in Bénédicte—of her mother eating more than her share of Bénédicte's ice creams and discussing, at great length, her constant digestive and eliminatory problems.

The following day Bénédicte reported a dream whose theme suggested that heterosexual desire and love could lead to death. During the past months she had spoken of her strong attraction to and admiration for a young man who was a clarinet player. Although the attraction appeared to be mutual, Bénédicte forbade herself to act upon her desire on the grounds that this friend was much younger than she. Moreover, since she had known his mother in the past, in her mind this cast him the role of a son. In other words, she experienced the relationship and its attraction as incestuous in nature.

BÉNÉDICTE In my dream I was admiring a rare and beautiful bird . . . enclosed in a clarinet. I watched it with fascination. Then I turned to tell you about it and saw a look of absolute horror on your face, because the bird was being crushed inside the musical instrument. His blood—it was a male bird—I somehow knew was flowing through all the holes and his body was being torn to pieces. I realized suddenly that he was going to die and . . . woke up.

A chain of associations formed in my own mind while listening to Bénédicte's account of her dream: The bird, whose body was being crushed while it lost its blood through the holes, evoked in me the thought that this image might pertain to Bénédicte's fantasies around her father's rectal cancer and death. This hypothesis was strengthened by the incest taboo associated in Bénédicte's mind with the clarinet player. The instrument might then became a dream representation of Bénédicte's own sex as an organ that would be dangerous for any man toward whom she felt a sexual attraction. Once again, there was a glimpse into a strange and terrifying primal scene imagined by a child. My role in the dream is to reveal its horror to Bénédicte. (The analyst usually gets this role!) Bénédicte's associations took this factor as their starting point.

BÉNÉDICTE My first thought . . . I want you to shock me, perhaps batter my mind, with your interpretations. Like yesterday . . . about my mother having killed my father by eating him. Maybe women can crush men to death as well.

JM [*Bénédicte now invites me to commit verbal violence; through my words I am to embody the castrating and murderous image that the small Bénédicte of the past attributed to her mother. While examining her transference feelings, Bénédicte began to think about the violence and fierce jealousy she felt for my other patients as well as about the anger she felt at discovering my husband's name on a mailbox at the entrance to my building.*]

BÉNÉDICTE In fact, I want to be not only your only patient, but the only person *in your life.*

JM To devour me?

BÉNÉDICTE Yes! Do I want to crush the life out of you? Good heavens, I'm exactly like my mother! [*The phallic castration represented in the dream hides a prototypic castration fantasy in which life itself is endangered.*] Under the mask of love, my mother sucked the blood from my veins. [*A long pause*] I'm shocked to discover that there's a part of me that wants to do exactly the same to the people I love — especially men. I've never allowed myself to love *and* desire a man sexually. But there's something different when my lover is a woman. In love I refind my body through the body of another woman — provided she herself loves her body and takes pleasure in lovemaking. Then there's no murderous exchange. That's one thing my mother did not manage to crush and obliterate!

Bénédicte remained silent as she reflected over the changing images in the dream and the thoughts that followed. Just before the end of the session she posed the poignant question, "But *whose* body do I live in?" Here Bénédicte touched upon her confusion regarding her sexual identity — and even her identity as a separate individual — that had plagued her since early childhood.

BÉNÉDICTE'S MIRROR REFLECTS A NEW IMAGE

A final fragment from this phase of her analysis illustrates the link between biparental identifications and the construct of sexual identity. In Bénédicte's case, this developmental task had been rendered more difficult due to the sudden loss of her father. The trauma could not be elaborated psychically because the mother herself was unable to deal with it. The following analytic fragments were noted in the fifth year of our work together.

BÉNÉDICTE [*As she lay down on the couch*] I scrutinize you all the time . . . your way of holding yourself . . . the way you walk and sit . . . your clothes, your hairstyle, your makeup.

JM What do you hope to learn from this careful scrutiny?

BÉNÉDICTE I want to know how you see yourself as a woman . . . what it feels like to be a woman. I don't know what a woman is . . . or a man either. This weekend, for the first time in five years, I tried to imagine your *body* under your clothes.

A heavy silence followed, as though she were afraid to continue. I also was struck by her emphasis on the "five years" of our analytic work, thinking of the secret calendar we all carry in our preconscious minds, and of the fact that Bénédicte was five years old when the truth of her father's death could no longer be denied.

BÉNÉDICTE But I couldn't go any further with the thought of your body, as though . . . I were afraid you would . . . disapprove.

JM What would I disapprove of?

BÉNÉDICTE The idea comes to me that you might have something to hide.

JM And what am I hiding?

BÉNÉDICTE Something like . . . a mutilation . . . or a shameful deformity.

The fact that, on several occasions, we had discussed the notion of woman as a castrated man led me to feel that the present associations were related to fantasies more primitive, or more specific to Bénédicte, than the so-called feminine castration. I invited her to try to imagine the nature of my deformity in more detail, to which she responded, "It's difficult to divulge all my thoughts since last Friday . . . things I have carefully avoided revealing from the very beginning of my analysis."

Bénédicte went on to recount how her friend Véronique had informed her, some years ago, that Bénédicte's pubic hair was distributed "in a masculine way." Her lover claimed she found it attractive, but this comment had evoked in Bénédicte a feeling of explosive rage and hatred toward Véronique. Bénédicte had suffered all her life from the impression that her body was monstrous and, as she often put it, "ambiguous." Véronique's observation had suddenly confirmed this longstanding fantasy.

BÉNÉDICTE   That's the reason I always wear tight-fitting jeans and clinging sweaters. If clothing floats around my body, it might give the impression I have something to hide . . . as though my female shape might not be evident, or as though I might be afflicted with a man's sex. Even if I consciously wished for a male body as a child, I certainly don't today. But the sudden appearance of these secondary sexual characteristics is just terrifying to me. I've not worn shorts or bathing suits for years and I've entirely given up swimming and sunbathing because of this unsightly hair.

In reply to my question about the "sudden appearance" of this "masculine" pubic hair, Bénédicte explained in detail that as far as she could recall, it had occurred shortly after the death of Frédérique's husband. For a number of years before his quite unexpected death, Bénédicte—who knew that Frédérique was very unhappy with her husband—ardently desired to take his place and had frequently fantasized ways of killing him. Since his actual death, she had often wondered whether the shock of reality replacing fantasy had produced a "hormonal change."

Just before the end of the session I pointed out to Bénédicte that she had talked about her own feeling of being mutilated but had not been able to explore further her fantasy of my "shameful deformity." Alone in her apartment that evening, the realization that both of our bodies were female and could be compared had given Bénédicte the conviction that she had a right to study her own body in more detail. The following day she described her experience.

BÉNÉDICTE Last night, after the session, I tried to imagine your body and its resemblance to mine, and to grasp what was so forbidden about this thought. I stood in front of the mirror and, for the first time in years, looked at myself in the nude. Would you believe it — there's nothing at all wrong with my pubic hair! Absolutely nothing! It isn't the neat and pretty triangle it could be, but there's no hint of anything masculine. And to think of all those years I've hidden my "monstrosity" from everybody!

We then examined Bénédicte's conflicted feelings following the death of Frédérique's husband. On one hand, a husband had to die before she could feel secure about her place in the world. In her imagination his death would allow her to possess what she had not felt entitled to take from her mother — her own femininity, through the gift of femininity from another woman. At the same time, a deeply unconscious fantasy pushed her to seek every possible trace of a living father figure, whom she could carry around in her mind. Through her illusory "hormonal change," she would appear to have carried out a fantasy of *incorporating* the dead husband of her lover. Did she, as a very small child, believe she had *become* her lost father by a similar process of primitive internalization? In seeking to possess the mental representation of two parents capable of conferring upon her the status of subjective and sexual identity, it appeared that the price to be paid was her own castration — the forfeiture of her femininity.

BÉNÉDICTE You were the first person ever to tell me that I had had two parents. I now see that I had kept traces of my father alive everywhere, both outside and inside myself. [*I thought to myself that Bénédicte's professional life and her love-life were both living monuments to her dead father.*] I also think that you, or any woman, should be wary of me, since I don't possess my own female body. It's only through the body of another woman that I regain mine.
JM In order to possess your own body — in order to be a woman — you have to disposess me? There cannot be two women?

It occurred to me that unconscious identifications are something like one's liberty. The latter loses its significance if it can only be handed over with permission. One has to reach out and grasp it for oneself! Consolidating a firm sense of one's own sexual identity requires the freedom to internalize the psychic representation of both parents. The confusing, restrictive, and traumatic circumstances that surrounded Bénédicte's understanding of her own sexuality had left her with only partial identifications concerning her gender and sexual role.

BÉNÉDICTE Yes! It's as though I have to take something away from you — but I don't know why. I still can't imagine what your deformity might be — or did I lend you my imagined monstrosity? Anyway, I had an important thought about that. I said to myself that I love you and that no matter what monstrosity or bodily deformity you might be hiding, it would make absolutely no difference to my feelings for you.

JM In other words, you have never been sure that this is also true for you — that you, too, could be loved — no matter what body, no matter what sex, you have?

BÉNÉDICTE [*An astonished silence ensued before Bénédicte was able to reply; when she did, her voice trembled through her tears.*] How strange . . . I never believed I could be loved, with my body, with my sex. Just as I am. Just because I am . . . me.

During the weeks that followed this phase of her analysis, Bénédicte found the courage to ask her mother to give her more details about her father and her relationship with him before his death. Her mother responded that this man could not possibly have any meaning for Bénédicte, because children of that age are unaware of their fathers! Faced with Bénédicte's insistence, she did add that her father had been the one who cared for her when she was teething or restless in her sleep. He also frequently helped with her bodily care, since he did not suffer from any repugnance about soiled diapers, as did her mother. "There you were, so excited, jumping up and down at the sight of him, with your diaper full of shit, and he would grab you up and hold you in his arms, as if it didn't matter at all. You see, he wasn't a classic father." [*As she recounted this touching recollection, Bénédicte's voice broke with a sob. I also felt close to tears.*]

BÉNÉDICTE I don't understand why I feel so moved by this.

JM Perhaps it's because, without realizing it, your mother has furnished the proof that your father loved you totally; your body and all its functions were precious to him — as you yourself were.

On the same occasion, Bénédicte also learned that her father
had died when she was 18 months old, not 15 months as she had
always believed. His sudden disappearance from her life, three
months earlier, had been equated with the time of his death.

This fragment of Bénédicte's analysis illustrates some of the
primitive elements that contribute to the origins of sexual identity
feeling and its relationship to acts of creativity. These elements
include identifications to both parents, which in turn require the
capacity to resolve the bisexual and incestuous wishes of childhood, to tolerate similitude and difference, as well as to assume
the psychic conflicts and mental pain of the past.

In Bénédicte's case the traumatic impact of the sudden disappearance of her father when she was only 15 months old was
intensified by her mother's inability to face the loss of her husband. Her attempt to deny that the father had ever truly existed
for her daughter had forced Bénédicte to accomplish a magical
mourning for her lost father by, in a sense, becoming him. Within
a relatively short span of time, she produced several fascinating
themes for upcoming books. I felt that only unusual circumstances could again cause this creative source to run dry.

I hope that this fragment of Bénédicte's analysis conveys something of the struggle that the little girl, caught in a web of traumatizing circumstances, was obliged to maintain in order to protect
her feeling of identity and her sexuality — as well as the extent to
which this struggle played a role in both stimulating and paralyzing her creative potential. Her sexual orientation and her creative
activity were both tributes to the dead father and attempts to
survive this loss.

In the three years that followed, Bénédicte and I weathered our
way through storms and setbacks, making surprising discoveries
as our work continued. However, traumatic circumstances brought
her refound creativity to an abrupt standstill. Once again, violent
psychic storms had to be braved before new shores came into
sight.

The continuation of Bénédicte's psychoanalytic voyage, recounted in the next chapter, illuminates further aspects of the
unconscious sources of inhibition in creative individuals.

CHAPTER 6

Trauma and Creativity

In the being we call man there lives also a woman, in the woman too a man. That a man should think of child-bearing is nothing strange but only that this should be so obstinately denied.

— Georg Groddeck

N EARING THE END of the sixth year of her analytic voyage, Bénédicte made some timid proposals about the need to terminate her analysis. I told her that we could conceive of terminating within the coming year, but that, meanwhile, we would explore the thoughts and feelings aroused by the anticipated separation.

Bénédicte was relieved by the suggestion of continuing for another year before terminating and admitted that the termination was her way of ending the treatment on her own initiative. She feared I might decide at any moment that our work together could come to an end! We were able to understand that her fearful anticipation of a dramatic end without warning was a way of reliving — and trying to prevent the shock of — her father's sudden disappearance by taking the separation into her own hands.

Although I would never end an analytic partnership "at any moment," Bénédicte was not altogether mistaken in her assumption that I had tentative thoughts about the termination of our work together sometime in the coming year. In addition to the fact that the reasons for which she had initially sought help appeared to be resolved, along with many phobias and inhibitions, she was also much more at ease in herself, in her work contacts, and in her general outlook on life. Also I feared that Bénédicte might be clinging to the analysis as a substitute for a more vital love-life, and that continuing analysis could mitigate against her turning to the outside world in this respect.

Some months later, however, a disquieting atmosphere began to pervade the analytic scene. Shortly before the spring vacation, Bénédicte made reference on several occasions to a "letter-poem" she had imagined giving me on the last day before the two-week break. This was a most unusual proposal for Bénédicte, since she never indulged in any "acting-out" of this kind. We discussed the possible meaning of her wish to give me the letter-poem but without uncovering its unconscious significance. At the end of the last session before the vacation break, she laid it on my desk and asked me not to read it until the next day (by which time she would already be in the south of France).

Reading it the next day, I felt uneasy; I slowly realized that it conveyed the impression of a halting movement toward death. Reproduced below, I have translated it from the French as accurately as possible, although the beauty of the lines is lost, to some extent, in the translation.

It is called "*Calencrier*", which is a play upon words: *Calendrier* means *calendar* and *encrier* means *inkpot*, so the composed word suggests the association between one's store of memories and creative writing.

Calencrier

J'ai onze ans de plus que mon père, c'est contre-nature.

J'ai cinquante ans et sans doute que je n'ai pas fini de prendre de l'avance sur lui qui en a trente-neuf à tout casser, je veux dire à tout jamais.

Je l'ai connu, mais ma mémoire pas. Sa mort a suivi de trop près ma naissance, de dix-huit mois m'a-t-on dit, pour que ma mémoire ait pu prendre ses habitudes. Mais un jour, celui de mes trente-neuf ans à moi, ma mémoire m'a joué un tour. De magie. Elle a émérgé de la surface, opaque pourtant, d'un miroir. Un miroir à main, laché aussitôt. Sept ans de malheur. Plus quatre. J'ai onze ans de plus que mon père, c'est contre-nature.

Calencrier. Sorti à l'instant de la plume de mon stylo à réservoir, ce sera désormais le titre de ma vie. Calencrier: jeu de mot. Justement.

Contre nature, elle aussi, l'encre est moins soumise que l'eau de la clepsydre. Elle remonte le temps, le suspend, le courbe en pleins et en déliés. Sous son empire, le temps n'a plus cours.

L'encre est moins visqueuse que le sperme, mais c'est elle, seule, ne fécondant que le papier, qui engendre. Etre l'enfant de l'encre qui paraphe son propre extrait de naissance. Ou ne pas être.

L'encre est moins épaisse que le sang. Elle ne coagule pas, vous tuant d'une embolie de la mémoire. Elle coule, fine comme les traits de l'alphabet ou des chiffres, et d'elle en découle la seule vérité: bleue nuit sur blanc.

La vérité est au fond du puits. Calencrier, puits du temps passé.

Here is my translation:

The Ink-Calendar

I am 11 years older than my father. This is not natural.

I am nearing 50 and, no doubt, I shall continue to grow older than he, who, all in all, is nearly 39, and will be 39 forever.

I knew him, but my memory did not. His death followed too closely on my birth; 18 months, they told me. Too soon for my memory to keep the trace.

But one day, in my thirty-ninth year, my memory played a trick on me. Of magic. It emerged on the surface of a veiled mirror. A hand-mirror that was quickly dropped. Seven years of misfortune. Then four. I am 11 years older than my father. This is not natural.

Calendar-ink, flowing at this very instant from my fountain pen. This shall from now on be the title of my life. Calendar-ink. Play on words. Exactly. Unnatural, ink is also less subjected to time than the water clocks of former years. Ink travels backwards in time, suspends it, shapes and bends it, in complete and broken curves. Under its rule, time no longer exists.

Ink is less viscous than sperm, but it alone has the power of fertilizing paper. To be the child of ink who pens her own certificate of birth. Or not to be.

Ink is more fluid than blood. It does not coagulate to produce a memory block. It runs sweetly like the trace of letters and figures, and from it emerges the only truth: blue-black on white.

Truth lies at the bottom of the inkwell. Calendar-ink, in the well of time long gone.

When Bénédicte returned after the vacation break, I continued to feel anxious about her. I also noticed that she seemed to be suffering some physical pain. She insisted it was purely psychological; I insisted she consult a medical specialist first and we would look at the psychological aspects later. The medical consultation revealed an ovarian anomaly. Following the careful predictions of two gynecologists, it was decided that Bénédicte should have her ovaries removed. It was obvious that both physicians suspected cancerous growth. This turned out not to be the case, but the appearance of the ovaries was disquieting and an ovariectomy was performed.

This mutilating operation precipitated a return of Bénédicte's writing block, in which she was as paralyzed in her thinking and in her professional activities as she had been prior to treatment. Because of her serious operation and its subsequent effects, I decided that the analysis was far from finished.

It had been agreed that, during her two weeks of hospitalization, Bénédicte could continue her analytic sessions, if she wished, by telephone. This she did, reporting dreams and discussing the themes of stories and plays that she would write when she was back home. However, once back from the hospital, she was again totally immobilized in her writing. The following notes, from three consecutive sessions, were taken a month after her return to analysis. I have chosen them in order to highlight the relation between illness that attacks the sexual body-schema and the creative process.

SESSION 1: OF BOOKS AND BABIES

BÉNÉDICTE [*She lies down and is silent for several minutes*] My operation is another hideous secret . . . like my father's death—but the most painful part was my mother's implied suggestion that he never loved me anyway!

Bénédicte goes on to make a link between her surgery and her father's operation for rectal cancer. A childlike part of her still maintains the fantasy that her mother was responsible for his death. Through this bodily and death-like link, as we shall see, she now reveals an unconscious fantasy that her mother is also responsible for her ovariectomy. Her associations reveal that this aspect of the internalized mother is fantasized as having attacked her sexuality and her ovaries, thus destroying her capacity to bear children.

Bénédicte's concern about the novel on which she is presently "stuck"—to which she "cannot give birth"—becomes doubly poignant at this time. Its title, *The Author of the Crime*, has led me to a number of free-floating hypotheses regarding the nature of *Bénédicte's* crime. For example, in typically childlike and megalomaniac fashion, she (like many an only child—and with a dead father as well) may unconsciously believe that she destroyed the parents' possibility of ever making another baby. As a result, it may well be the small criminal Bénédicte who now can no longer produce either babies or books.

I am becoming increasingly anxious about the inscrutable sources of the severe writing block that Bénédicte's castrating operation has resuscitated. Casting about in my mind for any ideas that might help me to understand Bénédicte's unconscious conflict better, I remember a remark Bion once made to the effect that "good writers make such a demolition of the breast, that only being a genius can make up for it"!

BÉNÉDICTE I'm thinking of yesterday's dream about the woman who was trying to get down from a train and who had apparatuses where one might have expected legs; they weren't yet attached, but they were intended to be used as legs eventually—and they were laced like the corsets my grandmother wore.

JM [*Her present associations to the dream all refer to men who are dead—her father, her grandfather, the husband of her lover Frédérique, etc. I point this out to her.*]

BÉNÉDICTE Yes, they're all men, and dead ones at that! Perhaps those apparatuses are men? Or penises? As though women need some artificial support if they have no men. Of course, that's the message I got from my mother.

JM [*She then recounts the story of an elderly male friend who had had a leg amputated and weaves her way through the underlying associative links—legs-penises-amputation-castration—recalling her operation and the poignant feelings and anxieties it has aroused.*]

BÉNÉDICTE I, too, am amputated.

Bénédicte now brings up a detail from her past that, to my mind, she had never mentioned in all her years of analysis. (At this point I must add that when I asked Bénédicte for permission two years later to use this fragment of her analysis for a publication, she said that she remembered distinctly having *recounted* the incident in detail. I was surprised I had forgotten it, since it reveals a deep longing for a child that had to be denied. I am therefore obliged to ask myself why I, too, implicitly denied, through my repression, Bénédicte's right to this desire! Had I fallen into unconscious complicity with the castrating mother? Did I want to be the *only* producer of babies, of books? This query still gives me food for thought!)

BÉNÉDICTE Did I ever tell you about my only "baby"? It was a mere promise of one, just before I came to Paris, after my short love affair with Adam, whom I talked about long ago. My periods stopped throughout the summer. There was every chance I was pregnant, yet I never gave it a thought. Crazy! The truth was, I didn't believe I *could* become pregnant because I'm not real in that way.

JM Martians don't have babies? [*I had proposed the Martian metaphor some years ago in response to Bénédicte's frequent assertion that she was neither male nor female, nor even sure she truly belonged to the human race. She considered herself a failure in all these respects.*]

BÉNÉDICTE Of course, not! At least not like human beings. [*Pause*] They showed me the X-rays of my two ovaries. I have a fantasy that in one ovary was Adam's son and in the other, his daughter. They had to be taken away from me, of course!

JM The twin dolls?

BÉNÉDICTE You know, that's what she did to me—she never ever wanted a daughter. All she wanted was a girl-doll!

Bénédicte's mother now appears as a little girl with doll-babies who might attack Bénédicte's womanly self and her wish for babies of her own. Whatever her mother's pathology may have been, there is certainly an element of projection here. It is the *little girl* who tends to imagine getting inside her mother's body to take away all her treasures: the babies, the father and his penis, the secrets of femininity. This common fantasy is no doubt transformed in Bénédicte's mind into one of the *avenging mother* who has destroyed *her* ovaries so that she cannot bear Adam's babies.

BÉNÉDICTE I have two novels waiting to be born . . . so desperate . . . I can't get on with either of them. I feel like an imposter when I'm with my friends; they all believe I'm working.

JM [Bénédicte also frequently refers to herself as an "imposter" in "appearing to be a woman." This material, which has been present from the beginning of our work together, returned in force following her surgery.] So you're holding on to your babies?

BÉNÉDICTE Huh! Guess I think I'm immortal, that there will always be time. One can wait too long to produce anything! Maybe you're right. I'm holding on. Then again, I often have the feeling that if I put forth all my fantasies and daydreams, there'll be nothing left.

Here we find a further elaboration of the fantasy that Bénédicte's creativity has been destroyed by the internalized mother. The metaphor now suggests a primitive fantasy of fecal loss. With irritation Bénédicte recalls her mother's endless concern throughout her childhood about bowel functioning—Bénédicte's and her own. Bénédicte's fantasy that "there'll be nothing left" if she allows all her stories to come forth suggests that she is experiencing a *regressive version* of her right to sexual and childbearing fulfillments: the fantasy of being emptied fecally by the anxious mother of childhood. She once again fears the loss of all her precious contents. In her projection of this unconscious fantasy, it is now the "public" that will empty her.

JM Is this a refusal to be generous, to give freely? As though you're impelled to hold back something precious?

BÉNÉDICTE Can you say a bit more?

JM I was thinking it's as though you're *constipated* with this novel. [*This was a loaded metaphor, not only because Bénédicte's mother displayed such concern about defecation, but also because of her father's death from rectal cancer. Any thoughts tinged with either anal sadism or eroticism, or references to fecal functioning, tended to recall the cause of his death.*]

BÉNÉDICTE I don't really want to talk about what's on my mind . . . well . . . Frédérique gave me her comments on the few pages I've managed to squeeze out . . . or down. She made me feel that what I've written, the whole story, is just a lot of shit! Frédérique said: "It's too tight, too fast . . . you make it too hard for the reader." [*Long pause*]
    Then there's another thing that makes me anxious. It's as though I

have to prevent the public from getting their hands on me! I have to keep my distance, be careful not to give too much away when I write. Frédérique's right about that. She makes it clear it's not just shit, but she says I leave no space for emotion. Mmm . . . the result is excessively . . . er . . . constipated.

JM [*It is interesting to speculate at this point upon the many aspects an anonymous public could unconsciously represent for a writer. If Bénédicte's books are equated with either children or feces, we are not surprised to discover that her public is felt to incorporate the negative aspects of her representation of her mother as the one who will destroy all her inner contents!*]

BÉNÉDICTE So I write and rewrite, and it gets shorter and tenser all the time. But there's a reader for me somewhere out there!

JM [*Two aspects of Bénédicte are talking at the same time. On one hand, she's an esoteric writer and should not attempt to be simplistic just to please an imaginary public. I tell her that we're well aware there's a sophisticated public "out there" for her kind of talent, but what she and I are trying to grasp, right now, are the emotional impediments to her creativity—such as the attributes she lends to her public which, in turn, inhibit her wish to give this public anything.*]

BÉNÉDICTE I didn't set it up this way . . . yet it's as though I don't want it to change. It's always more of the same. Like a destiny! As though, if I can't change the past, then I can't change anything in my novels either. [*Long pause*] I should have died at 40 . . . but I went on living.

I torture myself with another problem, too. It's as though I can't get beyond the beginning . . . the beginning never starts late enough in my story, so I rewrite it again and again. [*Long pause*] If I've started this last book the way I started my life, then of course I don't want my construction to stand. It has to fall down. *I'm not supposed to create!* Like the way I had to lose my ovaries. I love taking my endless notes, but when it comes to giving birth, then I have to abort. Am I being my own mother when she destroyed the first piece of writing I ever did? Must I destroy to fulfill my destiny? What else is missing?

Bénédicte has unwittingly supplied the associations that tended to confirm my unspoken hypothesis: Her inability to create anything at the present moment is due, in large part, to her projection of destructive tendencies onto the internal mother, unconsciously equated with and reprojected upon her public. Thus she represents herself as being in no way responsible for her attack on her own productivity. Whatever the pathology of Bénédicte's mother may have been, I wonder to what extent her own childlike destructiveness may be a reflection of her infantile envy. Although her mother would appear to be a good support for such projective fantasies, our analytic exploration can deal only with Bénédicte's own unconscious motives.

These ruminations now give rise to further free-floating thoughts concerning further possible reasons for Bénédicte's tendency to attack her creative potential as well as the link between this undermining tendency and her physical trauma. If she "births" her present *book-child*, does she fear she will destroy her own child-self — the one who was destined to fail, to fall down, to be aborted? — and thus lose her masochistic tie to the angry but profoundly important relationship with her mother? Does she feel guilty, not only for believing herself to be responsible for her mother's widowhood and single-child status, but also for having reduced her mother to the "unreal" person she always claims her to be?

Creativity and Transgression

In order to create artistic or intellectual "children," one must assume one's right to be both the fertile womb and the fertilizing penis. Therefore, there is always a risk that a creative act will be experienced unconsciously as a crime against the parents. Bénédicte's associations tend to reveal a similar fantasy but include the metaphor of her productions as "just shit," leading her to fear the irrevocable loss of all her stories and characters. The "crime" will now be detected through "soiling the page" and deliberately displaying it to the whole world.

I am reminded here of "Karen" (quoted in *Theaters of the Mind*), who was in analysis with me many years ago. A gifted actress, Karen, like Bénédicte, had grown up with a disturbed body image and confused feelings regarding her sexual identity. Like Bénédicte, Karen sought refuge in the arms of women lovers. She, too, held her mother responsible for having treated her body and its eliminatory functions as dirty. As a small child Karen truly believed that she alone produced feces, whereas her mother and her sisters merely urinated. Karen suffered crippling stage fright whenever she was to appear in public; her predominant fantasy was that the audience would see that she was merely "producing filth." In previous discussions of the unconscious significance of homosexuality as a partial solution to psychic conflict (McDougall, 1978a), I linked this kind of anal fantasy to a typical childlike representation of the internal father and his penis. I would add that this link is reinforced by the child's belief that he or she had no right to *any* erotic or narcissistic pleasure that was independent of the mother's will and pleasure. In both Karen's and Bénédicte's cases, it was clearly forbidden for them to take pleasure in their artistic activities *and* to exhibit the product, whether the works were equated with children, feces, or pleasure in any bodily production or erogenic zone.

Thus to Bénédicte's question, "What else is missing?" I reply:

JM It's as though, when you give birth, it's not only dangerous and forbidden, but there must be no pleasure in the giving. Only pain. You limit your pleasure [in French, *jouissance*] to taking notes. [Jouissance *has a double meaning in French: pleasure and sexual climax.*]

BÉNÉDICTE Yes, of course, it's a solitary pleasure . . . you're not supposed to do it.

Bénédicte elaborates on the "double-entendre" of what she had described, which on one hand referred to autoerotic activity and, on the other, to her belief that only her mother's pleasure counted. To do or be anything of worth on her own constituted a serious transgression in itself. Since any independence, such as spontaneous creative activity, represented a narcissistic threat to her mother, Bénédicte's own integrity was unconsciously threatened at the same time.

This symptomatic area is also closely connected with a measure of breakdown in the maturation of *transitional phenomena* (Winnicott, 1951). From Winnicott's concept it follows that if a small child dare not play in her mother's presence, fearing that mother will either withdraw interest from her as she plays or take over the game, then any thrust toward creative independence will be fraught with this double danger. *To create* is to claim one's right to separate existence and individual identity. Bénédicte and I had worked many a time on her belief that in writing, she was transgressing an unconscious taboo; she was being disloyal to her mother. Her destiny was to repair her mother by being a narcissistic prolongation of her and, in this way, be forgiven for the death of her father (magically slaughtered by the megalomaniac baby-Bénédicte).

In actual fact Bénédicte was ill-paid for her sacrificial aim, since she was invariably put aside in favor of her mother's lovers. These lovers were not only hated rivals; their existence reduced her identity to nothing. She had interpreted her mother's communications to mean that she, Bénédicte, did not exist except as a part of the mother herself and, thus, was not entitled to any wish other than the fulfillment of her mother's desires.

"We must look pretty for Mr. E, mustn't we?" her mother would fuss, as she dressed her daughter and herself in preparation for a visit from a suitor. From early childhood Bénédicte had refused to be the "girl-doll" she felt her mother demanded; indeed, she fought violently against conforming to anything she believed her mother expected from her. To have complied would have meant "to be nothing," the equivalent of psychic death.

In her adult life Bénédicte had always refused to join her friends in any activity she felt resembled the girl-doll role (such as getting dressed up for parties or trying on amusing clothing in a festive atmosphere). However, she did fulfill the goal of being *reparative* in her two important relationships with women lovers. With each, she had in fact replaced a dead husband and had acted toward them as she believed she should have acted toward her mother.

Bénédicte now struggles with a transference thought she claims is difficult to reveal.

BÉNÉDICTE I'm worried about you. "Myrtle" was holding down a stack of urgent mail when I left yesterday. Remember, I asked if things were going badly?

(Myrtle the Turtle, my favorite paper-weight, had once again come out of my office into the consulting room. Some two years earlier Bénédicte had complained that her mother had written her name on her birth register using a masculine instead of feminine spelling, a fact that had troubled her as a child in school. On leaving the consulting room that day, she asked me what I called my turtle. Probably because secrets and correct names had been such a sensitive issue, I told her that she was called "Myrtle.")

In reply to Bénédicte's query at the end of the previous day's session, I had simply said, echoing her question, "So things are looking bad?"

BÉNÉDICTE And I see all those books and papers stacked up under the window . . . as though you can't cope with everything you have to do. The difficult thought is this: You no longer have a man in your life. Even the umbrellas are gone. [*This reference requires some explanation. With her fine eye for detail and for drawing conclusions from her perceptions, Bénédicte had often remarked on the two umbrellas my husband left in a stand in the hallway. Her fantasy was that I had two male lovers and that the one who was "in session" planted his umbrella to warn the other of his presence. When both umbrellas were present, she claimed to be shocked at my sexual behavior. Now both umbrellas were apparently missing!*] So your men have deserted you, you're all alone, broken up inside, because you just can't do everything alone.

JM Like Frédérique and Véronique, whose men are dead? You killed them magically along with your father. Maybe it's my turn now?

This interpretation took her totally by surprise. After the session I noted that we have analyzed many versions of her as a husband-killer, so I now question whether there is an added dimension, something that I am not hearing in her associations. Does she imagine she's carrying her dead father within her? Or a dead baby she has had with him? Do the "son and daughter petrified in her ovaries" also stand for parts of herself that she felt were dead? Any or all of these possibilities would be experienced as her own fault to her megalomaniac child-self: She is responsible for the dead husbands as well as the women who are abandoned, unable to cope, devitalized.

Bénédicte often presents her mother as not being truly alive in relation to others. Does she feel responsible for paralyzing the life-force in her mother? To bring forth her novel may then confirm that its story is not a fantasy. Having rendered dead or lifeless the most significant objects in her inner world, is Bénédicte indeed the author of a real crime?

I then ask myself whether she is doing something similar with me when we to go "round in circles," as in the last few sessions. If she brings this novel to life as a result of our analytic work, not only will the "crime" be revealed, but she might suffer once more, as in childhood, from overpowering guilt and fear as a consequence of her dangerous acts. Suppose the novel were not fiction but truth! Such a fear would join the many other complex reasons for which it has to be kept "unborn."

SESSION 2: AMBIGUOUS IDENTITY, ANALITY, AND CREATIVE INHIBITION

BÉNÉDICTE How do *you* work? You're not only constructing my . . . our . . . analytic story, you're also doing something else of your own, aren't you?

JM [*Analysands often sense that, at certain phases in their analytic voyage, their analysts are particularly anxious to understand; they frequently appear to "know" when we are taking notes after their sessions. Bénédicte confirms some perception of my heightened interest. I do not reply to her query, attempting instead to elicit further fantasy.*] I, too, have an unconscious mind and hidden motives?

BÉNÉDICTE Yes, I do think about that sometimes. I try to imagine what you're doing with "us," what you're thinking and feeling about what is happening here. Anyway, I know what I'm feeling! You hurt me yesterday when you put into words what I seemed to be expressing about being so stuck in my work: You said, "constipation." That shocked me. But it was still harder when you suggested that I don't want to give. I particularly hated that, because I cherish an image of myself as someone extremely generous — whereas, in fact, it's quite untrue! I *can't* give! I'm *not* generous! But you aren't supposed to know that! [*Long pause*] I wonder how much this "withholding" affects my work? With each piece of writing it's as though the first spurt is enough. I don't want to give any more of myself, of my story. The reader is supposed to *know* what the rest of the story is about.

JM [*Although the aspect of anal retention plays a prominent part in Bénédicte's present predicament, her associations also imply an omnipotent demand for understanding.*] You should be understood without having to use words?

BÉNÉDICTE It's not that I'm not saying anything — there is a public in my mind. But I think it's true that I'm holding back most of my "contents." My mother tried to get everything out of me, as though all I had, all I was, belonged to her, not to me. So I'd die rather than give birth to, or produce, anything for her! [*Pause*] Then, too, I torture myself with the idea that the present novel, the constipated one, won't be up to everybody's expectations.

JM [*We catch a further glimpse here of the immense importance of public recognition as a factor in convincing the creator that he or she is absolved of fantasized transgressions.*] Still the shit fantasy?

BÉNÉDICTE Exactly! But there's a difficulty with my characters, too. They have the same problems I do . . . I've been going over this in my mind since yesterday. My characters can't do more than they're already doing. If they try to reveal a little more of themselves, they'll become like my mother — lousy actors. It's all I can do to keep them on the page. I've only two alternatives: Either I keep *me* together . . . that's to say, *my characters*, because they're part of me . . . or else we'll end up doing what my mother does — look real but, in fact, be completely phony. So my book-child is a bit flattened out, two-dimensional. What is missing?

JM To be or not to be — your mother? No third dimension? [*I am reminded of Winnicott's statements regarding the true and the false self. No doubt the True Self, in order to remain alive and available, imperatively needs the third dimension that is represented by the father and his importance to the mother. A mother who values her sexual and love relationship with her mate will not use her child as a narcissistic extension of herself.*]

BÉNÉDICTE That's right! In everything I've written, all my male characters are killed. I guess they only come into existence to resurrect my father; that done, they may just as well die. And there's always some shadowy plot underneath. It has to be shadowy because it must be expressed in a language different from my mother's. My language is either further ahead or further behind ("*au delà ou en deça*") everyday words. Perhaps it's Martian language? — like my Martian body — ambiguous, with a shameful defect that always has to be hidden. [*Pause*] I've never had a normal body.

JM What's a "normal" body?

BÉNÉDICTE It's the body of someone who *thinks* that the body she lives in is normal. Do you remember that Véronique once remarked on my pubic hair having a masculine distribution, and that I believed I'd suffered a hormonal change after the death of Frédérique's husband? You allowed me to discover that this was a delusion on my part. Meanwhile I looked desperately at other people's bodies. They seemed okay. Since then I've read that most people are unhappy with their bodies. It helped a little to think others share some version of my suffering.

JM [*Bénédicte went on to say that, although she now knew she was not the only woman to feel such anguish, her childhood experiences had done nothing to help her construct a better body image and, consequently, a better image of herself as an individual. Here we catch a glimpse of the link between Bénédicte's present-day trauma of the ovariectomy and the impact of the past psychic traumata that have given rise to her severely damaged, "ambiguous" body image. She now links this new insight to her writing block.*]

BÉNÉDICTE I wonder if this ambiguous feeling about my body and my sexuality affects my characters as well? Take the killer who's the central character—even *his* identity keeps changing! The reader will be constantly puzzled. Frédérique complained about that, too.

JM The reader has to guess what the plot is? Like you had to do throughout your childhood about the mystery of your father's absence?

BÉNÉDICTE Yes, that's one problem that always plagues me. But there's another hang-up, too. The killer's all set; he knows his crime is going to be just about perfect. The trouble is, he doesn't know *who* to kill. He spends all his time covering up the traces of his crime before it's even been committed. The crime should take place on a train, though I don't know why.

JM [*The destroyed "opera" of Bénédicte's adolescence floats through my mind. Bénédicte is silent for a moment, presumably because the train as the carrier of death has to remain repressed. Then, as though she were branched into my own psyche, she continues.*]

BÉNÉDICTE But who's the victim? I suppose it's got to be a suicide story. How banal! [*Pause*] What started me talking about the plot? Oh, yes, *bodies*. You must wipe out all trace of a body! Or at least it must pass unnoticed . . . just like I try to do on the street. It's my way of fooling everyone so they don't discover that I have a hideous, ambiguous body. That's it! The reader has to *guess*, with no trace or clue to help!

Not only must sexual differences and sexual identity be denied, but even separate identity—otherness itself—must be shrouded in mystery. The "trace," as we have already seen, represents the sudden disappearance of Bénédicte's father, which had to be denied. Yet his death left the little Bénédicte "without a clue as to who has killed whom, and what one's identity really is."

Furthermore, the *"manque à être"* in Lacan's terminology—the "something" that will always be missing for every human being—must also be denied. It is true that Bénédicte's childhood experiences did not help her accomplish any of the mourning processes involved in the task of becoming an individual. She is now trying to compensate for this through her writing—provided she can allow herself to work!

SESSION 3: THE TWO VOICES OF CREATION

BÉNÉDICTE [*In a triumphant tone, recounting the use she made of the weekend break*] From four pages it's now become seven and a half. I'd love to bring both versions so you could see what's missing in each. Of course, I know what you'd say: "*You* tell *me* what's missing; the missing part is inside you, obeying some unknown force." Deep down, I'm glad I can't and won't bring my work to you. The solution's inside me. You showed me that right from the beginning. [*Long pause*]

Chaplin's *City Lights*, with those tear-jerking techniques of his, comes to mind . . . the effects that I've sometimes produced without knowing how.

JM [*Bénédicte's stories are often strangely moving, in spite of her efforts to prune emotional impact to the minimum. She is non-plussed by the reactions of her readers, since she believes she creates concise statements intended to convey nothing other than the complexity of the drama and the interrelations between the characters.*]

BÉNÉDICTE I *won't* write tear-jerkers! My mother is the tear-jerker artist—one big elaborated lie! All her emotions are of this variety. I'll never write that way, even if, as Frédérique says, I leave no space for feelings. Falsity has got to be eliminated so that only what's real is left. [*A long and painful silence*]

You said the other day that I always "sing in a low key." That's just the way I feel it. If I moved into a higher key, the terror of false notes would paralyze me. I can't help wondering what you'd think of my present work. [*Pause*] I'd be so ashamed if you thought it wasn't well written. I think of the letter-poem I gave you just before the spring vacation. Not only shouldn't I have done it, but like everything else, it wasn't good enough.

JM Always the same attack on everything you create.

BÉNÉDICTE Yes. The voice inside me says, "Heavens! That's terrible!" But it only speaks up when someone's going to *see* my work. Then I start to feel ghastly, terrified and ashamed. [*We've worked for a long time on everything that Bénédicte projects onto her public—the parts of herself she gets rid of in this way. I begin to wonder which level of instinctual body-fantasy is coming to the surface now: the anal crime or the murderous one?*] I suppose I'm my own mocking public much of the time, but the shame is sometimes justified, too! It's simpler to be a graphic artist—like those engravings of yours.

[*Bénédicte refers here to the engravings in my waiting room done by Oliver, an artist friend of many years standing. She has often ruminated about the engraver and his work and my choice of these particular pieces for display. Was he a patient? Did he interest me more than she did? Could I help him better because, she felt sure, he was a man.*] Oliver, like all artists, expects the eye to be willing to accept the missing details and fill in the gaps. Why can't I expect the same for my writing?

JM There are two aspects to what you're saying. The first is a reasoned discourse on literary style. But we're trying to get to the destructive and shameful voices within you that you lend to the public and with which your work becomes identified. So you expect to be attacked.

[*After the session, reflecting over Bénédicte's destructive attitude toward her writing, I came up with the same hypotheses: that every child dreams of stealing the creative potential of the parents and that creative people are prone to feel guilty about having attacked and damaged their parents (or their internal representatives). However, these fantasies have never been close enough to consciousness in Bénédicte's mind to allow such interpretations, and I must be careful that she doesn't "run away" with an idea in order to please me! Nevertheless, in the above associations I felt she was offering me ideas that we could work on together regarding the theme of falsity. I decide to propose potential feelings of guilt about being responsible for her mother's failings.*]

JM You're very afraid of producing something false and shameful that would have to be hidden. You use these identical words to describe your mother, insisting that all your mother's productions are false. You seem to be not only afraid of becoming your mother, but it's as though she were *your creation*, and a terrible one at that.

BÉNÉDICTE Oh! That's a new thought! It's true I was ashamed of her. Could I have made her that way?

JM [*Bénédicte has never accepted any interventions suggesting that there was a period of her life when she might have felt dependent on her mother, loving her, needing her, wanting to cling to her. Possibly her need was so overwhelming after the disappearance of her devoted father, that the overdependence fostered envious and destructive feelings that were too strong for her to acknowledge. Through the link with her work, Bénédicte is finally able to elaborate on possible guilt feelings toward her mother.*] The other day you saw me as being all broken up, alone, without a man.

BÉNÉDICTE Yes, I guess you were *her*. Perhaps *I* broke her up and made her into that reconstituted falsity? It's true, I remember feeling that everything that was wrong with her was my fault. Because of me she had to move back to my grandmother's house, where she was so unhappy. She hated her mother, whereas I loved and needed my grandmother. If my mother hadn't had a child, if only she'd been a "regular widow," her life would've been different. She wouldn't have *had* to go back to her mother's. When she looked terrifying, or awful, I was sure I'd provoked that, too.

[*For the first time during our years of working together, Bénédicte has assumed the infantile megalomania that is universal to children — the belief that she is responsible for everything that had ever happened in her past. After a long silence, she continues.*] You know, when your own mother can't answer a question, everything falls down. Until then, she always seemed so intelligent. Then one day you ask the question she can't answer and suddenly you've turned her into an ass! If I hadn't asked any questions . . . well, what difference would it have made?

JM "Ask me no questions, I'll tell you no lies"?

BÉNÉDICTE That's it! If I hadn't asked the questions, I wouldn't have been told a pack of lies! Yes, *I* turned her into a liar. *I* did it to her. So what you're showing me is that my contention about *her* falsity is one of the false notes in *my* song? Does this have something to do with my blocked writing?

JM Maybe you're asking the wrong questions of your characters? [*I must admit, I did not understand what made me say this or what I had in mind, but the question stirred some important ideas in Bénédicte, as we shall see.*]

BÉNÉDICTE Yes! Before I trap them into words, I've already locked them up, pushed them back into a house where they cannot breathe or live — just like I pushed my mother back into her mother's house. And then after we left my grandmother's to live in the other house, I *did* feel ashamed of my mother most of the time, especially with all her lovers. *They* were the punishment for my crimes, for not keeping my father alive, for what I'd done to her. I brought her nothing but harm. The lovers were there to do what *I* couldn't; they did her good. She showed it in every way. Her whole appearance changed. That excessive and false emotional manner disappeared; she became an entirely different person, once there was a man around. Sure, they were stronger than I was and gave her what I couldn't — everything, I guess, that *I* wanted to be able to give!

[*Bénédicte laughs suddenly.*] I was so happy at my grandmother's. [*Her voice immediately becomes grave.*] Oh, I suppose I chose myself over my mother. I took away her husband and deprived her of her constant theater, her one desire, which was to be radiant, "on stage," with a man. She made the tragedy of her situation very clear — and, of course, I understood that *I* was the tragedy. I wasn't supposed to win, after what I'd done. I had to be a loser. Maybe . . . I wonder if that's what I'm still doing? When I write the way I do, is it a way of repairing *her*? Or when I'm blocked, of refusing to do so? You said that, among the missing things in those inner voices, was my father's voice. She had no answers—only false, secondhand ideas. I needed my father . . . I'm thinking of David . . .

JM [*David was a man with whom Bénédicte had had a lengthy relationship and with whom she has remained close friends. She refused to make a life with him, for many complicated reasons—some, connected to her deep need to recover a feeling of bodily and narcissistic integrity by loving a woman. The normal integration of the primary homosexual longings of childhood had gone awry; thus the missing identifications in her inner psychic world had to be sought in the external world. She derived great pleasure in making love with her few male lovers, but afterwards always felt lost and empty, "as if I do not get my body back." In other words, her lesbian love relations enabled her to feel like, to* become, *a woman. I began to ask myself whether her writing also served this same purpose.*]

BÉNÉDICTE David's way of looking at things, of making me listen to another viewpoint, was a *man's* discourse. I felt his presence and the force of his difference. What he was telling me was important and I had to understand it. Could this be the missing element in my work? The longing for this voice is part of the "low key," of course, but it is a longing that has to remain so muted, I'm not actually listening to it fully.

JM As though you can't "sing in different keys"? Listen to both? Be both man and woman in your writing?

BÉNÉDICTE Yes! I can't give my characters enough space—*because they're men*. You know, my terror of writing a soap opera is also connected with this problem. If I turned my father or my grandfather into a soap-opera character, without any reality, then I'd deserve to die!

JM So these male characters can't become fully alive? You might destroy them?

BÉNÉDICTE Oh—what a discovery! All my male characters are naturally good fathers, but above all, what they are . . . is *good mothers*! That's their true vocation! [*Long pause*] Perhaps I'm unable to bring a man to life . . . Is this the secret of my paralyzed writing? Is this the secret of my loving? Can I only recreate, only love, a woman?

These were Bénédicte's concluding remarks as the session ended. Since this session took place shortly before the summer vacation, the issues involved were explored through their expression in the transference and the extent to which I was a "bad" mother who was going to abandon Bénédicte for the coming weeks. On the return session, Bénédicte's first words were, "I've been writing all summer and it's going well." When I made reference to her novel, she surprised me by saying that she was not concerned with "that old stuff," and then told me that she had spent the summer writing a play with an all-female cast!

TRAUMATIC SOMATIZATION AND
THE ANALYTIC PROCESS

Bénédicte's analysis continued for another year, during which time we continued to explore the psychic significance of the ovariectomy in relation to Bénédicte's creative work as well as the possible "meaning" of the somatic illness in itself.

Before concluding our exploration of the elements that contribute to creative inhibition, it is imperative to reflect on the nature of trauma itself and on the clinical and theoretical problems involved when such an event arises in the course of a psychoanalytic treatment. An event may only be characterized as "traumatic" if it subsequently gives rise to psychic *reorganization* of a symptomatic kind. In addition, a present-day event, in general, will only prove traumatic to the extent it reactivates psychic trauma from the past.

Little has been written about the fact that toward the end of — or shortly following — a lengthy analysis, reports of serious somatic illness, though not a common phenomenon, do occur. My own research provides no more than a statement of the relative frequency with which patients who have come to me seeking a second analysis have described, in passing, illnesses that followed the termination of an apparently successful analytic adventure. In addition, a small number (including five of my own analysands over a 35-year span) became somatically ill as they *approached the end* of their analyses. Although the physical illness may have arisen in any case, it is nevertheless important to question whether unanalyzed archaic fantasies and unacknowledged psychotic anxieties are more apt to be mobilized with the approaching closure of a psychoanalytic treatment — and therefore to augment psychosomatic vulnerability.

Physical Trauma and
Creative Inhibition

What, then, is the relation of trauma to creative activity? As the above fragment of Bénédicte's analysis illustrates, creative acts can be conceptualized as a fusion of the masculine and feminine elements in the psychic structure. A lack of integration of either pole of the psychic bisexual wishes of infancy may readily cause creative paralysis. Similarly, any event that threatens to overthrow the delicate balance of bisexual fantasies in the unconscious mind may also precipitate inhibition of intellectual, scientific, and artistic creation of all kinds.

Given the bisexual underpinning of creativity, the question arises whether women's creative activity differs from that of men. In my clinical experience I have noticed that men suffering from *inhibition* in their artistic, intellectual, professional, or business pursuits unconsciously tend to experience the blockage as a form of *castration*; for women, the same paralysis is more often unconsciously equated with *sterility* — which in the unconscious is also experienced as castration. (This fantasy was clearly manifested in Bénédicte's case.)

It is understandable, therefore, that any traumatic disturbance in somatic functioning or bodily integrity — particularly when it affects genital and reproductive functions — can have a profound influence on artistic and intellectual inhibitions. This potential fragility is an integral part of the creative process.

I conclude my reflections on the mysteries of the creative process with the hope that I have been able to elucidate — and communicate — a few of the elusive elements that my analysands have helped me to understand.

PART III

Sex and the Soma

CHAPTER 7

Archaic Sexualities and the Psychosoma

$\mathbf{M}$Y PSYCHOANALYTIC RESEARCH has been increasingly concerned with conceptualizing the body-mind matrix and observing traces of the earliest forms of psychic structure in the psychoanalytic situation in order to better understand their enduring effects on the growing child and the adult-to-be. These traces are inevitably marked by the biparental unconscious and their projections onto this particular infant as well as by the internal and external events surrounding the baby's conception and birth.

In the dawn of psychic life, libidinal and aggressive strivings are practically indistinguishable from one another. What are later verbally identified as the emotions of "love" and "hate" are initially confused with each other. This confusion may persist into maturity, causing adults to feel profoundly disturbed in their relationships. The unconscious equation of love and hate sometimes gives rise to feelings of panic, but more frequently is met with total foreclosure of the psychic conflicts aroused, thus increasing psychosomatic vulnerability or, more rarely, precipitating moments of psychotic decompensation. This extreme response of decompensation, in which words lose their intimate connection to the world of things, is beautifully described by the New Zealand writer Janet Frame (1988), who transports us into a world of unreality:

> . . . the prospect of the sudden annihilation of the usual perception of distance and closeness, the bursting of the iron bands that once made rigid the container of knowledge, the trickling away of the perception of time and space, although at first the shape persists as if still bound, yet if you examine it you see the widening crevices in what was believed always to be the foundation of perception. Near and far, then and now, here and there, the homely words of the language of space and time appear useless, heaps of rubble.

If we assume that the early structural development of the psyche depends, to a large degree, on the mother's and the father's unconscious fears, wishes, and projected expectations for this particular infant, it seems feasible to propose that their value judgments will impregnate the growing child's mind with an enduring template of beliefs concerning his or her biological, sexual, and psychosocial identity.

Although these biparental transmissions play a determining role in shaping the infant's psychic structure, the child's innate resources are also a determining force that creates a margin of choice in the process of growing up. Daniel Stern's (1985) concept of a "core-self" in the newborn babe captures this creative aspect of the infant's psyche. In adult analyses we frequently find that the child within, instead of identifying totally with the desires and anxieties of the external (and, later, internal) parents, readily creates strong counter-identifications to the biparental demands. These counter-identifications contribute just as forcefully to the creation of an opposing personality pattern that differs from that of the parents and endows the character structure with a similar compulsive dynamism in order to maintain the sense of subjective and sexual identity.

Such a stance is not acquired without severe anxiety about the nature of one's identity and one's right to it. The psychic economy may even require a severing of the links between psyche and soma in order to keep at bay psychotic-type anxieties, such as the fear of bodily or mental fragmentation, as well as many neurotic fears. To what degree are fragilities in the psychic and somatic constitution of any given individual hereditary? Let us pause a moment to consider the question of "fateful" circumstances and the notion of a "psychosomatic destiny."

SOMATIZATION: FATE OR DESTINY?

In opposing the concepts of fate and destiny, I am drawing upon Christopher Bollas' (1989) notion of fate as accidental, an element over which the individual has no direct control, as opposed to the "destiny drive," which Bollas defines as "the urge to use objects through which to articulate — and hence be — the true self." Bollas regards the destiny drive as a contributory element to character structure, and as such, it may be used to deal with fateful events.

"Fate" is defined in most dictionaries as that which is inexorable or irrevocable, frequently "revealed" through oracles and prophetic declarations. In other words, fate depends on *verbal* pronouncements, to a large degree. "Destiny", on the other hand, implies a *potential*, suggestive of action initiated by the individual rather than words imposed from the outside. As Bollas puts it (1989), "one can fulfill one's destiny if one is fortunate." In Greek mythology, destiny is believed to emanate from a power that is superior to that of the gods. In *Vie de Racine* Mauriac (1950) writes, "We all weave our own destiny; we draw it forth from within ourselves as the spider with her web."

Destiny, then, could be viewed as an essential and determining element in our lives, but one that also allows for ongoing modifications throughout our life-course. Fate, on the other hand, encompasses those external events over which we have no control whatsoever. From a psychoanalytic standpoint, such fateful events would include the inevitable universal traumata of humankind: the exposure to otherness, sexual difference, aging, and death.

To the analytic ear, linking the notion of fate with verbal pronouncements rings associative "bells" to the effect of *parental pronouncements* (as well as their resounding silence), to which the child is nakedly exposed throughout infancy. From this viewpoint, the biparental discourse resembles a fateful heritage, which may prove as potent as an atypical, traumatic event in a small child's life. Destiny, by contrast, refers to the course of events over which the child potentially has some control.

The distinction between fate and destiny could be summarized in psychoanalytic terms as follows: *None of us is responsible for the blows of fate or the burdens imposed by the significant objects of childhood. Ultimately, however, we alone are responsible for our inner objects and the management of our psychic world with its powerful destiny drive.*

I would like to add to Bollas' concept of the destiny drive (which, I trust, I am not distorting) that this drive may also lead to a *misinterpretation* of the life forces in the service of the core (or true) self. In clinical work we often encounter patients whose destiny drive seems to be shackled to maintaining—at no matter what cost—primitive childhood solutions to the traumatic or fateful events and relationships of the past. It follows, then, that this inexorable repetitive force functions in the service of *psychic survival*—"survival as a being," as an individual subject, as an aspect of the true self—even in its apparently pathological dimensions.

I am taking issue here with Freud's concept of the "repetition compulsion" as exclusively serving the death drives. The compulsion to *maintain and repeat* deep unconscious patterns of behavior, even those that are manifestly pathological, is frequently revealed to be *on the side of life*.

Perhaps what I am calling the drive to survive psychically—that is, to keep intact one's sense of subjective and sexual identity—is an equivalent of Bollas' destiny drive. But I believe I am adding a further hypothesis to this important concept by suggesting that the creative driving force of the true self might also be accountable for certain pathological repetitions which, at the same time, represent an attempt to remain psychically and physically alive.

THE SOMA AND THE PSYCHE: FATE VERSUS DESTINY

Our somatic constitution appears to be part of our fateful heritage. Similarly, we might assume that our deaths are also biologically programmed; yet it is evident that many people die for the wrong reasons—that is, for reasons that supersede their biological clocks. Likewise, many respiratory dysfunctions, dermatological allergies, gastric sensitivities, and the like, are frequently shown to be inherited weaknesses. Thus these, too, might be considered to be physiological legacies of a fateful nature. Yet, to the extent that such apparently inherited factors are influenced by one's unconscious fantasy life, character structure, and specific psychic economy, psychic destiny clearly takes a hand in shaping and maintaining the somatic maladies that fate has dealt us.

This viewpoint therefore allows the potential for psychical—and, consequently, biological—change as a result of psychoanalytic exploration into the infraverbal archaic symbolism underlying somatic phenomena. As mentioned earlier, many analysands lose their lifelong allergies, their tendency to gastric ulcers, their high blood pressure, and their respiratory and cardiac dysfunctioning as an unexpected side effect of lengthy analyses. The very fact that we label a physical illness as a *psychosomatic* phenomenon suggests that both fate and destiny play a role. These reflections may become clearer with illustrations drawn from my work with analysands who brought their psychosomatic dramas onto the analytic stage.

My interest in psychosomatic phenomena was initially awakened by clinical observations that puzzled me. One of my first adult patients, Louise, complained that whenever she felt obliged to undertake one more ritual visit to her mother, her *asthma* became progressively worse as she drew closer to the city of Strasbourg where she was born and where her mother still lives. Then I noticed that Jean-Paul's *ulcer* recurred regularly before every vacation break. I began to wonder whether the illnesses of Jean-Paul, Louise, and others might have a hidden symbolic meaning? If so, what was that message?

Coming to a slightly different observation, I realized with shock that another analysand, Pierre, had had yet another seemingly *fateful* accident on his motorcycle, this time resulting in a detached retina. Later he revealed that he had had continual accidents as a child. Like many other patients who shared his vigorous, sporting, and aggressively intellectual approach to life, Pierre appeared to suffer from apparently self-inflicted bodily harm.

I began to ponder the possibility of a psychodynamic relationship between "accident prone" individuals like Pierre and those with psychosomatic manifestations like Louise and Jean-Paul.

Furthermore, I asked myself what role disavowed suicidal tendencies, unacknowledged rage, or displaced erotic wishes of a highly conflictive nature might play in all of these cases.

THE SECRET CALENDAR AND THE SYMBOLIC MEANING OF SYMPTOMS

Another apparently fateful element, which has come to my attention frequently in the course of my clinical work, is the "secret calendar" that every human harbors in the deepest layers of his or her psychic structure. This secret calendar is particularly evident in regard to the age, date, time, or season at which certain serious somatic illnesses first occur or return. The body's memory appears to be involved here, too. It is evident that the body and its somatic functioning are, to a remarkable extent, under the sway of the repetition compulsion. But, in addition, there is frequently a profound and fateful conviction in the individual that he or she is destined to fall ill, or even die, of a specific illness and at a specific time — as though an unconscious "contract" had been signed with the earliest caretakers of infancy. In such patients I frequently observed a phenomenon that seemed to indicate that they could *survive*, but that they must pay for this right by rendering their lives emotionless in order not to violate the interdiction to be fully *alive*. Similar clinical observations inspired psychoanalyst and psychosomaticist Paul Lefebvre to write a paper called "The Faustian Bargain" (1989), in which he describes patients who seem to have understood from their parents that "they could survive, but not beyond a certain age."

Sometimes such fantasies, and the somatic events themselves, can be understood as a product of hysterical conversion, but more often they appear to initiate that form of psychosomatic explosion I call "archaic hysteria." This concept (McDougall, 1989) was exemplified in my work with Tim who, at the age of 40, repeated the fateful heart attack that his father had suffered at this identical age — but Tim survived. The reasons he overlooked the cardiac-inducing dangers, which he incurred almost voluntarily in the face of a life-threatening illness, were traced back to yet another element in his psychic economy that had its fateful origins in earliest infancy and appeared to have been carefully constructed to deal with his *mother's* terror of any expression of emotion.

In attempting to conceptualize the dynamic meaning as well as the psychic effort involved in the production of psychosomatic symptoms, I studied the work of members of the Paris psychosomatic researchers, from which came the enlightening concept of "operatory thinking" (a pragmatic and delibidinized way of communicating with others and with oneself). Their theories aroused considerable interest in the Boston school of psychosomatic researchers inspired by Peter Sifneos and John Nemiah. Elaborating on the work of the Paris school, they added the concept of "alexithymia" (a condition in which afflicted individuals cannot describe their affective experience or distinguish one emotion from another). Both schools of research slowly evolved theories of causality that appeared to favor principles of the neurosciences rather than of dynamic psychology.

Although I found their work stimulating, I was still left with a nagging question: "Must I accept the theories of these eminent psychosomatic research workers who propose that diseases such as ulcerative colitis, bronchial asthma, gastric ulcer, high blood pressure, thyrotoxicosis, gynecological and cardiac pathology, and innumerable dermatological and respiratory allergies are *devoid* of symbolic meaning?" It did not seem feasible to me that these illnesses could be totally detached from the love-hate dramas of early infancy. The research of the psychosomaticists appeared to indicate that these patients were suffering from predominantly neuroanatomical defects—in other words, a fateful affliction. And therefore incurable. Was it not possible that the same somatic phenomena might have arisen, not so much in response to genetic dictates, but *to a need for defense against literally unspeakable (and, hence somaticized) psychic pain?*

In my earliest speculations about the potential meaning of the somatic phenomena to which my analysands unwittingly drew my puzzled attention (for these were never the reasons for seeking treatment), it was immediately obvious that such manifestations could not be subsumed under the categories of *neurotic* hysterical phenomena (McDougall, 1982, 1985b). Working on the basis of psychoanalytic (as distinct from, but not excluding, neuroanatomical) theories of causality, I observed buried conflicts of a *psy-*

chotic rather than a neurotic nature, such as: that loving was the equivalent of devouring or being devoured; or, at a slightly more sophisticated level of emotional relating, that both love relationships and sublimatory interests were unconsciously equated with urinating or defecating as a privileged form of amorous exchange and also of professional production.

In many cases, continuing analysis of these primitive erotic fantasies, which were frequently manifested in the transference relationship, led to the disappearance of somatic symptoms as well as the attentuation of intellectual and creative inhibitions — surprising both myself and my patients!

In Chapter 6 we explored the relationship of archaic sexual fantasies to creative and innovative activity. Here we will focus on the links between primitive sexualities and the varied phenomena of somatization in adult analysands.

SOMATIZATION: REFLECTIONS OF ARCHAIC
AND PREGENITAL SEXUALITIES

In my continuing clinical observations, I noted that current experiences that incited conflict, mental pain, or unusually pleasurable excitement frequently precipitated a return of the psychosomatic phenomena. In some instances, such events also appeared to initiate a somatic explosion for the first time. I found that the research work on alexithymia was pertinent to my reflections in trying to conceptualize the role of the psychic economy underlying psychosomatic states. Rather than finding confirmation that operatory thinking and alexithymic phenomena were due to some kind of gradual disorganization or neuroanatomical defects, I discovered that, as far as my own analysands were concerned, they had been the target of overwhelmingly *affective* experiences that had failed to achieve *psychic* representation, so that only the *somatic* pole of the affect was observable (McDougall, 1985a).

As my patient Tim put it, when he came back to see me some years after the end of the analysis, "I know that in the first years of our work together, I appeared totally emotionless; I was the perfect operatory character. But I was so submerged with feeling that if I'd let it show, if I hadn't been so 'supernormal,' I'd have gone crazy." In fact, a turning point in Tim's analysis had oc-

curred when he realized how concerned I felt over his life-
threatening behavior, leading him to the surprising conclusion
that I wanted him to live (McDougall, 1985a).

Asthma and Primitive Eroticism

Let us now return to the story of Louise, whose asthma attacks
increased in severity as she drew nearer to her mother's home
in the north of France. She sought analysis because of marital
disharmony and sexual frigidity. Although underlying oedipal
conflicts played a predominant role in the first two years of her
analysis, here I shall refer only to material pertaining to her psychosomatic symptoms and their link with early emotional states
and primitive fantasies.

From babyhood, Louise suffered from asthma as well as eczema. She seemed to have "inherited" her illness from a long
line of asthmatic forebears — an inborn fragility, according to her
pediatrician. Specialists decreed, and her mother readily agreed,
that Louise was fated to suffer from asthma and eczema for the
rest of her life, like the mother herself. Louise was an only child
and described her mother as having always taken meticulous *physical* care of her throughout childhood. This included forbidding
Louise's father to approach her when she was only a baby and
toddler, on the grounds that his presence excited her and thus
exacerbated her asthmatic tendencies. Her mother also complained that the father drank too heavily. But Louise recalled
with tenderness and nostalgia the times they were allowed to play
together, the jokes her father used to make, and the games they
concocted, as both laughed uproariously.

Because of her delicate condition her mother forbade Louise to
take part in sports or any of the normal physical activities of
childhood. But Louise was a rebel. From early childhood she
remembers secretly disobeying her mother in manifold ways. For
example, having been severely chastised for masturbating, Louise
learned in latency to withhold her urine in such a way as to produce an orgasmic sensation. While pretending to be reading, she
would achieve this erotic effect in her mother's presence, with a
secret sense of triumph.

Because of her own strong drive to be herself, Louise refused to
form a close identification with her mother on any level. In puberty, unbeknownst to her mother, she even joined a dance class

offered to the pupils of her small private school. Her secret was kept for a year, during which time Louise showed unusual talent for ballet and, interestingly, there was no marked increase in her asthmatic attacks. Receiving the end-of-the-year school report commenting on Louise's dancing prowess, the mother became enraged at her daughter's deception (no doubt because of her deep conviction that this activity threatened her daughter's very life), and her fury left an enduring imprint on Louise. Her mother was only slightly appeased when the family doctor said he thought Louise's breathing, if anything, was rather improved. Furthermore, the dance teacher staunchly supported Louise's participation in the ballet school as well as her expressed wish that she might one day become a professional dancer. (In spite of her mother's dire warnings, Louise fulfilled this wish.) As the analysis proceeded, we came to the understanding that through the experience of dance, Louise had finally been able to invest her body with libidinal interest and affection, no longer regarding it, as her mother did, as a sick and fragile object. At the time Louise entered analysis in her mid-twenties, she was a performer in a well-known Paris cabaret.

Although Louise had sought psychoanalytic help for marital problems, her mother constantly stepped onto the analytic stage. When Louise was expecting her first baby, her mother issued fearsome warnings about the ill health Louise would suffer after the birth, and added severe disapproval that Louise was not yet married to the father of her baby. Her mother suddenly appeared in the maternity ward the day after Louise's little son was born and publicly declared that Louise was to be "damned for eternity" because of her misdemeanors. Although Louise proclaimed (aided by the other young mothers on the ward) that her mother was a bit crazy and that, henceforth, she would keep her at a distance, I noted that she nevertheless constantly sought her mother's company, inviting her to Paris or arranging to go to Strasbourg to be with her.

It slowly became evident that the secret underlying the confused tie between Louise and her mother was lodged somewhere in the recurrence of the asthma attacks at the approach of each new encounter between them. As we constructed their underlying significance in the course of the analysis, it became clear that the asthma attacks (1) brought reassurance to Louise that her body truly belonged to *her* and not to her mother, and (2) were also the result of Louise's determination to turn feelings of rage against her own body and self rather than vent them on her mother.

After three years of analytic work with Louise, a further hypothesis concerning the relation between primitive eroticism and psychosomatic manifestations began to take shape in my mind. It became clear, from Louise's own associations, transference feelings, and fantasies, that the asthmatic attacks (as well as the outbreaks of eczema) were closely connected to *sexual fantasies* marked by oral and anal contents and permeated with both erotic and sadistic features. This interconnection was foreshadowed by Louise's early discovery that withholding her urine in her mother's presence resulted in erotic gratification.

As our analytic voyage continued, we were able to reconstruct that, on one level, Louise's urine unconsciously represented a penis substitute which she placed between her mother and herself and with which she obtained sexual pleasure. Louise also made a connection between her father's excessive beer drinking and urine. At another level, her masturbatory "invention" constituted a pregenital sharing of secret sexual pleasure with her mother as her chosen partner. This was a most unexpected revelation for Louise and led to uncovering homosexual and primal-scene preoccupations that had been dormant until then.

A further fantasy, discovered much later, was one in which fecal eroticism and anal aggression played important roles. For example, Louise became aware that she could not *touch* her mother following an angry exchange between them, "as though my mother were then covered with filth."* In light of this gradual reconstruction of fecal fantasy, attached both erotically and sadistically to her mother's image, we further analyzed the underlying content of Louise's hitherto inarticulative homosexual tie to her mother—which, like the anal-erotic material, had only found expression through her psychosomatic outbursts. This fundamental

---

*Clinical observation has led me to observe that anal and fecal fantasies are typically more difficult to bring into consciousness and to verbalize, particularly in their erotic dimension, since they are more deeply counter-cathected than erotic and sadistic wishes with oral and phallic content. Therefore, fantasy constructions around these unconscious themes emerge more slowly than oral- and phallic-level fantasies. In this context the original research of Wrye and Welles (1993) is highly pertinent.

elaboration of primitive erotic desires and homosexual wishes coincided with the attenuation of Louise's asthma attacks as well as
the disappearance of her sexual frigidity. The pregenitally loved
and hated mother-figure had slowly lost her hold on the rebel-
lious, but deeply attached, daughter.

The overwhelming importance of the mother-child interpsychic
and intrapsychic relationship in Louise's psychological structure,
as well as the extent to which her father was excluded or denigrated
by her mother, surfaced frequently in my later work with polysomatizing patients. Tim, Isaac, Georgette, and Paul (described in McDougall, 1978a, 1985b, 1989), all displayed similar parental particulari-
ties. It became progressively evident to me that these primitive
erotic ties, although a vital element in the early organization of
psychic structure, could nevertheless contribute to the creation of
psychosomatic rather than psychological reactions to overwhelming
circumstances. This was particularly the case for those in whom
the representation of the mother was interpreted by the child as an
engulfing force that sought total mastery of her offspring's physical
and psychic self. These children experienced themselves as libidinal
or narcissistic extensions of the mother. Such an apprehension
tended to arouse inchoate terror of the psychic death implicit in
the relationship. At the same time the child felt a megalomaniacal
satisfaction in recognizing the mother's desperate need for him or
her. Thus the bond between mother and child, impregnated with
primitive pregenital strivings, tended to perpetuate itself, despite
every appearance of external rebellion against it.

This analytic work with Louise early in my career led me to be
particularly attentive to archaic sexual fantasy, with its violently
sadistic and masochistic affect tone, in other analysands displaying polysomatizing tendencies or severe character disturbances.
Repressed fantasies, permeated with oral, urethral, and anal excitement, were revealed with surprising frequency.

Enuresis and Primitive Eroticism

Another interesting example of primitive sexual love connected
with urethral eroticism was furnished by Nancy (who was
mentioned in the Introduction). Nancy's case also illustrates
what I have come to consider to be a lopsided oedipal constellation.

Nancy was a constantly ill child with a particularly grave asthmatic condition. Her father was made a prisoner-of-war when she was 18 months old. She had one sister two years older than she. During the five years of her father's absence, Nancy slept with her mother and, as she put it, "innundated Mother every night with streams of urine." Her mother appeared to accept this urinary acting-out with kind complicity. Nancy's grandfather, however, who had come to stay with them in the father's absence, would come in every morning and sing a song whose theme was that of "the little fiancée who did '*pipi au lit*' and lost her lover for ever." If the bed was dry, there was no song. In Nancy's words, "Although I had to prevent Grandfather from singing, at all costs, at the same time, for some reason, it was also wonderful that he came in every morning, even when he sang. His presence alone was deeply reassuring to me." I suggested that perhaps she had understood Grandfather's tactic as a way of communicating to her that it was forbidden to "make love" every night in this fashion with her mother. This interpretation catalyzed many other associations, including Nancy's current lack of sexual pleasure in making love with her husband.

Nancy's mother constantly denigrated and criticized the father in his absence. When Nancy was six and a half years old, her father returned; her continual illnesses as well as her asthma attacks all disappeared. Nevertheless, Nancy remembered insisting on "sleeping in Mother's bedroom—oh, I mean, of course, my *parents*' bedroom—because I believed that I needed to hold Mother's hand throughout the night, otherwise I couldn't sleep. Besides, Mother insisted on it, too." From Nancy's recollections it appeared that this arrangement was as much a product of her mother's separation anxiety as of her own—a situation that clinical experience has led me to postulate as being present in many psychosomatic sufferers.

Nancy's enuresis continued until she was nine years old, ceasing abruptly when her baby brother was born. This event seemed to have shattered Nancy's illusions about being mother's chosen sexual partner and brought to an end the pregenitally expressed love affair with her mother. Nancy, at last, had a room of her own and, from then on, not only was her bed dry, but she had no further recollections of her earlier insomnia.

OPPOSING MATERNAL REPRESENTATIONS

From the child's point of view there is a paradoxical demand in this type of mother-child relationship. On one hand, there is a longing to continue the blissful pregenital love affair with the mother, as expressed through symptoms connected with bodily dysfunction (allergies, insomnia, encopresis and enuresis, bulimic or anorexic tendencies, etc.). On the other hand, there is an inarticulate, stifled rage against the archaic libidinal tie that is interpreted as an omnipotent demand on the mother's part. I find this affective conflict to be typical of child psychosomatic sufferers (and many adult ones, as well). The most powerful and dynamic elements affecting the psychosomatic couple formed by the mother (which includes the place of the father in her inner world) and her nursling are the mother's unconscious needs and fears. Perhaps it would be more accurate to refer to the biparental unconscious, since there are clinical signs throughout these analyses of the father's complicity in leaving his child totally in the hands of the omnipotent mother. It is important to reiterate that each child brings his or her own solution to the problem of separating from the mother and coping with the parents' unconscious communications. The element of destiny is revealed by the way in which the child resolves the conflicts of these influences. The outcome is not necessarily a psychosomatic one.

In attempting to summarize the maternal representations revealed by my more severely somatizing patients, I noted that two opposing characteristics were frequently attributed to the inner maternal object. On one hand, the mother was often described as *refusing close bodily contact* (thereby forcing premature *symbolic* communication for defensive reasons, leading to precocious physical and mental autonomy in some cases). In the (re)construction of early psychic trauma, this representation of the internal mother is experienced as the mother's terror of being devoured, absorbed, emptied out, by her baby. (Isaac and Tim experienced the mother-child relationship in this manner.)

On the other hand, the mother in the internal world was just as frequently perceived and remembered as one who was *overly close and dependent* in her physical and psychological demands upon her infant, as exemplified by the cases of Louise and Nancy. In these situations the mothers are recalled as being particularly interested in their children's physical pain but unable to hear or deal with their psychic pain.

PSYCHOSIS AND PSYCHOSOMATOSIS

Feelings of confusion or depersonalization surge forth at precise moments in the analyses of all my patients whose psychosomatic vulnerability is very marked — and, more particularly, when pregenital or archaic sexual longings are aroused, since these are comprised of violently destructive wishes as well as the desire to merge with partners or to exchange bodily substances. Neurotic anxieties concern the adult's rights to sexual and narcissistic enjoyments, whereas psychotic anxieties threaten the individual's sense of identity, of bodily integrity, of life itself. Neurotic fears concern the genitals and the erogenic body, whereas psychotic anxieties are more related to narcissistic terror concerning the whole physical and mental self. In other words, in these analysands, certain aspects of mental functioning are closer to psychotic than neurotic organizations.

Nevertheless, as their analyses progress, seriously somatizing patients do achieve access to their unconscious fantasies and forgotten memories. Often, when the somatic symptoms have been present from babyhood, they are combined with severe childhood phobias, which are not well-articulated fantasies (for example, like those of "little Hans," in Freud's 1909 paper). Beyond the realm of pregenital libidinal aims, with their attendant anxieties, is the realm of archaic and mortal eroticism that is expressed in phobias such as a terror of water and empty spaces, or in relationships with others, the fear of dissolving, exploding, or being invaded and imploded. Additional anxieties are attached to anguishing expectations of being emptied out or vampirized, of falling into nothingness, or of being crushed by overwhelming forces. Needless to say, the projective dimension of these anxieties is represented in the unconscious as a wish to vampirize, empty out, or crush *the other* (the mother, the father inside the mother, the other siblings), and these will also come to light eventually and require analytic exploration.

Quite recently, Nancy (who is still in analysis) was able to tell me for the first time why she has always hesitated before entering

my consulting room, a tiny stumbling movement that has continued throughout the last five years. She often used metaphors of
vampirization, but now mentioned her fear of being "possessed"
by strange forces. I commented that she seemed afraid to walk
into the consulting room without a ritual hesitation, as if she
would be accused of "taking possession" of my room. The projective identification was immediately evident to her and she was able
to acknowledge her desire, as well as her fear, that I would take
psychic possession of her, as she felt her mother had done to her.

In the course of our analytic work with patients, it is important
to consider the way in which we capture subtle, nonverbal communications, such as Nancy's hesitation, and are then able to trace
the gradual coming into consciousness of the as-yet-unverbalized
apprehensions that are struggling for expression. These experiences have been firmly excluded from consciousness, in large part,
because of the violent, archaic, and pregenital erotic fantasies
of sexual and love relationships, in which sex is unconsciously
conceived to be a violent and mutually disintegrating experience,
and love as equivalent to death. The struggle to find words to
contain and communicate these early events is an inaugural experience in any individual's life and opens the way to an extraordinary
voyage of psychoanalytic discovery.

CHAPTER 8

The Smell Self and the Skin Self

To live one's life in a body
that one cannot feel, is, I believe,
the loneliest loneliness.
— James Lynch

LET US NOW LOOK at two further vignettes that exemplify, in a different manner from those quoted in the last chapter, the relationship between archaic sexual fantasy and psychosomatic symptoms.

Although familiar with the somatopsychic importance of the skin in many patients suffering from different forms of allergy, in reflecting on the mysterious somatic dramas and childhood experiences of my "allergic" analysands I was also struck by the overwhelming importance often given to odors. Tiny infants always seek the breast through their sense of smell; pondering this fact I reflected that every baby surely knows the smell of the mother's sex, no doubt distinguishing the parents, among other signs, by their different *odors*. It seemed probable that a propensity to allergic reactions might begin to be organized psychically in the context of a disturbed mother-infant relationship.

With several of my patients, I was further inspired by the observation that the toxic allergens, in infancy, had been smells, tastes, or tactile experiences eagerly sought after and *positively invested* by the infant. One of my analysands, who had allergic reactions to different forms of "environmental toxins," suffered particularly from the pervasive smell present at gas stations. On enquiry, she learned from her mother that, as a little girl, she would lean over automobiles in gas stations with an ecstatic air, proclaiming that "the smell was so lovely." She had to be dragged away from these enticing odors.

In patients with marked allergic reactions who showed a particularly acute awareness of odors, I noted that a conflictive relationship with the "environmental mother" of early infancy was always revealed. This led me to postulate that early attractions to specific odors were learned to be forbidden or dangerous and therefore had to be *counter-invested*. However, because the "learning" occurred at a time when verbal communication was still rudimentary, the major protective response was a somatic one.

Forbidden Fruits

This vignette is drawn from the analysis of "Georgette" (discussed at length in a previous work (McDougall, 1989). At the beginning of her analytic voyage, Georgette had casually complained about an extensive array of psychosomatic symptoms, including cardiac, gastric, and gynecological disturbances, respiratory pathology, rheumatoid arthritis, and severe eczema. The symptoms slowly subsided but tended to resurface before every vacation break. Georgette's severe separation anxiety, as well as the somatizations if precipitated, caused her to dread any discontinuity in our analytic work. For her, this was equivalent to a severance of our relationship. In such circumstances she feared that, in her solitude, she would again become prey to her body's violent protests.

In the seventh year of analysis, however, Georgette began to look forward to vacation breaks, a feeling she had not experienced before. At this point, almost all her psychosomatic symptoms had disappeared, but she still suffered from severe allergic reactions whenever she ate certain fruits, fish, and shellfish (in French "*les fruits de mer*" — allowing for a play on words: the fruit of the *mother*). I had come to call all these foods the "forbidden fruits."

Before continuing with the session notes, I would like to mention that in Georgette's case, as with other polysomatizing patients, many different odors appeared to cause allergic reactions. She was also acutely aware of her own body odors. In the first years of our work together, Georgette doused herself with perfume for fear that any of her natural body odors might become perceptible. Many anal-erotic and anal-sadistic fantasies came to light during this phase of the analysis. We later discovered that she perfumed herself profusely with the additional hope that my other analysands would notice it (which, indeed, they did, often complaining that the scent could be detected even at the entrance of the building, three floors below). When we were able to talk about this behavior, she proclaimed that she wanted the "others" to recognize that this was "*my* territory." The dominating presence of her perfume was intended to convey the illusion that she had the right to exclusive possession of the analyst-mother.

Then, through dreams and associations, Georgette's smell sensitivities revealed their link with sexual odors and, in particular, a fear that the female sex had a disturbing odor. On one occasion she longed to taste an oyster "because of its lovely smell." This experiment gave rise to a violent edemic reaction, and the following night Georgette dreamed of a woman's body in the form of a clam shell. In her associations she remembered that, at school, the slang word used by the village boys to refer to a girl's sex organ was *clam*. Analysis of these important signifiers, while enriching Georgette's enjoyment of her sexual relationship with her husband, had not effected any change in her violent allergic reactions. These, we later discovered, were related to more archaic libidinal fantasies, whose meaning had been long foreclosed from consciousness.

In view of Georgette's extreme anxiety over the clam dream and its associations, I interpreted this material by saying that it seemed as though the little girl in her wanted to smell, touch, taste, and, indeed, to eat her mother's sex — as a primitive means of becoming her mother and possessing her sexual organ as well as her sexual privileges and imagined body contents. However, it appeared that these desires were highly forbidden and, therefore, she received a somatic message to transmit the danger she was courting.

There is little doubt that such incorporative fantasies, in which one becomes the other by eating either the person or the part that is desired, represent archaic libidinal longings of a universal kind. The persistence of these primitive erotic longings into adult life, in the form of psychosomatic manifestations, would indicate an early breakdown in the processes of internalization and symbolization. I now leave it to Georgette to recount the use her psyche made of these tentative interpretations.

GEORGETTE [*In the first session following the summer vacation*] I have something important to tell you. I no longer have any allergies! During the vacation I ate everything—everything that is in the sea [*mer* and *mère*]—fish, oysters, lobsters, clams, mussels. I couldn't get enough. What a feast, and not the slightest allergic outbreak! I even ate strawberries and raspberries—everything that has made me suffer for the past 40 years. [*A long pause*]

I thought of what you sometimes said about the "forbidden fruits" . . . my mother's fruit—her breasts, her sex, her babies—that the little girl in me wanted to devour so that I could become a woman. It feels profoundly true and I don't know why the idea frightened me for so many years. [*Another silence*] One day I was talking to my husband about how much I now love the "fruits *de mer*" and instead I said, "Oh, how I love the fruits *de père*!"

JM [*This slip of the tongue attributes the forbidden fruit to the father instead of the mother—an important and hitherto shadowy dimension in Georgette's psychic world. I ask her to explore the interesting idea of a connection between shellfish and her father, and she suddenly recovers a forgotten memory.*]

GEORGETTE How strange . . . how could I have forgotten? My father adored fish and shellfish. He consumed them all with great gusto— mussels, shrimp, clams, oysters. Oh! I've remembered something else. I must have been about three. I was watching my father, with great fascination, eat a clam or a mussel, and he offered me one. I can still see him parting the two little lips . . . then he squeezed some drops of lemon juice into it and gave it to me to eat. I swallowed it down—it was delicious! How come I didn't remember all these years that shellfish were my father's passion? That seafood was his "special territory"?

JM [*Struck by Georgette's use of the words* passion *and* special territory *to describe her father's gustatory preferences, I decide to interpret the image of the primal scene that she has painted for me with surrealistic vision of a child's eye: The father opening the "lips" of the shellfish and depositing a drop of lemon juice therein.*] The little lips of the shellfish and the drop of lemon juice . . . could this be a childlike image of your two parents together?

GEORGETTE I feel confused . . . everything is getting mixed up in my mind.

JM Father and mother?

GEORGETTE Yes! And that special smell . . . my father had a smell that frightened me. *That*'s why I wouldn't let him kiss me when I was a child! That's another thing I'd forgotten. Now I'm thinking of something that embarrasses me to say [*Pause*] My father, who ate shellfish all the time — is this crazy? — would have the smell of my mother's sex . . . maybe I thought he devoured her sex. [*Long silence*] But there's another thought that's even harder to say. Well, here goes! I was telling my friend Eva yesterday about my great discovery that, for me, shellfish represented the female sex and she replied that sperm also smells like shrimp.

JM The "fruits *de mer*" . . . where both sexes meet? Is that the thought that is difficult to explore?

GEORGETTE I guess that they were not a *couple* in my mind.

At this point I remind Georgette how often she has mentioned the persecuting quality of odors. It now seems evident that, through her allergic reactions, she is refusing the sexual odors that had once been so attractive to her as well as refusing their implication — that her parents existed as a *sexual couple*. The rituals of closing her mouth and holding her breath that she had practiced secretly throughout her childhood were no doubt intended, as she always affirmed, to ward off death. But I also wonder if these rituals were a way of denying the sexual relationship between her parents, which, for the little Georgette of the past, was experienced as a threat of death.

GEORGETTE Yes, I'm beginning to see this!

JM To look?

GEORGETTE Yes and to understand . . . the odor! It was the *smell of their room* that I had to avoid at all cost!

For the first time in seven years Georgette is able to recognize that her parents slept together in the same bed, at least until she was three years old. Later in the session she recalls a dream she had reported in the first week of her analysis with me, in which she was looking at a pair of crystal earrings but was not able to put them on. Since this was one of her first dreams, I had picked up on *pair, ears, earrings*, her being unable to *use* them, but no further associations came to her mind. Now she proclaimed with delight, "I know what those crystal earrings really were — the beads that decorated the lamps in their bedroom!"

A new and vital link has been forged in the chain of forgotten memories in Georgette's inner world. The oedipal dimension can now be added to all that we have reconstructed of Georgette's passionate love-hate attachment to her mother's body and person. The narcissistic mortification and despair, which the child Georgette had undoubtedly experienced at the birth of her sisters, is now encapsulated in the forgotten memory — a screen memory, destined to be repressed — in which her father avidly enjoys (under the guise of the "fruits of the sea") the mother's sex, giving rise to their mutual fruit, the little sisters.

Faced with her own infantile wish to eat her mother (which represents every infant's earliest attempt to internalize and libidinally possess the mother-universe), the amorous little cannibal could turn neither to mother nor to father for any confirmation that she, too, would be a woman one day and would have the right to her own erotic desires and sexual fulfillment. For many reasons (of which I have indicated only a few), Georgette had "no place" to go. In her representational world there was no model of a loving couple, through whose example she could discover her own future as a woman.

After the birth of her little sister (which almost certainly precipitated a sudden disinvestment of Georgette in her mother's eyes), any attempt to cling to her psychically absent mother would be experienced as doubly dangerous: On one hand, Georgette's demand for fusion spelled psychic death; on the other, she was terrified of her own destructive wishes, fearing that she might omnipotently destroy (devour) father, mother, and little sisters — fruit of the mother's womb and the father's seed — and consequently, lose her own right to live.

Instead, these fantasies were safely buried in the taste of raspberries and strawberries and in the smell of shellfish and seafood — tastes and smells redolent with the somatic memories and archaic libidinal longings of an infant, only secondarily acquiring verbal and oedipal significance. In other words, these "forbidden fruits" are not true symbols but *symbolic equivalents* (Segal, 1957), which have not been transformed into the language signifiers for the different aspects of the "breast mother."

Without the earlier substratum of psychological distress, these same elements might have been used to create hysterical rather than psychosomatic symptoms. The forgotten memory of the father offering his little daughter a clam, with all it epitomized of her father's procreative role in the primal-scene, could not have produced, in itself, the severe psychosomatic regressions that have plagued Georgette throughout her life. The preverbal signifiers of early infancy, as yet incapable of verbal symbolization, have instead given rise to a series of symbolic equations that Segal (1957) likened to a psychotic mechanism. We could also propose that the "forbidden fruits" were still psychically registered as a "pictogram" (Aulagnier, 1975) or, in Bion's (1963) terminology, as "beta elements," untransformed by the absent mother's "alpha" functioning. Lacking word-presentations, the psyche was left with highly dynamic but destructive *thing-presentations* (Freud, 1915a). There was no "signal anxiety" in the face of psychic conflict. The thing-presentation alone emitted warning signals. Since they were not contained in words, these warnings mobilized uncontrollable unconscious forces whenever the psyche detected a menacing situation (such as annihilation experiences or feelings of murderous rage).

To these muted preoedipal warnings were added oedipal interdictions of both a homosexual and a heterosexual nature. Having achieved verbal capacities by the time of the oedipal conflicts, these were subsequently *repressed*, potentially providing a fund of elements for the construction of neurotic symptoms. Consequently, this absence of strong neurotic defenses exposed Georgette to the risk of somatic explosions, should she transgress her bygone incestuous longings in the form of the wish to eat the "forbidden fruits." As in infancy, psychic distress responded only to the pictographic thing-presentations of bodily sensations. These somatic ills were later invested with sadistic fantasies turned against her own body and self. Through her somatizations, the amorous *and* the destructive infantile wishes were kept completely hidden from conscious as well as preconscious awareness. But, as Freud (1923) observed, affects readily bypass the preconscious layers of mental functioning. In the face of deeply disturbing affect, Georgette's psyche sent only primitive somatopsychic signals.

When the conjunction between threatening affects and their somatic expression is established during the early structural development of the psyche, these pathological somatopsychic links may last a lifetime, offering the individual no means other than somatic disorganization for reacting to external and internal tensions. Because of the body's tenacious memory, combined with the absence of verbal cognitions, situations charged with archaic affect are excluded from more evolved forms of mental representation and affect-recognition. Paradoxically, psychosomatic maladies, even when they are life-threatening in nature, can be envisaged as serving the purpose of psychic survival.

In Georgette's case, her survival techniques required her to stifle all hostile thoughts aroused against her first love-objects. In place of a psychosexual history, Georgette had constructed a *psychobiological* one; her unrecognized emotional conflicts were manifested in the serious anorexia that lasted throughout her childhood and adolescence, as well as in the "refusal to breathe" expressed in her asthmatic attacks from babyhood onward. To these were added the mute rebellion that resulted in heart pathology, gynecological disturbances, ulcers, edemic reactions, and neurodermatitis. Georgette believed that the desired *and* feared fantasy that there could be "only one body for two people" was her mother's law. Refusal to comply with this law would incur the shattering of her fusional relationship with her mother and the loss of her mother's love. Only the terror of psychic death could compel Georgette to relinquish this fusional bond. Thus she found comfort in her body's suffering, since it reassured her, through corporeal limitations, that she possessed her own body. She no longer feared the destructive aspects of the wish to merge with the mother-universe, which had threatened the integrity of her physical image and her sense of individual identity. It could be proposed, therefore, that Georgette's psychosomatic manifestations conveyed her profound determination to survive. Her continual somatic productions on the psychoanalytic stage allowed us to decode the soma's primitive "language" and to translate these mute communications into psychic representations that could, for the first time, find expression in words.

The Scream of the Skin

A second clinical illustration may give further insight into the hypothesis that psychosomatic maladies represent (among their other psychic functions) a defense against archaic sexual longings. The analytic vignette that follows is drawn from the analysis of a patient whom I quoted in previous works (McDougall, 1978a, 1982). I took many notes on Jean-Paul's analysis because, to begin with, I didn't understand his mental functioning. Also, I was fascinated by the way he used language — which was poetically, but without ever being able to express his feelings clearly. In fact, he was terrified that allowing his thoughts and emotions to run freely would make him go crazy.

Jean-Paul was 39 years of age when he first came to see me. I had told him on the telephone that a consultation was possible, but that I would have no place available for another year, should he contemplate beginning an analysis. A good-looking man, director of a small enterprise, he surprised me by not once looking into my eyes while he talked, all the while searching hesitantly for the words he needed to communicate his reasons for seeking help. Other than that, he appeared composed and spoke in a measured voice with little trace of emotion.

JEAN-PAUL I've come to see you because there's something wrong with the way I live.

JM [*I invited him to tell me more about his way of living.*]

JEAN-PAUL Well, I feel okay at work — as long as there's no hostility in the air. When that happens, I'm seized by a strange feeling. My arms shake. I suppose it's a kind of panic. Anyway, when it happens, I can no longer think . . . or even utter a word.

JM [*As if this experience, which he found difficult to describe, were linked to his bodily health, he switches to that topic.*]

JEAN-PAUL I have a long history of digestive disturbance. I was in my early twenties in the middle of my university courses. My life was a desert. I lived in absolute solitude, which, for some reason, I associate with the pain. Although I was in constant pain, I didn't give it much thought . . . used to tell myself that if you're alive, you have to expect misery.

JM [*I learned later that Jean-Paul had suffered for 15 years from a severe form of peptic ulcer, which he had done nothing about, other than "trying to find a position that was comfortable for walking, studying, or eating." Eventually, the ulcer perforated. Still not looking at me, Jean-Paul changes topics once more, as if he believes this misery were a punishment for his sexuality.*]

JEAN-PAUL My sexual life was a desolation. Masturbation filled me with a sense of horror because of all my father's dire warnings about it, so I felt dirty, degraded, valueless. I had short-term relationships with women, but these never led to any real friendships. I was too tied up to be with a normal woman. [*Long pause*] I met my wife, Nadine, at the university where we were both studying political science. We've been married 12 years. She criticizes me all the time, but the worst of it is that she rejects me sexually. I must admit, I'm not that easy to live with either.

JM What are you hoping to gain from an analysis?

JEAN-PAUL Nothing is as it should be in my life. Everything soft, color-ful, and musical escapes me. [*Suddenly looking at me, he lays his hand on his heart.*] It's all blocked — here.

JM Here? [*Imitating his gesture*]

JEAN-PAUL Yes, it's uh . . . well, how would you say it . . . [*struggling to find the words*] . . . it's like sobbing in my heart (*sanglots dans mon coeur*). [*After a short silence, during which he continues to stare at my walls, once more carefully avoiding any eye contact, he continues in the same emotionless voice.*] The gastric problems keep recurring, but there's nothing to be done about it. I've had them for 18 years. Like my skin allergies, they're something I just have to put up with.

While saying this, Jean-Paul scratches the back of his hand, then makes a movement as if to touch his sex. He looks at me briefly and says, "Well, when can we begin?" I repeat what I said on the telephone: that I would have no space available for another year yet. Undaunted, he asks, "And how much will it cost me?" I tell him my fees. He throws me another rapid glance and says, "I have a friend who pays less than that for his analysis." I offer to give him names of analysts whose fees are lower than mine. He replies in an offended voice, "No, thank you! So, we shall see each other in a year's time?"

To my surprise, he abruptly rises. As he marches toward the door, I suggest that he call me some time in the following year if he was still sure he wanted to begin analysis with me. He does not look back.

My first impression after this initial interview is that Jean-Paul suffers from depression, but reading my notes some months later, I realize that he was truly unable to express *feelings* of depression in words. Instead he sought to communicate them in a concrete way, laying his hand on his chest and saying, "It's all blocked here," as well as through a condensed metaphor, "It's like sobbing in my heart" — the way that poets and little children communicate.

Exactly one year to the day, Jean-Paul telephoned me to ask when we were going to start! I understood later that this was part of his way of functioning; without realizing it, he enjoyed a magical belief that everything he wanted would occur automatically. I was a part of Jean-Paul himself and therefore there was no need to inform me of his decision to keep the tentative agreement made one year ago. In the years to come, we discovered that he had experienced his mother as someone who had total rights over his body; he, too, believed he had omnipotent rights over her and her body. This conviction was reinforced by the fact that she had breast-fed him until the age of four.

During the first years of our work together, Jean-Paul was either silent or vituperating against his wife and her lack of enthusiasm for their sexual relationship. He dreamed rarely and produced no fantasies. However, he frequently mentioned his ulcer and various dermatological problems, and I began to "hear" these communications as dreams and to wonder if, indeed, they *took the place* of dreams and fantasies.

I was a relatively young analyst at that time and understood little about the underlying significance of the somatic complaints of my different patients. With Jean-Paul, I frequently had the feeling that something was escaping me, and I began to take extensive notes. I also encouraged him to try to capture feelings and fantasies and to search for any links between these and his somatic outbreaks. On numerous occasions I had pointed out to him that he frequently suffered from an outbreak of eczema and a return of the ulcer just before vacation break. Little by little, we found traces of long-forgotten childhood and adolescent attempts to deal with his overwhelming anxiety, not only about his sex and his body, but about his whole feeling of identity. In the safety of the consulting room he was now able to allow himself to be deluged by a sudden eruption of ideas; he attempted to grasp and describe strange perceptions and sensations which, in the past, had apparently been forcefully *ejected* from his consciousness (and therefore unavailable as elements for dreaming). He thus taught me a great deal about the psychic economy that underlies psychosomatic phenomena.

I made frequent interventions intended to enable Jean-Paul to perceive the way in which he functioned psychically: by eliminating any thoughts tinged with affect as well as discarding any free-floating fantasies. As our analytic voyage continued, fantasies began slowly to take the place of somatic communications. After three years of intensive work, Jean-Paul was free of gastric pathology—with rare exceptions, such as the announcement of vacation breaks. At the time the following session notes were taken, our work was approaching its fifth year.

SEPARATION, SADISM, AND SOMATIZATION

While an impending separation never aroused an affective reaction of any kind in Jean-Paul, invariably there was a recrudescence of his gastric symptoms. Not only did these somatic outbursts occur with a regularity that even *he* could not deny, they were also accompanied by other nonverbal manifestations. For example, Jean-Paul could never remember my vacation dates and, on more than one occasion, he had turned up for his regular session after my departure. This time he had carefully noted that our work for the year would cease on July 11th, but this did not prevent his announcing, in the second to last session, that to his intense regret, he would have to miss the session of July 25th!*

JEAN-PAUL No session on the 25th? Well, well! Madame has decided to take her holiday? Leaving *tomorrow*? Anyway, I couldn't care less. [*Pause*] In case you're wondering, I'm thinking about my penis. Large, suntanned, very good-looking, I assure you.

JM [*Here Jean-Paul announces a theme which has appeared on several occasions—elaborate fellatio fantasies, in which I am to participate and find sublime pleasure. The fantasies are strictly non-genital, limited to partial objects: mouth and penis.*] Do you think there's a connection between our upcoming separation and these erotic fantasies that link us together—and perhaps deny the separation?

JEAN-PAUL Perfectly absurd! So you're going on vacation? Fine! I'd be crazy to make a fuss about so little. [*Pause*] My penis isn't as good-looking as I boasted . . . a bit misshapen and dark-colored. When erect, it looks like a pick.

Jean-Paul cannot tolerate the idea that he might be disturbed about the vacation break. By offering me a flattering view of his penis, he believes he has changed the subject under discussion. My intervention, suggesting that the two themes might be related, is received as a narcissistic hurt. In any case, the imagined exchange

---

*A full account of this vignette is given in McDougall, 1978a, Chapter 10.

between us shifts subtly into a sadistic one, revealing the counterpart to his erotic fantasy.

JEAN-PAUL I see myself attacking your mouth with my sex. It leaves a brown, terrifying stain on your breasts. [*Pause*] My arms are jumping again, as if they had electric shocks in them. It's annoying!

JM [*The vision of buccal aggression is no doubt also related to my interpretation, which Jean-Paul experiences as an attack on his phallic narcissism. The physical sensations in his arms appear to me to be the residue of an affect that had been stifled and that had failed, therefore, to achieve psychic representation.*] Can you think of anything that might go with this sensation of electric shocks in your arms?

JEAN-PAUL You might tear my penis to pieces with your mouth. Good God, what have I said now [*clasping his hands over his mouth*]!

Jean-Paul's difficulty in containing and working through any ambivalent feelings, whether about himself or other people, is evident in the above associations. His penis is "split" into two contrasting images: On one hand, his sex organ awakens fascination and admiration, only to become ugly and dangerous a moment later. The analyst is fantasized as erotically receptive to his "good-looking" penis, then as violently castrative, tearing his penis to pieces with her teeth.

In this phase of Jean-Paul's analysis, castration anxiety could only be expressed in pregenital terms of penis/breast and mouth/vagina—both mutually gratifying and mutually destructive—while the "brown, terrifying stain" foreshadows fantasies of fecal attack. The part-objects are neither good nor bad but *idealized* and *persecutory*. Faced with this primitive form of sexual exchange, Jean-Paul does not deal with it by use of repression but by foreclosure; the whole conflict is simply eliminated from the symbolic chain. Based on our former sessions, I anticipated that this would give rise to either delusional projections or somatization.

JEAN-PAUL I've had terrible gastric pain the last two weeks—and I *don't* want to talk about it. It's so childish that this always happens before the vacations. And eczema between my fingers, too! But that's due to sexual frustration. Nadine rejects me totally these days.

JM [*In an attempt to render his somatic manifestations more accessible*

*to verbal thought, and with the hope of warding off the constant
blocking of affect that effaced so much of Jean-Paul's psychic reality
and hampered our work, I attempt to link these afflictions to fantasy
content of an affective kind.*] Nadine and I both reject you: She
refuses sexual relations; I abandon you for the vacation and tear
your penis with my teeth. Instead of getting aggressive, you present
yourself as sick, helpless, totally incapable of harm.

JEAN-PAUL But I have no aggressive feelings about either of you. Besides, I *adore* women!

JM Maybe there are two parts of you speaking there—one that adores
women and another that is afraid of their aggression?

JEAN-PAUL That idea upsets me . . . I feel something shrinking in my
stomach.

JM Can you imagine "something" in the place of this shrinking sensation?

JEAN-PAUL Nadine! When she won't make love, I imagine my penis is a
white hot pick stuck in her stomach. She wriggles like a worm and
can't get off. [*Pause*] That thought gives me considerable pleasure!

JM [The "pick-penis" . . . the castrating mouth . . . the abdominal attack fantasized as the pick in Nadine's stomach and, at another moment, the "something" that shrinks inside his own . . . the confusion
between inner and outer, between self and object—all invaded my
imagination and I wonder vaguely if this were "ulcer imagery." Finding no adequate interpretation, I decide to wait.]

JEAN-PAUL Your silence frightens me. [*Pause*] I'm thinking of my fear
of crowds—Bastille Day—they can celebrate it, but I assure you, you
won't find *me* in the streets. I'm always afraid the crowd will turn
nasty.

Here Jean-Paul gives an interesting example of projective identification. As Bion (1963) points out, this mechanism is an archaic
form of thinking. Jean-Paul now attributes his own hostile feelings to the anonymous "crowd," feelings which he can neither
contain nor elaborate at the level of verbal thought. In place of
the attack on "woman" with his "pick penis" (perhaps against the
content of her abdomen—a "crowd" of babies?), it is Jean-Paul
himself who is threatened with attack from the crowd. His next
associations suggest that the defense afforded by projective identification is fragile and tends to break down, leaving somatic sensations and feelings of depersonalization in its wake.

JEAN-PAUL The other day, as I left here, there was a crowd gathered in
the street. I felt dizzy and said to myself, "Now imagine something

quickly so you can get across that street." So I thought of my penis, standing up, strong and clean . . . like a positive statement. [*This endeavor to surmount overwhelming anxiety through eroticization recalls his earlier attempt to deal with unexpressed feelings about the vacation break by eroticizing the transference.*] But my idea didn't work. Right away, I saw my penis all brown and horrid and covered with sores. So I wasn't protected. Just then, my head split into two; I *felt* it. Such horror . . . it made me want to throw up.

Submerged in his inexpressible conflict, Jean-Paul seems to have suffered a brief moment of depersonalization. "My head split into two" is a thought produced by primary-process thinking, as it might have appeared in a dream. This condensed image reflects Jean-Paul's confusion between himself and others, as well as the inextricable merging of libidinal and destructive impulses. His highly invested gastric area provides him with yet another somatic metaphor in place of representations and emotions: The conflict presents itself as a wish to vomit.

It was tempting to imagine that Jean-Paul's destructive and cannibalistic fantasies were the cause of his gastric pathology, but everything pointed to the contrary conclusion: that his very inability to allow himself to experience such impulses and put them into words left him with "nameless dread" (Bion, 1962), which he could neither contain nor think about. His ulcer pathology could be regarded as having a *protosymbolic* meaning (which, as a result of the analytic process, was slowly acquiring fantasy content). At the same time, his gastric response to mental conflict might also be conceived of as a *psychosomatic regression* to that early stage of undifferentiated affect, in which gastric hyperfunction is stimulated by both erotic excitement and destructive rage. I made rough notes to this effect—perhaps because Jean-Paul's confused and excited monologue stirred in me the need to bring some order into my own thinking. In any case, he brought me back abruptly to his discourse.

JEAN-PAUL Now I'm completely lost—and I wonder if your head isn't as muddled as mine with all these thoughts.

JM So my head is now "split in two"?

JEAN-PAUL Ha! That's truer than you think. All week I said to myself, "There we are, gastric pains are back again, and that could be really serious. And eczema as well! Just wait until I tell her how ill I am and that it's all her fault." I promised myself you'd go off on holiday, torn apart by guilt for conducting this analysis so badly!

JM [*Jean-Paul continues to elaborate at length on the pain and anxiety he hopes I will suffer during the vacation. I am delighted to observe that, for the first time, he is reacting with some trace of affect when faced with our separation. However, it was not Jean-Paul who was to suffer, but me.*] So I may go off on vacation on condition that I carry you in my thoughts, "torn apart" inside with anxiety? Do you think this is a way of getting rid of your own inner anxiety, by giving it to me instead?

JEAN-PAUL Bitch! *Mon Dieu*, what have I said now [*clasping his hands over his mouth*]? I'm sorry . . . the word just slipped out, you know. You aren't angry with me, I hope? [*Pause*] Say something! I'm afraid!

JM Of dangerous words? Thoughts that can kill? [*Here I am referring to an earlier session in which he was afraid to imagine things in case they came true.*]

JEAN-PAUL Ah . . . yes! Just now, I didn't want to say it, but I was thinking about . . . well . . . a fascinating detective novel . . . the criminal was a strangler. But he only strangled women. Exciting desire. Ah, if only I were crazy! You know, there's something special about strangling . . . almost a caress. [*Pause*] Do I scare you?

JM [*Jean-Paul's flourishing fantasies of violence and physical attack on women are in such striking contrast to his earlier statement that he "adores women" and would be incapable of aggressive thoughts about them, that I ask him whether the "exciting" idea of strangling women might not be a way of having erotic contact—while, at the same time, keeping their dangerous aspect under control. This intervention leads to sudden free associations concerning masturbation, never previously mentioned, and points in the direction of prepubertal fantasies of sadistic intercourse.*]

JEAN-PAUL What you said there gave me a strange feeling—reminds me—when I was about nine, I used to strangle my penis. It hurt terribly, but I also got terrific pleasure from it.

JM [*Thus I learn for the first time about Jean-Paul's attempts to master castration anxiety through the invention of a sexual deviation in which his fear (that his penis would be "strangled" because of forbidden sexual wishes) became the very source of excitement and pleasure. The repressed fantasies revealed in this masturbation activity begin to take their place in a chain of archaic primal-scene images: the devouring and castrating mouth . . . the strangling vagina with oral and anal qualities . . . the "strangler-strangled" relationship in which Jean-Paul would strangle the woman's neck instead of his own penis—and thus, through projective identification and the lack of*] *distinction between self and object, could contrive to approach eroti-cally, and at the same time control, the dangerous female and the frightening impulse.*]

JEAN-PAUL Say something! Frankly, I don't feel you're very well-disposed toward me today.

JM The bitch-woman with a sex that strangles?

JEAN-PAUL Now there's an important idea! [*His whole body, which has been taut and rigid for the last ten minutes, relaxes visibly. Further new associations come to the fore, bringing forth a classical symbol of the dangerous female genital.*] What you just said makes me think of my terror of *spiders*. I loathe them. There was one in my office the other day, near the ceiling. I was paralyzed with fright . . . couldn't understand a word my secretary was saying.

The spider-woman, devouring and strangulating, with her para-lyzing effect, now stands out clearly behind the "adored" image. In Jean-Paul's unconscious fantasy the sexual relationship is rep-resented as a duel in which he confronts terrible odds: He faces the archaic maternal image alone, with no signs of a phallic symbolic paternal object with which to identify or from whom protection might be sought. Perhaps, Jean-Paul must "tame" his sexual ob-jects by massive seduction? Or dominate them by fantasies of sadistic attack?

He then recounts a series of spider memories. As a little boy he had adored insects, *especially spiders*, and would play with them for hours. This period, in latency and early puberty, coincided with the time of his penis-strangling invention. While talking, Jean-Paul suddenly becomes aware of his contradictory feelings about spiders: the favorite companions of his childhood, today a source of phobic anxiety. After this session I note once again how objects or activities that were highly invested with forbidden erotic and sadistic meaning in childhood have to be counter-cathected in adulthood, and that the solution to this conflict may take many forms, ranging from neurosis to psychosis to psychosomatosis.

JEAN-PAUL How did I get on the subject of spiders, anyway?

JM The "spider-woman" who is not very well disposed toward you today?

JEAN-PAUL Wow! I get a picture of my sex positively mangled by you. [*Pause*] When I feel like making love and Nadine rejects me, I get urticaria around my genitals.

JM As though you produce urticaria in place of lovemaking? What does urticaria make you think of?

JEAN-PAUL Ugh! Ants, worms, things wriggling everywhere. Horror. Just talking about it makes me itch all over. When Nadine refuses to have sex for days on end, that's just the way I feel—as though I were covered with insects. I itch everywhere, even in the places where there's no urticaria. My hair gets greasy and sticks to my scalp. I feel dirty and have to keep taking showers.

JM [*Traces of hysterical conversion and obsessive-compulsive behavior are briefly visible but poorly organized. Insect games from the past and childhood primal-scene fantasies are now replaced by skin sensations and anal fantasy; Jean-Paul's skin itself seems to become enraged when Nadine pushes him away, and his entire body-image is imbued with fecal imagery.*] What do you think this skin language signifies?

JEAN-PAUL It reminds me of my mother and her horrid skin eruptions. It used to make me itchy just to look at her. [*Jean-Paul twists his hands in the air, scratches at his skin, and rubs it as if brushing insects.*]

JM [*I reflect on the images Jean-Paul conveyed of his mother, in which she was seductive and frustrating at the same time. He now seems to be living out a regressive fantasy of being inside her skin (a desire to fuse? to undo separation?) and of being punished for his invasion (a fantasized castration carried out on his own skin?). Whatever answers we might find, it seems certain that Nadine's present coldness, coupled with my imminent departure, has contributed to reactivating the interdiction of Jean-Paul's archaic erotic longings toward his mother.*] So you're getting into your mother's skin?

JEAN-PAUL God damn! Becoming my mother is no solution! Besides, the idea is horrendous. Having sexual desire for her doesn't bother me—I've always known that I found my mother sexually attractive. What eats me up is the idea of *being inside her skin*. I feel crawly all over.

Here Jean-Paul provides some inkling of the primitive nature of his desire to become one with his mother, no doubt activated by the unacknowledged threats of separation and abandonment (my vacation, Nadine's sexual rebuffs). The original object of desire, the mother's body and genital, is endowed with oral-castrative and anal-exuding toxic fantasy as an archaic line of primal defense. But the self-object confusions—due, in part, to the particular nature of Jean-Paul's relationship with his mother and the poorly structured oedipal organization to which it gave rise—could only lead to displacements, condensations, projections, and counter-projections in a never-ending cyclical series: the mother's body . . . its contents . . . her skin . . . the penis-neck to be strangled . . . the crowd-woman . . . the spider.

Jean-Paul's internal struggle with his mother and her particular investment of him would seem to have found—and subsequently lost—a multitude of psychic expressions, which were childhood attempts at self-cure in the face of mental pain and confusion. Some of these solutions were only just returning to his awareness; many were clearly abandoned without any compensation in the form of new psychic constructions: For example, the insect theater, half eroticized and half sublimated, had given way to a sexual perversion, a hysterical conversion, a phobia, an authentic sublimation (Jean-Paul is an expert amateur entymologist), and a psychosomatic malady.

JM Our time is up for today.
JEAN-PAUL Okay. I just want to say that I'm beginning to see that there's something wrong in my relationships with women. Nadine, you, my mother—I've plenty to occupy me for the summer vacation!

In my notes I speculate that the chasm between Jean-Paul's real body and his imaginary somatic self is becoming narrower and that the "delusional" body, with its deranged somatic functioning, was on the way to becoming a symbolic one. With the wish to comfort myself about this difficult analytic voyage, I added that "hopefully he is becoming capable of neurotic rather than somatic solutions to psychic stress."

Reflecting on the significance of the archaic sexual imagery that played such a predominant psychic role in the analysands quoted in this chapter, I had noted that eroticization is a privileged means of combatting very early traumatic experiences. When such a defense fails, or is only partially operative, the archaic sexual impulses, with their contradictory aims and self-other confusions, are then foreclosed from consciousness. This foreclosure leaves the psychosoma with only one recourse: somatic explosion as its sole means of defensive expression.

The rediscovered fantasies are no doubt part and parcel of

everybody's repressed erotic infantile wishes. The question remains as to why, in these analysands, their suppression gave rise to somatic rather than psychological expression. The presence of similar unconscious fantasies in individuals whose psychic destiny is guided by a different dynamic substratum and a more fluid psychic economy, could have led to the creation of phobias or obsessional and hysterical conversion symptoms in the place of psychosomatic disorders.

In the next chapter, continuing clinical vignettes from Jean-Paul's analysis illustrate, in striking fashion, the slow recession of psychosomatic communications of his inarticulate conflict and the ensuring growth of neurotic constructions in their place. Links that provided the articulation of psychosomatic phenomena with language had been forged.

CHAPTER 9

From the Silence of the Soma to the Words of the Psyche

> *. . . one of the most integrative and therefore*
> *supportive things that we have to offer a patient*
> *is the power of verbal symbols to contain and*
> *organize thoughts, feelings, and sensations . . .*
> *That is, symbols help create us as subjects.*
> — Thomas Ogden

THE PRENATAL TRANSACTIONS between the mother and her fetal infant, coupled with the impact of the biparental unconscious on the body-mind matrix of the new life, produce a faint blueprint of the psychic structure of the nursling-to-come. Clinical observation (Morgan, 1992) confirms that parental projections onto the unborn child, as well as the occurrence of affectively-charged external events during the mother's pregnancy, play a role in the mother's contact with her fetal baby. Following these prenatal influences, the early transactions between mother and nursling may together determine the tendency to somatic rather than psychological reactions to internal and external stress. Since primary psychic structures are created through the psychic representation of *prelinguistic signifiers*, it is important to explore the relation between this forgotten language and psychosomatic symptoms.

THE PROTOLANGUAGE OF SOMATIZATION

The risk of somatization is greater *for everyone* whenever there is an unusual increase in internal conflict or external pressures.

There is scarcely any patient in psychoanalytic treatment, or any analyst either, who does not display, at one time or another, somatic disturbance due to psychic distress. We are all likely to somatize when internal or external circumstances overflow the containment provided by our usual defenses against mental pain and overwhelming excitement, or depontentiate our habitual ways of discharging stressful emotional experiences. As analysts, however, we are more concerned with those patients whose psychosomatic manifestations constitute a prominent part of their overall clinical picture, especially when their psychic structures display a relative poverty of other forms of psychological defense.

My interest in attempting to understand the unconscious significance of psychosomatic manifestations in the course of psychoanalytic treatment derived from an overarching interest that dated back many years: an interest in detecting factors that appeared to *escape* the analytic process. These include conflicts, anxiety situations, fantasies, and character patterns that are never mentioned in the course of the analysis, but through which unacknowledged mental pain and psychic conflict — whether stemming from inner pressures, outer environmental tress, or even tensions created by the analytic process itself — are discharged via some form of *action* outside the analytic situation. Typically, the analysand does not question this particular behavior, because it is felt to be intrinsic to his or her way of being or manner of coping with stress, and the analyst therefore remains unaware of it. Action symptoms of this kind short-circuit the work of psychic elaboration that is required to construct psychological symptoms. They depend less on language and thus can be thought of as a regression to an earlier phase of mental organization — the ways of thinking that characterize infancy. Throughout the lifespan, we all have access to this form of primitive mental functioning. Symptoms — whether they be neurotic, psychotic, character organizations, action patterns, addictions, or psychosomatic manifestations — are, *without exception*, the result of infantile efforts to find solutions to mental pain and psychic conflict.

We are all obliged to develop psychic organizations and mental structures that deal with the physical and mental forms of pain that await us from birth onward. Success in this endeavour depends on two interrelated factors: the capacity for the development of symbolic functioning, and the extent to which personal history and early environment facilitated rather than impeded this development. What is important here is discerning the extent to which the parents' unconscious problems rendered the task of growing from infancy to adulthood more difficult than it already is.

The two challenges that confront every human being—the complicated process of acquiring and assuming a sense of *individual identity*, followed by coming to terms with one's *gender identity* and assuming a future sexual role—both involve a mourning process. As already noted, individuality and monosexuality are major narcissistic wounds to the megalomaniac psyche of the child, but there are rich compensations. Overcoming the claim of fusional rights involves renouncing the omnipotent expectation of a magical fulfillment of one's wishes, as occurred in infancy, when wishes were met without having to pass through the code of language. However, this renouncement is rewarded with a sense of self-identity and freedom from the counter-fantasy of being omnipotently controlled by the mother. Overcoming bisexual and incestuous wishes involves renouncing the impossible desire to be and to have both sexes, as well as the demands attached to the oedipal crisis in both its heterosexual and homosexual dimensions. This loss is compensated by the gift of sexual desire and satisfying adult love relations.

Somatic symptoms invariably involve a breakdown in an individual's capacity for symbolization and therefore in the capacity for elaborating mentally the impact of stressful experiences. When anxiety, distress, unacknowledged rage, terror, or unusual excitement are *somatized* instead of being recognized and processed mentally, the individual is submerged in a primitive form of thinking in which the signifiers are *preverbal*. In other words, there is a regression to infantile methods of dealing with affective experiences. A baby can only react somatically to either physical or mental stress, when this stress is not metabolized by the mother's handling and care. Somatizations might be conceptualized as forms of preverbal or protosymbolic functioning which, therefore, constitute a "protolanguage." This chapter explores the psychic economy underlying somatization and the primitive symbolism and "protocommunication" that is mutely seeking expression through psychosomatic symptoms.

THE BODY-MIND MATRIX

In the newborn infant, body and mind are not yet experienced as separate, nor is there any distinction in the nursling's psychic experience between its own body and self and that of the mother's body and being. Mother is not yet another human being; yet, at the same time she is much more than that: She is a total environment, of which the infant is but a tiny part. We might posit the existence of a universal fantasy in the psychic experience of the infant, in which there is only *one body* and only *one mind* for two people.

It is normal for mothers to share the illusion of fusion and oneness with their babies in the first weeks of life. But some mothers, for a variety of unconscious reasons, prolong this fusional fantasy and unconsciously experience their children as an integral part of themselves long past early infancy. Ignoring or overriding their infants' signs and signals, they impose their own interpretation of the nurslings' needs and wants. In other words, it is the *mother*'s separation anxiety that is the problem and not the child's. (Infantile sleeping disorders, one of the earliest forms of infant psychosomatic disturbance, are an example of one response to this form of mothering.)

The mother's anxiety subsequently tends to inhibit a second important psychological need in every infant, one that parallels the baby's wish to maintain the illusion of fusional oneness with its mother: namely, the drive toward *separation*. A mother who wishes to remain as one with her baby, due to unconscious conflicts and unresolved problems stemming from her own childhood experiences, tends to remain deaf to the baby's signals that indicate a need to differentiate from the mother's body and self. Indeed, she may even prevent her infant from taking any spontaneous action that has not been initiated by her.

In former works (McDougall, 1989) I have referred to all that we are able to learn about the mother-infant dyad from psychosomatically ill infants. This dyad includes the father and the role he occupies, in both real and symbolic ways, in the mother's life.

BODY-LANGUAGE AND THE
LANGUAGE OF THE BODY

The verbalization of body experience and the corporealization of language raises many a complex question. To begin with, the assumption of a dissociation between body and mind is an arbitrary one. This concept of mind-body duality, a legacy of Cartesian philosophy, can cloud our perception, skew our theoretical conceptualizations, and even distort our clinical work. Likewise, the assumption that the body has no "language," as some theoricians claim, is also dangerously biasing for a psychoanalyst. Perhaps body-language is the *only* language that cannot lie! At least, it is safe to say that the body, as well as its somatic functioning, are gifted with remarkable *memory*.

The infantile psyche is manifestly articulated in a prelinguistic mode, yet the first transactions between mother and baby take place in an atmosphere that is verdant with language: that of the "mother tongue." From birth onward the tiny infant is surrounded by environmental influences that are organized by a system of verbal signs and meanings. At the same time, *another language* is being transmitted. The infant's body, along with all its sensory perceptions, is in constant contact with the mother's body (her voice, smell, touch, warmth). The baby receives these nonverbal communications in the form of bodily inscriptions, although accompanied by speaking individuals.

This pairing of the sensory with the verbal is surely the reason that somatic experiences are usually translated into verbal expression in ways with which everyone can identify. The same identification occurs whenever we recount important emotional experiences. The words used to convey emotion are invariably rooted in sensory metaphors: we *tremble* with fear, we are *crushed* with sorrow, *weighed down* with cares, *choked* with anger; our hearts *beat* with pleasure or are *pierced* with grief. An affect is never a purely psychic phenomenon nor a purely somatic one.

In a certain sense, somatic experience is interwoven with the symbolic world from birth, but as yet there are no verbal signifiers. The celebrated principle of Lacan to the effect that "the unconscious is structured like a language" can be a confusing rather than helpful metaphor when examining the early preverbal interaction between psyche and soma and the infantile origins of psychic structure. Over the years I have become skeptical of those disciples who contend that the symbolic world of language is the sole valid container for understanding the psychoanalytic process — particularly when the conceptualization of primitive states of mind is concerned.

Most of us share Freud's fascination with words. As Pontalis points out in a thought-provoking paper, Freud displayed a remarkable confidence in the power of language. Words were invested with magic and, indeed, were "magical in their very origin." It is also noteworthy that Freud never wavered from this position, even after his discovery of the shattering effects of what he called "the demoniacal power of the death instinct." Even this all-powerful drive could not attack the written word! Although Freud witnessed dislocation, fragmentation, and relentless destruction in the internal psychic world of his patients, colleagues, and friends — and in the war-ravaged world of external events — his faith in language held fast in the midst of every catastrophe (Pontalis, 1990).

In this context the biblical phrase "in the beginning was the word" comes to mind. Perhaps this reverence for language is the legacy of a paternalistic religion. In the beginning was the voice — but even before the voice, in the intrauterine world, there was already sound and rhythmic beating — the dawn of music. Freud himself admitted that, with few exceptions, he could not comprehend music, that he was insensitive to its power. Clearly he could not, or did not, allow such a primal penetration into his heart and soul. Is it feasible to suggest that Freud erected a phallic barrier of words, equating language with the paternal order (as does Lacan), in order to protect himself from the voice of the siren, the power of the primitive mother?

Whatever the answer, everyone knows that a mother gives more than words and phrases to the baby she holds in her arms. The very timbre of her voice is imbued with her bodily self and its emotions. Our words are capable of caressing — and just as readily, of wounding — another person. The sound of a voice may be warming to the heart or chilling to the ear; it may have the same effect as a gesture or a way of looking at another person. Within the infant-mother dyad, the mother's voice permeates the bodily self of the infant, whereas looking — the visual world —

tends to create a distance from the other, as do words themselves. It is also possible to shut out visual perceptions by merely closing one's eyes or turning one's head away, whereas there is no simple recourse for closing one's ears!

Didier Anzieu (1986) has accorded great importance to the early "skin self" ("*le Moi-peau*"), in which he includes many other senses. I would add to this fruitful concept that of an early *olfactory self*—and, indeed, a respiratory, a visceral, and a muscular, self—as eloquent sources of *preverbal signifiers* that flow between mother and nursling and that make a fundamental contribution to the early structural development of the psyche. In this context it must be emphasized that it is not the perceptions in themselves that are of primary interest to us, but *the way in which they are registered psychically*.

It is also important to recognize that these early signifiers cannot be repressed in the manner in which repression is defined by Freud (1915c); that is, as a psychic mechanism maintaining representations in the unconscious that are linked to drives through the medium of verbal thoughts and memories. Since preverbal memories cannot be dealt with in the same fashion, there is a constant risk that their dynamic force will be vented in the sudden eruption of hallucinatory experiences or somatic explosion.

The unmediated nature of preverbal forcefulness eludes awareness and any attempt to capture psychic representations of highly-charged affective experiences. Thus patients in whom this type of psychic economy *predominates* are handicapped in representing mentally the impact of external events and relationships as well as demands arising from their inner world. Their conscious contact with their own psychic reality tends to be impoverished, resulting in an apparent incapacity to dream, a blockage in waking fantasy life, expression of conflict through action rather than through mental elaboration, and so on. As already indicated, behind a normopathic facade lie psychotic anxieties that eventually find expression in words and images. The nature of these anxieties recalls the experience of overwhelming dread against which autistic children attempt to protect themselves, in particular, by refusing to participate in symbolic communication through language. In polysomatizing patients it is the soma that behaves in an "autistic" fashion and "refuses" verbal elaboration of the terror that is submerged or foreclosed from conscious awareness.

In this respect Ogden's (1989a) concept of an "autistic-contiguous" position has helped me (1) to conceptualize the relation between polysomatizing phenomena in certain analysands and their use of language; and (2) to understand my own countertransference feelings, in which I felt as if I were being held in an "autistic position" or, inversely, as if my body were not differentiated from my patient's. In this primitive fashion my analysands were "communicating" the way in which *they* had managed to survive early psychic trauma in interaction with the biparental unconscious: by relying on the autistic-contiguous position in relation to both inner and outer worlds. This allowed me to further my understanding of the defensive value of "pseudo-normality" which I had always considered as a sign of deep, unrecognized distress (McDougall, 1985). I had observed that this protective shield helps these analysands go about their daily lives and frequently permits them to engage in highly intellectual pursuits or run important enterprises with great efficiency. (Although not *all* normopathic patients somatize, years of clinical experience have taught me that their psychosomatic vulnerability is extremely high.)

The analyst's task with these analysands is multi-fold: First, attention is directed to discerning the anonymous terror (what Bion, 1962, referred to as "nameless dread") hidden beneath the analytic associations, and then to helping analysands find the courage to perceive their feelings for themselves. As the overwhelming anxiety slowly becomes perceptible, the analytic frame provides a safe environment that enables patients to imagine what fantasies might accompany such emotion. Finally, it becomes possible to *name* the formerly nameless dread, against which such patients have defended themselves all their lives. The fantasies can then be linked to present-day conflicts which, in turn, reveal their underlying significance. Unconscious anxieties of this kind usually have their origins in traumatic events that occurred in earliest childhood before the acquisition of language.*

---

*However, similar nameless dread may also arise in patients who have experienced unassuaged terror at a time when they were totally verbal, if the events were of such magnitude that their capacity to use verbal thought was temporarily extinguished—for example, due to the horrors of war or genocide.

WHEN SADISTIC EROTICISM
BECOMES VERBAL

The session notes that follow were taken from my work with Jean-Paul, discussed in the previous chapter, some three years later. Around this time, Jean-Paul was visibly more relaxed. He could now look at me, and although he still dived like a shooting star onto the couch, his whole attitude was distinctly less tense and bizarre.

During the preceding week's sessions, Jean-Paul had engaged in a series of daydreams in which he imagined himself hollowing out "large black craters" in women's breasts, a theme inspired by a poster he saw daily of a woman with naked breasts. The focus was accompanied by another preoccupation, in which Jean-Paul, in his quick glance at me before flinging himself on the couch, would perceive me as "smashed up" or "physically ill."

JEAN-PAUL Are you tired? If you only knew how anxious that makes me! I'm always terribly afraid of finding you looking worn out. I don't know why. [*Long pause*]

JM You may remember that last week you imagined yourself digging black craters in women's breasts. Might not this sort of activity make a woman look tired and worn out?

JEAN-PAUL Now that irritates me, because it has nothing to do with reality. I'm not at all interested in fantasies!

JM You see me looking worn out, rather like the other day when you described my face as "dislocated." Might these impressions arise in place of imagining or feeling something concerning me?

JEAN-PAUL I sometimes "see" strange things just before falling asleep, and it terrifies me." [*Jean-Paul rarely has memories of dreaming.*]

JM As though there, too, you might "see strange things" to avoid fantasies or letting yourself imagine just anything, like in a dream? Maybe if you refuse to let such thoughts come up, they appear in front of you like real perceptions?

JEAN-PAUL But I've every reason to stifle my mad ideas. They cause me much greater panic than the strange things that I imagine I am seeing. My thoughts are truly horrible! . . . Something important has changed, though. I can now look people in the *eyes*, and I'm no longer afraid of their looking at me. It still troubles me, because I see them all smashed up much of the time, but that doesn't worry me like it used to. So what if they look like that . . . [*long pause*] . . . or is it *me* who makes them look that way?

JM The way you saw me just now?

JEAN-PAUL Yes, it's exactly the same! *I have a destructive stare. Mon Dieu*, why do I do that? What do I reproach you with? . . . I've got it! . . . Your interpretations! I hate them—particularly if I feel they're important and useful to me. [*Pause*] I can't take it when you think of things first.

JM As though you were afraid of being dependent on me? That I might possess something you could need?

JEAN-PAUL Exactly! Especially if it's something I could have thought for myself. At those moments, I'd like to tear you to bits.

JM [*Remembering that Jean-Paul was breast-fed for nearly four years*] Like a small boy who's hungry might feel furious to have to depend on his mother, depend on her breasts, in order to be fed? Would that make him want to "tear them to bits"?

JEAN-PAUL You know, I think that's very true. And I hate you for that! *Merde alors*, why should I have to *need* you?

JM [*At the following session Jean-Paul again describes his image of my face broken up.*]

JEAN-PAUL Oh, *là*! Now *you're* the one who's getting it. But I mustn't even think such things or you might really fall ill. I'm terribly afraid of such thoughts, you know.

JM Afraid your fantasies might be magical and fulfill themselves?

JEAN-PAUL There you go again! Okay, let's plunge on. Why is it so terrible to imagine you with black craters in your nipples, anyway [*tossing his head from side to side*]? I know why! It's because, for me, the breasts are the most beautiful, soft, and sensual part of a woman's body. I just can't bear to see myself attacking them.

JM [*His voice trembles and he seems to be on the verge of tears. This might well be considered to be an approach to the "depressive position" as defined by Melanie Klein (1957).*]

JEAN-PAUL I feel as if I destroy everyone. Nadine . . . my mother . . . I look at them and I see them looking grotesque, deformed, aged. But with you, it's the worst of all. To *you* I mete out death. It's truly horrible. [*Long pause*] I really don't understand anything anymore. Why is everything erotic invariably full of horror for me? I want to make love, but instead I imagine scenes of torture. Ouch! I'm beginning to have terrible gastric pains! I harden my whole body, tighten my insides, to *prevent* such horrible thoughts. If I tense up enough, maybe they won't come to mind. But that's a bit crazy. What's wrong with these thoughts, anyway?

JM [*While exploring this idea, Jean-Paul suddenly realizes that his sharp gastric pain has disappeared. He is astonished by this "miracle," and he begins to question his way of using his body to prevent himself from thinking.*]

JEAN-PAUL But it would mean total confusion to allow just any thoughts to take possession of me. Disorganization . . . illness! I couldn't stand it . . . I'd go crazy.

THE EYES OF ATTACK

In the weeks following the sessions just described, Jean-Paul continued to have sudden "visions" and pseudoperceptions, but he was now able to examine them more thoughtfully and with less fear that he was going crazy. The following vignette illustrates the gradual "neurotization" of his conflicts.

For some time Jean-Paul had become aware of "blind spots" in his field of vision; his preoccupation with this phenomenon, which he referred to as his "scotoma," reached hypochondriacal proportions. After a visit to the ophthalmologist, he reported that there was nothing at all wrong with his eyes: "I just don't see things the way I should."

The important change reflected in this remark was that, for the first time, Jean-Paul was using his body-images *metaphorically*. That is, he was beginning to "desomatize" his self-perceptions. He still had pseudoperceptions, but he now questioned them. Further on in the session, he spoke of a woman at work who appealed to him sexually and whom he referred to as "the young mother." The following excerpt from the session provides an unusual example of sudden repression during the analytic work itself.

JEAN-PAUL I can't stop thinking about her breasts and her fragility. I have to be careful of my thoughts about her . . . um . . . ah . . . where was I? Funny, I've completely lost the thread of my thought. A void. Just as though I were up against a blank wall. *Bon Dieu!* There's my scotoma back again!

JM [*Sudden repression is followed by the reappearance of the hysterical manifestation!*] What were you thinking just before the scotoma appeared? When you said you felt you were up against a blank wall?

JEAN-PAUL Haven't the vaguest. Don't even remember what I was talking about.

JM The young mother who seems so fragile. . . .

JEAN-PAUL Oh, *là là*! Do I dare let myself think just *anything* about her? Well, I see myself undressing her, and I'm biting her breasts, and I start to make love to her furiously, like a madman, and I sodomize her, and I eat her feces . . . Listen, I can't do this!! If I follow your system of saying everything that comes into my mind, I'll go quite crazy. Good heavens—the scotoma has disappeared!

ARCHAIC HYSTERIA AND
ITS TRANSFORMATIONS

Symptoms such as Jean-Paul's "scotoma" might well be described as a primitive form of hysteria—a defense against pregenital wishes that remain blocked and encapsulated rather than elaborated as fantasies to be subsequently repressed. The "black craters in the breasts" appear to have been transformed into the "blind spots" in Jean-Paul's eyes. In the above session, however, Jean-Paul no longer faced the terror of nameless dread. He was now able to find words and mental representations capable of expressing his painful affective states. These newly identified states began to reflect common infantile sexual theories with their accompanying pregenital impulses. In the sessions that followed, I noted that Jean-Paul frequently observed the "scotoma" whenever he was angry or filled with violent erotic fantasy.

JEAN-PAUL The scotoma makes me anxious. I'm sure it's a way of *not seeing*—that is, of not knowing something—but the trouble is, I don't know what! At such moments I'm filled with terrible anguish, a frenetic primordial dread, that descends on me, especially after making love—I simply can't look at the woman then. She becomes a vampire.

JM Yet you were the one who had daydreams of eating up the woman who attracted you sexually—the young mother: You wanted to eat her breasts and her excrements. Do you think that the frightening and destructive aspect of your own fantasies might make you afraid that the woman is going to vamparize *you*?

JEAN-PAUL Oh, I don't know about that! [*Pause*] God almighty! I've got palpitations just thinking about it . . . exactly the same palpitations I get now when I make love . . . or even think about making love. [*Pause*] I'm thinking once more of that Polanski film about vampires and that scene where the man carried off the pretty girl. *Tiens*! The vampire was a *man*!

JM Are *you* the vampire, then?

JEAN-PAUL [*Laughing with astonishment and delight*] Of course, it's me!! How come I never thought of it? I'm *sure* all this has to do with my sexuality.

JM [*Jean-Paul was finally becoming aware that, in his childlike vision, making love was equivalent to destroying the partner—or being destroyed.*]

JEAN-PAUL Why does all erotic pleasure turn into poison for me? I can see those black holes in the breasts again—just like dead holes, as though the breasts were stung by hornets. Yes, that's what they are— poisonous bites into the nipples. [*Long pause*] I think I've always associated eroticism with death. Lately, I'm afraid to make love to Nadine. I get an image of those hornet holes and suddenly I lose my erection. I mean, I can't make love in that dead hole!

JM [*Jean-Paul gives further evidence that he is now constructing neurotic symptoms in place of psychosomatic ones—this time in the form of a temporary phase of sexual impotence—a problem he had not experienced when his sexual life was considerably more mechanical and affectless than it is now.*] As though you wish to avoid being the *hornet* who attacks the breasts or who goes into the dead hole?

JEAN-PAUL That's it! *I'm* the hornet! *I'm* the one who's dangerous; even my eyes can destroy. The vampire, now that's an image of my father and also some part of myself.

Thus we arrive at the beginning of Jean-Paul's oedipal analysis. His psychosomatosis, previously inaccessible to verbal thought, was gradually becoming an analyzable psychoneurosis.

The analysis lasted ten years. Since its termination, many years have elapsed. I have had news from Jean-Paul several times in which he tells me, among other things, that his gastric ulcers and skin allergies have not returned.

Jean-Paul's true illness was not his gastric ulcerations or his neurodermatitis, but the profound split between psyche and soma, between his verbal everyday self and his emotional self; a split that had been constructed in order to prevent deep pain and psychotic terror, as well as archaic sexual fantasy, from emerging. His mind sent only primitive messages about these dangers, but as the analysis continued, his "delusional" body, with its deranged somatic functioning, slowly became a symbolic one—a psychosomatic unity—which kept him in touch with his inner life while allowing him to become conscious of the impact of the outside world upon himself. The incoherent somatic messages were translated into psychic representations and the life forces within him sought many new avenues of expression. His relationship to his children changed radically and his love-life became richer and more satisfying. Eros had finally triumphed over the destructive and death-like factors that, until his analysis, had invaded and dominated his life.

FROM "BIO-LOGIC" TO "PSYCHO-LOGIC"

How does the biological body eventually become a psychological one — an integrated body-image that can be named, erogenetically invested, and cognitively explored?

From the beginning of somatopsychic life, there are double messages that pass between psyche and soma. As Freud put it, the soma "imposes the need for work" upon the psyche by means of what he called its "representatives." These representatives, or messages, report states of need and demands for satisfaction. In turn, the psyche sends messages to the body, usually originating in a conflictive experience, because no acceptable solution to the somatic message has yet been found. The soma must then reply to this emotional message. And so on. Of course, physical and mental needs are not yet dissociated in the tiny infant. In the adult, however, this distinction has usually been achieved.* The vignettes taken from Jean-Paul's analysis revealed that he frequently confused somatic and psychic experiences, treating them as one and the same thing.

Apart from the experience of corporeal suffering (and even this can be totally excluded from conscious recognition), it is clear that the body we live in, the body of which we are consciously aware, is essentially a psychological construct. Those aspects of the body and its somatic functioning that do not achieve psychic representation do not exist for us. This applies also to emotions. Affects are the most privileged links between soma and psyche; any radical cutting of these links increases not only the eventuality of character pathology but also of psychosomatic vulnerability.

---

*This confusion also characterizes patients suffering from chronic pain syndrome, who typically equate physical and psychical pain. But, in these cases, the body-schema as a whole provides a stage for psychosomatic production.

In summary, psychosomatic symptoms express a form of primitive body language, a *protolanguage*, which was intended to communicate a message to the outer world in the early life of the individual. (To the extent that there is an image of an "other" believed to be capable of decoding and responding to this protolanguage, the term *communication* is valid.) It is important for psychoanalysts to realize that, as analyses progress, this protolanguage, with its protosymbolism, begins to be used as a symbolic language, so that the boundaries between "purely psychosomatic" and "purely hysterical" manifestations eventually become less distinct (Sachs, 1985). Under the impact of the analytic voyage, all analysands learn to experience their somatic symptoms as communications, to pay attention to them in an attempt to identify the internal or external pressures that have precipitated them, and thus invest them with metaphor and meaning. Many a patient will use a somatic symptom as the embryo around which to build a protective neurotic wall. In this way the mute somatic communications secondarily acquire symbolic status. Consequently, these messages are accessible to direct communications with the inner and outer world, through the decipherable language of neurosis.

Apart from this neurotic overlay that is often in place before an analysis begins, psychosomatic manifestations resemble dream processes in many ways. Freud regarded dreams as employing a regressive mode of expression of an archaic kind. I have frequently referred to psychosomatic disorders as "dreams that never got dreamt." Might we not envisage many a psychosomatic expression as a regressive and archaic form of communication, a primitive body language which the nervous system is programmed to transmit. The task of the analyst is that of creating—with the analysand—a glossary for translating this *bio-logic* into *psycho-logic*, finally enabling the anarchic, psychosomatically expressive body to become a symbolic one.

PART IV

Deviations of Desire

CHAPTER 10

Neosexual Solutions

> *I hereby appoint myself Aesthetician. And there-by — as self-assured as an art critic — pronounce as truth my conviction that the construction of erotic excitement is every bit as subtle, complex, inspired, profound, tidal, fascinating, awesome, problematic, unconscious-soaked, and genius-haunted as the creation of dreams or art.*
>
> — Robert Stoller

IN 1984 I WAS INVITED to present a paper at the Congress of the International Psychoanalytic Association in Hamburg, Germany, on the subject of "identifications and perversions from a predominantly clinical point of view" (McDougall, 1986a). My first thought was that this clinical focus would allow me to evade the complex issues involved in defining what is and is not *perverse* in human sexuality. However, my relief rapidly receded. Given the clinical material that would be suited to this purpose, I realized that it would be factitious to make any clear-cut distinction between "theoretical" and "clinical" psychoanalysis. Clinical vignettes *prove* nothing. They only serve to illustrate a theoretical conception. By the same token, theoretical advances are the fruit of innumerable clinical experiences that have stimulated us to recognize impasses and to question our existing concepts. Moreover, there is the ever-present risk that our theoretical beliefs unduly influence our technique, to the degree that our analysands may employ much of their analytical process in an attempt to confirm their analysts' theoretical expectations! For all of these reasons I feel obliged to articulate some idea of what I understand by the term "sexual perversion."

WHAT CONSTITUTES A "PERVERSION"?

I take a critical view of this terminology, since the word *perversion* always carries a pejorative connotation, implying a degradation, a turning toward evil. (One never hears that so-and-so was *"perverted* to the good life.") Over and beyond this moralistic implication in the vernacular usage of the word, our standard psychiatric and psychoanalytic classifications of clinical entities are equally questionable. To designate someone as a "neurotic," a "psychotic," a "psychosomatic," or a "pervert," may have little real pertinence, particularly since the variations of psychic structure within each so-called clinical category are innumerable. The remarkable aspect of human beings in their psychic structure — as in their genetic structure — is their *singularity*. Psychological symptoms are attempts at self-cure, to avoid psychic suffering; this same intent applies equally to symptomatic sexuality. Taking this more constructive view of the underlying meaning and purpose of symptoms, and the reasons for which they came into being, we invariably discover that they are childlike solutions to conflict, confusion, and mental pain. Faced with the difficulties of being human, as well as the unconscious conflicts of our parents, we must all contrive ways of surviving, both as individuals and as sexual beings, and the solutions we find tend to endure for a lifetime.

For some 25 years I have endeavored to find a satisfactory definition of "perverse" sexuality from a psychoanalytic viewpoint — of what is and is not symptomatic with regard to sexual acts and sexual object relationships. Take homosexuality, for example, is it to be regarded as a symptom under all circumstances? Or, under all circumstances, as another nonsymptomatic version of male or female sexuality? Analysts are sharply divided in their opinions on this question. Leavy (1985), Limentani (1977), and Isay (1985), for example, express ideas that differ from those of Socarides (1968, 1978).

Most of the so-called perverse sexualities, such as fetishism, sadomasochistic practices, voyeurism, and exhibitionism, are com-

plicated attempts to maintain some form of *heterosexual* relations. Indeed, the clinical issues of heterosexual relations are no
clearer than with homosexual acts and object choices. The poly-
morphous nature of non-perverse adult heterosexual activity
needs no emphasis. Our analysands describe an infinite variety
of erotic scenarios, including cross-dressing, the use of fetishistic
objects and adornments, sadomasochistic games, and so on,
which surface as interludes in their lovemaking, perhaps igniting
erotic pleasure within a stable love relationship. These practices
cause no conflict, since they are not felt to be compulsive or to be
exclusive conditions for sexual pleasure.

Then there are those heterosexual patients who have *only* fetishistic or sadomasochistic scenarios at their disposal in order to
engage in a heterosexual relationship. As with certain homosexual
patients, we might wish that these analysands were a little less
restricted and less subjected to inexorable conditions in their sex
lives, but if these erotic theater pieces are the sole conditions for
allowing access to sexual relations, we should be wary of wishing
for them to lose these heterodox versions of the objects of desire,
simply because we may regard them as symptomatic!

Most people experience their erotic acts and object choices as
ego-syntonic, whether or not they are judged by others as "perverse." Specific varieties of sexual preference become an analyzable problem only to the extent that the individuals concerned
regard their normal form of sexuality as a source of *suffering* and
therefore experience it as ego-dystonic. This problem arises with
those gay men (and, to a lesser extent, with lesbian women) who
feel that they should be heterosexual because of family opinion,
society's norms, religious principles, and so on. In such circumstances a fierce inner conflict may arise, accompanied by feelings
of guilt or shame, in spite of the fact that the sexual acts or
relationships in question are the only ones that bring pleasure,
and sometimes the only ones that hold the promise of a love
relationship. A few homosexual analysands may come to discover
that they are "latent" heterosexuals and would be happier in pursuing heterosexual relationships. But they are not the majority.
Most gay men and women find it vitally important to maintain
their homosexual identity and orientation. In view of what is at
stake, one cannot but feel they are right. It should also be noted
that there are as many varieties of homosexual acts and types of

relationship as there are heterosexual acts and relations. There are also what might be called "deviant homosexualities" that require fetishistic additions, such as shoes or whips, or sadomasochistic conditions of pain or humiliation, in order to achieve satisfactory sexual engagement.

Whatever the sexual pattern may be, the analysands themselves rarely wish to lose their erotic solutions. A number of patients, under the impact of the analytic adventure, develop richer erotic and intimate relationships. However, should this fortunate outcome not occur, then to lose one's only system of sexual survival would be the equivalent of castration. And more than that. In many cases, these intricate and ineluctable erotic scenarios serve not only to safeguard the feeling of sexual identity that accompanies sexual pleasure, but frequently reveal themselves to be techniques of psychic survival that are required to preserve the feeling of subjective identity as well.

WHY NEOSEXUALITIES?

To emphasize the innovative character and intensity of the investments involved, I refer to deviant heterosexualities and deviant homosexualities as "neosexualities." This nomenclature utilizes the concept of *neorealities*, which are created by fragile borderline patients in an illusory, or even delusional, attempt to find solutions to overwhelming conflicts.

In both heterosexual and homosexual deviations, the need to reinvent the sexual act can usually be traced to disturbing childhood events or misleading communications regarding sexual identity, sexual roles, and the concepts of femininity and masculinity. In these cases, adult relationships with partners require complicated maneuvers, conditions, and accoutrements in the manner of stage sets.

Analysts who regard homosexuality as a pathological formation and "a sexual perversion like any other" often question the validity of differentiating between neosexual inventors and homosexuals. Freud (1905) himself made a distinction between the homosexualities and the heterosexual forms of deviant sexualities. He referred to homosexuality as "inversion" and the deviant behavior of fetishists, exhibitionists, sadomasochists, etc., as "perversion." As he defined them, both referred to a "deflection of the original sexual aim or goal." Freud's differentiation between *inversion* and *perversion* is pertinent, because there are frequently important structural and dynamic differences between the two types of psychosexual organization. At the same time, many analysts have observed similarities in their oedipal structures. For example, these analysands often report an unduly close relationship with the mother, sometimes with incestuous overtones, and the father is experienced as denigrated or excluded from his symbolic role in the oedipal constellation. Others report a history of seduction by the father, in which the mother appears to have played a role by virtue of her complicity; or a history of neglect by the mother, in which she, for whatever reasons, emerges as having disinvested this particular child. Further complicating the clinical picture, a certain number of analysands, whose sexuality is neither homosexually oriented nor deviant in the sense of a neosexual invention, also present similar parental patterns!

The majority of homosexuals are uninterested in neosexual inventions and, in general, heterosexual deviants have little interest in pursuing homosexual relations. Perhaps the one area that is characteristic of both homosexual and neosexual patients concerns the psychic economy that governs their sexuality. This economy is frequently marked by a sense of urgency and compulsivity, giving the impression that their sexual lives fulfill the role of an addiction. This important aspect is explored in the following chapter.

The variations in psychosexual structure are so great that we are obliged to talk in the plural — of heterosexuali*ties* and homosexuali*ties*. To these must also be added the category of autoerotic sexualities, since many sadomasochistic, fetishistic, and transvestite practices are played out in solitude. These acts could be considered as deviant forms of masturbation, in that fantasy alone does not suffice; the condensed erotic dramas must be put into action.

PERVERSION AND SUBLIMATION

It is interesting to note that Freud (1930) defined sublimation in exactly the same terms he used to define sexual perversion! This is understandable in that many sexual deviations are veritable *creations*. They sometimes resemble complicated theater pieces that are minutely planned days or weeks in advance. I recall an exhibitionist who would photograph, from different angles, the exact spot where he intended to exhibit himself in the *Bois de Boulogne*, taking into consideration the footpaths and motorways along which his potential "partners" would be expected to appear and participate in his spectacle. The scenario was planned much as a painter might plan an important exhibition of his work, or a producer his stage set. Another analysand, a fetishist whose theater piece, to my mind, deserved the title of "The Anonymous Spectator" (McDougall, 1978a), would write out the scenes he imagined for many weeks before putting them "on stage." Then would come the triumphal opening performance—in front of the mirror—in which he played all the roles: that of the anonymous public looking into the mirror where "a mother was beating a little girl," as well as that of the chief actor reflected in the mirror, getting whipped on the buttocks. As was the case with the exhibitionist, the forethought and meticulous planning that went into the scenario before it was ready to be made "public" often seemed to be more invested than the act itself.

A pedophilac patient, whose case I followed in supervision, also demonstrated creative planning. He would wander for days through the sex shops and stand at the gates of different scholastic establishments, weaving fantasies in response to the sight of this or that young adolescent with whom he imagined himself engaged in passionate relationship. It was also important that the chosen boy be interested in the arts, as was the analysand himself, and this quality was incorporated into his fantasies. His acting-out was highly restricted; it had to follow a certain pattern in which he was convinced that it was the adolescent who wanted the relationship and who had initiated the process of seduction.

For all of these individuals, their elaborate constructions represent not only their one means of sexual expression, but also a dimension of their daily lives that is as vital to their psychic equilibrium as are their sublimatory activities. (The exhibitionist worked in the field of artistic publicity; the fetishist was a professor of philosophy; the pedophile, a teacher of music.) It is feasible to propose that their sexual constructions, like the sublimated libidinal investments that gave quality to their professional work, sprang as solutions from the same primitive sources of psychic conflict.

One common characteristic I noted in those analysands who had constructed complex deviations was that they frequently were unable, or even terrified, to imagine the slightest change in their ritualized scenarios. They often appeared unable to daydream freely around sexual themes. In humankind's psychic economy, one of the leading functions of daydreaming is to be able to accomplish in imagination that which is believed to be forbidden or impossible to enact in reality. Thus a restricted capacity to use fantasy, such as is manifested in many deviant sexualities, evidences some breakdown in the important introjections that take place in what Winnicott (1951) named *transitional phenomena*. There is a consequent inability to create freely an illusion in the space that separates one being from another, and to use a variety of illusions to support absence, frustration, and delay. I shall return to this important point in the discussion of addictive sexuality in the following chapter.

In all other respects, neosexual creators differ little from so-called normal people, who invest their sexual drives and relationships, as well as the sublimation of these in their professional work, with equally vital significance.

What Is a "Perverse" Fantasy?

In the realm of erotic fantasy life, everyone is free from external restraint; the only inhibitory factors are those enforced by internal parental figures. We must ask ourselves whether there is any such thing as a "perverse" fantasy—and if there is, then we must be prepared to define what might be meant by a "normal" erotic fantasy. In my view the only aspect of a fantasy that might legitimately be described as perverse would be the attempt to force one's erotic imagination on a non-consenting or a non-responsible other. In general, I would reserve the term *perversion* as a label for acts in which an individual (1) imposes personal wishes and conditions on someone who does not wish to be included in the perverse individual's sexual scenario (as in the case of rape, voyeurism, and exhibitionism); or (2) seduces a non-responsible individual (such as a child or a mentally disturbed adult). Perhaps in the last resort, only *relationships* can aptly be termed *perverse*; this label would then apply to sexual exchanges in which the perverse individual is totally indifferent to the needs and desires of the other.

From this standpoint the pertinent question is not which acts and preferences are deviant, but *under what circumstances* is deviancy to be regarded as a simple variation of adult sexuality in the context of a significant object relationship and when is it to be judged symptomatic? I would apply this question to heterosexualities, homosexualities, and autoerotic sexualities alike. The quality of a relationship cannot be assessed from purely external signs. There are qualitative a well as quantitative psychic factors to be taken into account: The qualitative aspects concern the individual's dynamic psychosexual structure; the quantitative factors refer to the role of sexual activity in his or her psychic economy. Human sexual patterns, as Freud was the first to point out, are not inborn; they are created. The ego-syntonic aspect of sexual choices and practices reveals the presence of a system of powerful identifications — and counter-identifications — with introjected objects of a highly complex kind. These inner object representations and introjective constellations give rise to significant differences, from both the dynamic and the economic viewpoints, in the sexual and love relationships of neosexual inventors.

The introjective images slowly reveal themselves on the psychoanalytic stage, like so many players in a theater. The parental discourse on sexuality that continues throughout childhood plays a cardinal role in every individual's psychic structure. But over and beyond children's interpretation of their parents' communications, as well as of their striking silences, are the powerful identifications and defensive operations that children construct in relation to what they understand about their parents' *unconscious* sexual conflicts and erotic desires and of the roles they (the children) are covertly required to play. The unconscious demands often contradict what is consciously communicated, creating confusion and conflict in children's minds. These same conflicts and confusions are later manifested in the analytic situation and may require some years to disentangle.

What Does "Object Choice" Mean?

Nobody freely *chooses* to engage in the highly restricted and exigent conditions imposed by compulsive neosexual inventions, or the loneliness of a life that is largely confined to autoerotic creations. Likewise, few people have the impression of "choosing" to be homosexual in a predominantly heterosexual society, or for that matter, of "choosing" heterosexuality in order to conform to the social majority. With regard to deviant heterosexual, homosexual, and autoerotic inventions, these so-called choices represent the best possible *solutions* created by the child of the past in the face of contradictory parental communications concerning core gender identity, masculinity, femininity, and sexual role. These solutions are experienced by the child or adolescent as a *revelation* of his or her form of sexual expression, along with the sometimes painful recognition that this sexuality is somehow different from that of others. There is certainly no awareness of choice.

However, several authors (in particular, those concerned with research into the nature of homosexual identities) have distinguished a pattern that is regarded as a "choice": for example, the distinction made by Burch (1989) between the "primary" lesbian and the "bisexual" woman who chooses a lesbian love-life after some years of heterosexual relationships. Perhaps the "bisexual" woman in Burch's formulation is not so much *choosing* but finally *assuming* her desire and her identity as lesbian. This acceptance, of course, is a conscious choice, but does not necessarily mean that the individual "chose" the profound libidinal investments and orientations that are involved and which, perhaps, have been strongly counter-cathected until their late acknowledgment. This possibility does not invalidate or exclude the thesis that there are marked differences in psychic structure between these two groups.

In this and the following chapters, I address two major theoretical-clinical issues concerning sexual deviancy: first, the etiological and qualitative considerations and, second, the quantitative aspects as manifested in the psychic economy. Both topics are intimately concerned with the processes of internalization in deviant sexual organizations, which invariably involve a measure of failure in integrating and harmonizing the various incorporations and introjections that are structured from birth onward.

ETIOLOGICAL AND QUALITATIVE FACTORS
IN DEVIANT SEXUALITY

Freud's early formulations (1905) conceptualized perversions
and inversions as vicissitudes in the sexual drive due to fixations
to early stages of libidinal development. But by the 1920s Freud
(1915b, 1922) had connected the mystery of their creation to the
internal oedipal organization and the fantasies of the primal
scene. There is no need to recapitulate the well-recognized significance of superego identifications in the psychosexual structures.
However, it is important to remember that these structures, which
are largely created through the vehicle of language (verbal expla-
nations, encouragements, and prohibitions promulgated throughout childhood), are themselves founded upon an archaic substruc-
ture that precedes the acquisition of language. While it is tempting
to accept the facility of Freud's conceptual framework regarding
the important (and clinically confirmed) role of the phallic-oedipal
phase in deviant sexuality, this explanation is not sufficient; Freud
himself came to question the adequacy of his theories in this respect.

In attempting to conceptualize the internalizations that take
place in the earliest sensory exchanges between mother and infant,
the terms *incorporation* and *introjection* are more appropriate
than *identification*. At this stage of development the mother's
unconscious fears and wishes play a predominant role in the early
structural development of the psyche. It is only as symbolic communication slowly takes the place of bodily contact between the
child and its parents that sexual identifications and counter-
identifications become a permanent part of each child's psychic
capital. At the same time, the body-schema becomes consolidated.

It is the mother who first names erogenous zones for her children, communicating, in manifold ways, the libidinal and narcissistic investment or counter-investment that these zones — and
their associated functions — are to receive. The very existence of
certain organs and bodily functions can be virtually denied in
some families. Because of her own inner distress about zonal investments and sexual prohibitions, a mother may readily transmit
to her children a body-image that is fragile, alienated, devoid of
eroticism or even mutilated. Clinical observation has convinced

me that those children who are destined to require sexually deviant behavior in adulthood initially created their erotic theater as a protective attempt at self-cure: Confronted with overwhelming castration anxiety stemming from oedipal conflicts, at the same time, they were faced with the need of coming to terms with the introjected image of a fragile or mutilated body. Thus they protect themselves from a frightening sense of inner libidinal deadness. These protective measures frequently give rise to a fear of the loss of the body representation as a whole, and with it, the terrifying loss of a cohesive sense of ego identity.

Much has been written, yet much still remains to be said, about the fundamental representation of the penis, which, in accordance with its nature as an introjected part-object, determines the role and the organizing power of the phallus as a symbol. As already noted, the phallus does not refer to the part-object itself but to an effigy of the erect penis, which, as in the fertility rites of ancient Greece, symbolizes fertility and sexual desire. As such, the phallus belongs to neither sex; instead it organizes the introjective constellation and fundamental fantasies that determine the adult psychosexual organizations for both sexes. When divested of its symbolic value, the phallus can be reduced to the status of a part-object and then split into two distinct penis-images in either sex: a detached persecutory object that must be avoided or hated, and an idealized and unattainable object that must be pursued relentlessly. While both of these penis-representations provide a dynamic source of unconscious fantasy and influence the later choice of sexual acts and object-choices, neither representation has a fundamentally symbolic role any longer.

Sometimes even before her baby's birth, a mother may consciously or unconsciously regard her infant as a libidinal or narcissistic extension of herself, destined to repair a sense of personal inner damage. This type of maternal investment frequently leads to a wish to exclude the father in both his real and symbolic roles. If, in addition, the father chooses to accept a passive role, then archaic, baby-like, libidinal wishes and terrors may not be worked through and harmoniously integrated into the sexual representation of the adult self, thus creating what might be called *symbolic havoc*.

In summary, I propose that individuals who, in the service

of libidinal and narcissistic homeostases, create a neoreality and neoneeds in terms of sexual acts and objects, have short-circuited the elaboration of phallic-oedipal castration anxiety. At the same time, by disavowing the problems of separateness and infantile sadism, they have also circumvented what Melanie Klein termed the "elaboration of the depressive position."

CHAPTER 11

Neoneeds and Addictive Sexualities

> *. . . we were driven to the conclusion that a disposition to perversions is an original and universal disposition of the human sexual instinct and that normal sexual behaviour is developed out of it.*
>
> — Sigmund Freud

IN THIS CHAPTER I explore the psychic economy of reinvented sexualities when they perform the function of a drug. In emphasizing that the objects of need are innate, whereas the objects of desire are created, Freud was proposing that the sexual drives are anaclitically derived from self-conservation needs. Therefore, they must first become detached from the original external object and find *autoerotic satisfaction* before reaching the stage of "object choice" (Freud, 1905). In other words, the primordial erotic act is not suckling but thumb-sucking.

When sexuality continues to function as an *anaclitic activity* — that is, when the individual must use another person in the way he or she used the mother in babyhood — sexual relations remain tied to an external object that is detached from essential introjects, perhaps because these are missing, highly damaged, or too threatening in the internal world. This adhesive attachment prevents the individual from identifying with these introjects, thus impeding or precluding any attempt to maintain stable sexual relations linked to feelings of love. The lack of such a stable introjective constellation disenables the individual from playing a self-sustained caretaking role toward him- or herself in times of stress. The incapacity to assure oneself, through identification, of both maternal and paternal caretaking functions, while it may not necessarily affect one's sense of core gender identity, will frequently prevent the integration of structuring oedipal identifications. Instead, narcissistic needs and fears predominate. When sexual desire arouses terror, this lack of essential introjects leaves a vacuum, so to speak, for the creation of a *sexually addictive solution* to the psychic conflict and mental pain. When the parental introjects are "good enough," the individual may find *neurotic* (rather than addictive and deviant) solutions to sexual conflicts. (In neurotic solutions, sexual pleasure is hampered by problems such as impotence, premature ejaculation, vaginal frigidity, or clitoral insensitivity.)

To the notion of neosexualities I would add that of "neoneeds," in which the sexual object, part-object, or practice is sought relentlessly in the manner of a *drug*. Such individuals have recourse only to inanimate, erotically-invested objects (whips, handcuffs, shoes, and so on), or to the addictive securing of partners who risk being treated as inanimate or interchangeable objects. Before proceeding further with our exploration of addictive sexuality, let us first examine the nature of addictive behavior in general.

WHAT CONSTITUTES AN ADDICTION?

The etymology of *addiction* refers to a state of slavery. Although the addict may *feel* enslaved to tobacco, alcohol, food, narcotics, psychiatric drugs, or other people, these objects are far from being the goal of the addictive guest. On the contrary, the object of addiction is experienced as essentially "good"; sometimes it even becomes the sole pursuit that is felt to give meaning to the individual's life. The psychic economy underlying addictive behavior is intended to dispel feelings of anxiety, anger, guilt, depression, or any other affective state that gives rise to insupportable psychic tension. This tension may also include affects that are pleasurable but which give rise to feelings of excitement or liveliness experienced as forbidden or even dangerous. (It is said of the alcoholic that he is always late for the funeral and always late for the wedding!) Once created or discovered, resource to the addictive substance or act is kept close at hand to attentuate such emotional experiences whenever required, if only for a short period of time.

In passing, we might well remind ourselves that we all tend to indulge in addictive behavior when events overthrow our usual means of dealing with stressful situations to the point that we are unable to contain and think about them constructively. At such moments we are liable to eat, smoke, or drink more than usual, take pharmacological drugs, engage in fleeting adventures, and so on, in order to escape briefly from the painful affective situation.

I first became intrigued by the underlying psychic economy in addictive behavior when I treated the mother of a little boy who was psychotic (McDougall & Lebovici, 1960). Sammy's analysis had been interrupted by the offer of a placement in the Orthogenic School in Chicago, and his mother then asked if *she* might now come and talk about *her* problems. She was on the verge of being alcoholic and wanted to understand the reasons for her compulsion to drink whiskey so often. I still remember my surprise when she tried to explain the circumstances that surrounded her irresistible urge to drink. "Sometimes I don't know whether I'm sad or angry or hungry or wanting to have sex—and that's when I begin to drink." Although it may seem self-evident, this was my first inkling of the notion that one of the goals of addictive behavior was to get rid of feelings!

I greatly furthered my understanding when I myself decided to stop smoking, thereby confronting the pressures that prompted my own addictive habit. I discovered that I reached for a cigarette whenever I had to accomplish a disagreeable task, whenever I was happy or excited, whenever I was sad or anxious, after dinner, before breakfast. In fact, I realized that I created a smoke screen over most of my affective states, thus neutralizing or dispersing a vital part of my internal world. I was devastated by this discovery and promised myself that I would apply my insight to an attempt to conceptualize the psychic structure of addictive behavior.

In preparing my first lecture on the subject for the Paris Psychoanalytic Society, I discovered that the words *addict* and *addiction* did not exist in French. "Why, they aren't even in the *Robert*, our most up-to-date dictionary!" said my good friend and highly cultivated colleague, J. B. Pontalis. My first task was therefore to take issue with the time-honored French equivalent, "*toxicoma-*

nie," which literally means "a crazy desire for poison." I explained that to pursue an addictive object was not a conscious wish to poison oneself; on the contrary, it was an act that carried the illusion of doing something to help oneself through the difficulties of everyday life. I then offered the English equivalent, backing up my statement with the etymological argument. (*Addiction* has since become a standard word in psychoanalytic writings in France, although "toxicomania" is still retained as a psychiatric diagnostic term with strict definitions.) I ended my lecture by noting the important questions that, to me, remained unanswered: Why didn't we choose less toxic means of dealing with emotional experience? And what were the sources of addictive solutions to mental pain?

THE ORIGINS OF AN ADDICTIVE ECONOMY

The early mother-child relationship may be decisive in laying the foundations of certain patterns of psychic functioning. A "good-enough" mother — in the Winnicottian (1951) sense — experiences a feeling of merging with her baby in the earliest weeks of its life. However, as Winnicott points out, if the fusional attitude persists beyond this time, the interaction becomes persecutory and pathological for the infant. In the state of total dependency on their mothers, infants tend to conform to whatever is projected upon them. A baby's motility, emotional liveliness, intelligence, sensuality, and bodily erogenicity can only develop to the extent that the mother herself invests these aspects positively. She may just as readily *inhibit* the narcissistic enhancement of these aspects in her infant's somatopsychic structure, if her baby is serving to palliate an unfulfilled need in her own internal world.

This mother-baby pattern then affects the development of transitional phenomena (transitional activities and/or objects) and engenders fear in the infant of developing its own psychic resources for dealing with tension. The growth of what Winnicott (1951) terms "the capacity to be alone" (that is, "alone" even when the mother is nearby) may be endangered, so that the infant constantly seeks the mother's presence in order to deal with any affective experience, whether arising from inner psychological or outer environmental impingements. Because of her own anxieties or unconscious fears and wishes, a mother is potentially capable of instilling in her nursling what may be conceptualized as an *addictive relationship to her presence* and her caretaking functions. In a sense, it is the mother who is in a state of "dependency" with regard to her infant.

Consequently, there is a potential risk that the small child will fail to establish an inner representation of a caretaking maternal (and later paternal) figure, performing functions that include the capacity for containing and dealing with psychological pain or states of over-excitement. Unable to identify with such an inner representation, the child remains incapable of self-soothing and self-care in times of inner or outer tension. An attempted solution to the lack of the self-caring introjects is inevitably sought in the external world, as it was in early infancy (Krystal, 1978). In this way drugs, food, alcohol, tobacco, and so on, are discovered as objects that may be used to palliate painful states of mind — fulfilling a maternal function that the individual is unable to provide for him- or herself. These addictive objects take the place of the transitional objects of childhood, which embodied the maternal environment and at the same time liberated the child from total dependence on the mother's presence. Unlike transitional objects, however, addictive objects necessarily fail because they are *somatic* rather than *psychological* attempts to deal with absence, and therefore provide only temporary relief. For this reason, in earlier writings (McDougall, 1982) I referred to addictive substances as "transitory" rather than as "transitional" objects.

WHAT DO NEONEEDS ACCOMPLISH?

In summary, the addictive solution is an attempt at self-cure in the face of threatening psychic states. These psychic states fall into three categories, which determine the amount of "work" the addictive solution must accomplish and give some indication of the severity of the addictive proclivity:

- An attempt to ward off *neurotic anxieties* (conflict around adult rights to sexual and love relations and to narcissistic pleasure in work and social relations)
- An attempt to combat states of *severe anxiety* (frequently of a

paranoid nature) or *depression* (accompanied by feelings of inner death)
- A flight from *psychotic anxieties* (such as fear of bodily or psychic fragmentation; a global terror of facing a void in which the sense of subjective identity itself is felt to be endangered)

It is evident that deprivation in the world of internal object representations cannot be repaired by substances or objects encountered in the external world—hence the compulsive recourse to the addictive object. If, as sometimes happens, psychoanalytic treatment seems inappropriate or counterindicated, we must recognize that for certain addictions (for example, alcoholism) organizations such as Alcoholics Anonymous may fulfill a vital therapeutic function by providing a caretaking community with which each member is surrounded—creating, so to speak, a new family environment with more adequate maternal care than had been available in the past.

ADDICTION AND DEFIANCE

In addition to the desperate need to discharge insupportable affective pressures, all forms of severe addiction seek to repair a damaged self-image that invariably includes an attempt to settle accounts with the parental figures of the past (sometimes projected onto society as a whole). This defiance is threefold:

1. There is a *defiance of the inner maternal object* (experienced as absent or lacking in the capacity to soothe the troubled child hidden within). The addictive substitute will always be available as a stand-in for the missing maternal functions. (In essence, the message is, "You can never again abandon me; from now on, *I* control *you*!").

2. There is a *defiance of the inner father*, believed to have failed in his paternal functions and therefore dismissed. This attitude is typically projected onto society ("I don't give a damn what you think about me or my actions—you can go to hell!")

3. There is a final *defiance of death itself*, which takes two forms. First, there is an omnipotent stance ("Nothing can touch

me—death is for the others"). Then, when this grandiose form of defense breaks down and the sense of inner deadness can no longer be denied, there is a yielding to the death impulses ("Perhaps the next fix [bout or encounter] will be the overdose—so what?—who cares?").

THE ADDICTIVE OBJECT

The "choice" of an addictive object is rarely a question of chance. Each selected act or object tends to correspond to particular developmental periods in which there was failure to integrate helpful, caretaking introjects. In addition, the chosen object reveals the search for the "ideal state" the individual hopes to attain through the sought-after substance, person, or act: plenitude, exhaltation, potency, painlessness, nirvana, and so on. Anyone who has worked with drug addicts knows that it is of little use to suggest that they change their object of addiction for one that is less harmful. For example, to suggest to a heroin addict that he or she take up overeating instead will evoke only astonishment and further alienation due to a feeling of being completely misunderstood.

As already indicated, objects of addiction are not limited to substances; other people can also serve this purpose. There are individuals who "feed" on others as narcissistic need-objects when they are faced with menacing affective experiences (usually of a depressive nature) that they are unable to contain or think about alone. A relationship established for these reasons frequently creates a demanding dependency and an infantile feeling of helplessness. Other individuals forage for aggressive interchange in relationships, constantly provoking quarrels with others. Such encounters often conceal a paranoid dimension. Indeed, the aggressive interchange serves, momentarily, to keep persecutory anxiety at bay. Still others exploit their sexual partners as tension-releasing devices, in which the partner may have little or no importance.

The addictive dimension of human sexuality, whether in a heterosexual, homosexual, or autoerotic context, may also be conceptualized as a breakdown in the internalization of parental functions as outlined above—in particular, of the environmental mother, who is experienced by the helpless infant as unable to modify its physical or psychological suffering. In this eventuality, sexual relations can come to represent a dramatic and compulsive way of preventing one's narcissistic self-image from disintegrating. The sexual act itself is used not only to dispel affective overcharge and to repair a damaged narcissistic image of one's gender identity, but also to deflect the forces of infantile rage from being turned back upon the self or against the internalized parental representations. Thus a drug-like utilization of sexuality becomes necessary to suspend feelings of violence as well as to anesthetize, if only temporarily, a castrated image of the self, a threatened loss of ego boundaries, or feelings of inner deadness. In this way, partners and sexual scenarios become containers for the addicted individual's dangerous and damaged parts, which are then overridden, in illusory fashion, by gaining erotic control over a partner or through a game of mastery within the parameters of a sexual scenario. At the same time, the partners become substitutes for the missing or damaged parental introjects and are used to repair the fragile sexual image constructed by the child of the past from negative biparental communications. The addictive solution to psychic pain once again reveals its twin narcissistic aims: *repairing a damaged self* while maintaining the illusion of *omnipotent control* through recourse to the addiction.

COMPULSIVITY AND ADDICTIVE SEXUALITY

As analytic work progresses with analysands who use sexuality as a drug, primitive emotional states, infiltrated with oral and anal sadism and eroticism, are invariably disclosed. The psychotherapeutic process may help the sex-addict learn how to distinguish anxiety from depression in the context of the transference relationship, thus circumventing the compulsion to discharge such affects through immediate action. Becoming aware of the distinction between anxiety (terror of the future) and depression (pain from the past) also alerts the individual to his or her difficulty in being able to support and contain intense affects for any period of time. The analytic process seeks to establish the basis for the development of psychological rather than addictive ways of dealing with depressive moods, anxiety-arousing situations, and narcissistic wounds, particularly when these affective experiences are associated with frightening aspects of current sexual and love relations.

Case Illustration: The Neosexual in Search of an Identity .

Jason, a surgeon in his early forties, sought help because, as he put it, he was "a grave obsessional neurotic." This diagnosis had been provided by the psychiatrist whom he had consulted for his problems. Jason then discussed his "case" further with a friend, also a psychiatrist, who cautioned him: "Whatever you do, don't have an analysis—you're a very ordinary kind of hysteric. Psychoanalysis won't help you. You'll only be wasting your time and money." Beyond these third-person negative pronouncements, I detected Jason's defiant challenge to me as the analyst and to the analytic process.

Jason explained in detail how his severe obsessional symptoms handicapped his sexual and social life (whereas his professional life seemed free from the symptomatology). Prominent among his obsessive ruminations was a constant preoccupation with minority groups, for whom he expressed a positive prejudice. "Am I as good as an Arab?" "Am I as good as a Black?" "Am I as good as a Jew?" In our initial interview he revealed that these preoccupations were also intimately connected with his sexual life. "Many women offer themselves to me. If they're Arab, Vietnamese, African, etc., I always accept and my obsessions are put to rest for a short while." He added cryptically, "When there's no mixture, there's no problem."

I asked him if he could expand on this notion and he explained that sexual relations were complicated with women who, like himself, did not belong to these ethnic groups and may have had lovers of different ethnic backgrounds. However, if the woman, of a different ethnic background from his own, had a man of the same race as her partner, he had no need to question her endlessly. In his early twenties he had married a young French woman whom he desired because, so it seemed, she had once had a brief affair with a famous Jew. "For years I tortured my wife every night to give me details about her former love affair with X. The interrogation would go on for hours. Then I would convince her to put on split panties and I would tie her up and rape her. But the sex wasn't so good. The questioning took too long."

Throughout his marriage, which came to an end after 10 years, Jason had innumerable "adventures" directed by the same ethnic bias. He then talked about another woman with whom he had a long-lasting relationship. She had had a nebulous affair with a well-known celebrity who was black. She, too, was submitted to endless questioning before he was able to make love to her. It appeared that the women would eventually avow or invent whatever they deduced he wanted to hear. Jason claimed that the torture was as great for him as for his lovers and that one day this compulsion would surely drive him mad.

During our initial interview I gained a glimpse into what lay beneath his concern about ethnic differences. Jason spoke briefly about his early family life. "There were endless quarrels between my parents because my mother is British and my father French. He looks a little dark and a little Jewish, but he's just a goy." Jason's only sibling was a sister four years older than he. Throughout childhood both had suffered from their mother's constant, denigrating remarks about their father. As a little boy, Jason remembered feeling humiliated by his mother's accent and her hatred for French people and for many aspects of French culture. Insults would fly across the table, the father retorting that she was "an ugly English bitch."

"My mother talked openly about my father's infidelities in front of us both," Jason continued. "I know he had daily adventures with his clients, especially women of other races." After a pause Jason added, "All I had was masturbation. Perhaps that's why I masturbated many times a day during my adolescence. In fact, I still masturbate on an average of twice a day." He added that his mother's image of true virility was that of her own father, who had lost a leg on the field of battle.

From this first encounter I deduced that, from childhood, Jason had displaced onto the difference between his parents' nationalities, not only his obsession with women of different ethnic backgrounds from his own, but also his anxiety concerning the difference between their sexes. It also appeared that Jason endowed ethnic differences and constant sexual activity with phallic significance; the father, with an idealized penis. The place of the woman was less clear. It was evident, however, that Jason's choice of a *woman* analyst with a marked *English accent,* who also *lived among the French,* was no accident! Even though he would have to wait a year before our analytic work could begin, he refused other referrals. Already I suspected that I was destined to pay for all the shame and psychological damage for which Jason held his mother responsible.

As agreed, the analysis began a year later, on a four-times weekly basis. Although Jason spoke of many professional and phobic concerns, for the purposes of this chapter, the clinical material presented is limited to different aspects of Jason's sexual behavior and the internal structures that gave rise to his neosexual inventions.

SEXUAL IDENTITY CONFUSIONS

At the time of our first meeting, Jason had revealed only those components of his sexual activity that caused him suffering. Later he described how he had begun cross-dressing during latency (in his older sister's clothing, particularly her dance clothes) and would masturbate in front of the mirror, clad in this attire. His numerous other erotic inventions appeared to be largely ego-syntonic. For example, in one highly invested sexual game, he would insist that his girlfriend wear an artificial penis and penetrate him anally. At other times he would tie up a consenting partner, while whipping her and penetrating her anally with his finger and, if possible, his whole hand. These practices revealed evident perturbation in Jason's sense of sexual identity, as well as a measure of confusion between his and his partner's body.

Now in our second session, Jason discusses what he describes as his "homosexuality."

JASON For years I went to group sex parties, especially to watch what the men did with their penises. There's something phoney about my relationship with women. Although I work wonderfully well in surgery with women patients, outside the hospital I probably hate them. In fact, I'm convinced I'm a homosexual, except that I've never wanted sex with men. All this has to do with my English bitch of a mother . . . I suppose you wonder why I want to do my analysis with you?

JM Perhaps because I'm a woman and an English bitch?

JASON It's true that your accent reminds me of my mother, but there's
something about you that's different. You make me feel I exist. [*To
my surprise, his eyes fill with tears.*]

Although I was well aware of what awaited me in the transference relationship to come, I was nevertheless startled by such early
manifestations. At the first session on the couch, Jason addressed
me as "Joyce," an extremely uncommon practice in France, and
also used the familiar form *tu,* which is reserved for family, intimate friends, children, and dogs. I was destined to fall into all of
these categories at one time or another! Throughout the analysis I
always addressed Jason using the formal *vous.* His way of attacking the analytic frame led to many an interpretation about his
narcissistic fragility or need to be seductive. To add to the confusion, Jason frequently addressed me by *his* name and would also
use *my* name when referring to himself: "Yesterday after the session, I was again seized with terror on your street; everyone was
threatening me. But I said to myself, 'Now, *Joyce,* you know
you're just lending these people your own violence. They mean
you no harm.'"

Although I will focus mainly on the psychic economy underlying Jason's erotic inventions, there were many other thought-
provoking dimensions to his analysis. Particularly relevant is one
detail from the overall picture of Jason's inner world. It seemed
that as a child he may have suffered from certain psychotic manifestations that lasted about a year. He would hear voices com-
manding him to make insulting remarks to friends of the family,
particularly his mother's women friends. Obeying the voices led to
regular thrashings by his father, which were only intensified when
the little boy protested that it was not he, but the voices, that were
at fault. I assumed that at this period of his life, Jason had managed to expel from his mind all violent and erotic thoughts concerning the different introjected images of his mother, and that
these had returned in classic Schreber-like fashion in the form of
auditory hallucinations. According to Jason, his father proclaimed that he would be thrashed until he stopped hearing voices.
This paternal "therapy" was finally effective!

Jason and I concluded that around this time, the auditory phenomena were replaced by compulsive questioning of his mother

and her friends—interrogations that often lasted for hours. Jason's questions frequently concerned the comparative prices and utility of articles of female clothing, such as fur coats. When similar questioning occurred in the analytic situation (and I must admit, it had the power to drive me crazy), I sometimes had the impression that I, too, was hearing voices! We were able to reconstruct Jason's childhood concern with sexual differences and, in particular, the formation and functioning of the female body. My interpretations of this concern in numerous contexts led Jason to recall in detail his mother's daily cross-examinations at the dinner table, in which she would interrogate his father as to how many women he had had intercourse with that day. Apparently she would spy on him, and if she saw him talking in animated fashion to a woman, particularly someone of different ethnic origins from her own, she became convinced that a sexual relationship was to take place. Jason's obsessive interrogation of his lovers reenacted this childhood pattern, in which he identified with his mother's endless questioning of the father's sexual exploits.

In the early years of his analysis, Jason firmly believed that his father had intercourse with four or five women a day; as time wore on, and his need for this belief diminished, he was able to say with conviction, "You know, I realize now that my mother was pathologically jealous. I think she had homosexual problems. I had forgotten that my father frequently protested that no man could engage in continual sexual activity, such as my mother imputed to him." These insights and recovered memories were facilitated by the ongoing analysis of Jason's homosexual fears and wishes. As time went on, it became clear that his violent complaints against his mother were not limited to her constant denigration of his father and his supposed sexual infidelities. In addition, he experienced his mother as unable to understand any viewpoint other than her own. Some of the most dramatic and poignant moments of his analysis occurred when he expressed his conviction that he did not truly exist in his mother's eyes. "I hammered on the walls of my mother's mind and the only response I got was an echo."

When similar fears were evoked in the transference (for example, if I were silent for some time), Jason would suddenly scream at me, asking if I were asleep or dead. He would shout so loudly that I could hardly distinguish what he was saying. When I asked if he were trying to keep me awake and alive by his screaming, he answered that he had to shout in order to reach me because, being English, I would never understand what he was communicating. We were able to interpret this extraordinary manner of speaking as expressing the excruciating feeling that he could not "reach" his mother, could not make her understand his suffering as a child, making him feel as if he were not truly alive, or as if she were not alive to him. (Other, more favorable, versions of his mother were to come later.) In essence, the primary goal of Jason's compulsive sexual practices and relationships appeared to be the need to protect some feeling of security and narcissistic reassurance about his masculine identity.

Some two years into our analytic voyage, Jason's obsession with ethnic differences and his complicated sexual practices began to lose part of their compulsivity, but he then found himself faced with catastrophic anxiety of psychotic dimensions, which he described as an experience of "nothingness" or "deadness." He called these experiences his "voids" (*etats de vide*).

By this time Jason no longer shouted in a deafening manner, and he rarely confused our two names, but he was clearly frightened of losing his mind, of losing his professional skills, or of perpetrating "crazy" acts in order to fill up the voids. These states of depersonalization occurred intermittently for nearly two years, and required constant interpretation, extra sessions, telephone contact on occasion, and psychiatric drugs as a temporary measure. We analyzed the taking of medication as a way of seeking a transitory object to palliate the void in his psychic world — that is the lack of an introjected image of a caretaking mother. Following our elaboration, Jason abandoned the recourse to medication.

At this phase of our work together Jason behaved in a manner that Mahler (1968) described as the practicing sub-phase, in which children return to home base for reassurance before setting off once again, since the internalized mother image is readily lost. Jason's incessant masturbation also increased during this time. We were able to understand that, first of all, this recourse provided a tangible means of assuring himself that the most dangerous of the various maternal introjects had not destroyed his manhood; and secondly, masturbation gave him the feeling that he existed and that his body had definite limits. In addition, the feeling of inner deadness would disappear momentarily. The game of being penetrated by an artificial penis fulfilled a similar function.

Particularly intense during this period was our analysis of Jason's phallic-oedipal anxieties—as well as their primitive prototypes in the form of separation anxiety and the fear of annihilation—which contributed to our understanding of the strength of his sexual addictions and obsessions as well as their underlying fantasy content. A clinical fragment taken from the third year of our work together exemplifies this process of uncovering.

JASON When I make love to a black woman whose own man is black, there's no problem, no obsessions, because I get his penis by taking his woman and I feel like a man for a short while. Men who are black, Arab, Vietnamese, Jewish, all have real cocks. But I still feel intense panic with my women friends who haven't had such relationships in a continual fashion. The hours of interrogation have come back again. Why?

JM If the woman hasn't had one of these powerful penises in her, then she's a castrate, just as you feel yourself to be. When you can force her to admit that she's had such adventures, you are able to penetrate her, but then your envy and hatred of her rises up and has no bounds, as we've often seen. [*I am referring here to transference affects as well as envious childhood feelings toward his mother. We had understood these feelings as an attack upon an idealized image of femininity in which the all-powerful woman is felt to possess both sex organs and the magical powers attributed to each sex.*]

JASON Yes! That reminds me of the times when I whip women. It isn't intended to hurt them; it's to prove that they *aren't* hurt and *aren't* going to die. At those times I have a phony penis that can make the woman have an orgasm. It's a great system!

JM And when you don't have this whip penis, then it's the woman who has to pass you the powerful penis she took from another man?

JASON Yes, I guess that's what I thought as a kid. [*Long pause*] But I still don't know why I've always longed to be a woman.

JM Perhaps because it's women with their female sex-organs who attract men and their penises?

JASON And I don't know why I've never wanted sex with men either, because I *am* a homosexual! [*He begins shouting*] Now don't deny it!

JM Why would I deny it?

JASON Well, that asshole, Dr. R [*an analyst whom Jason had seen for a short time prior to our work and for whom he expressed little es-*

teem], silly ass, said that I wasn't a homosexual because I'd never slept with men!

JM [*Jason desperately needs to have his homosexual longings recognized, since he feels that his need for masculine identification was forbidden by his mother.*] There are two Jason's talking here. One is homosexual and wants to receive the gift of a man's penis in order to become a man; the other is heterosexual and wants to make love to a woman while holding the fantasy of getting a man's penis from her — as if the woman must give you permission to possess your own penis.

JASON All those little games with my girlfriends and the dildo: You once said these games represented my mother with my father's penis tied around her, which she was letting me swallow anally. [*A long pause before he begins shouting.*] MY MOTHER HATED MY FATHER! SHE WOULDN'T LET ME BE LIKE HIM, AND SHE WOULDN'T LET ME LOVE HIM! ALL I COULD HAVE WAS *HER* FATHER, THE WONDERFUL WAR HERO WITH THE MISSING LEG! [*He begins to cry.*]

By this time in our analytic voyage, we both understood that one of Jason's childhood sexual theories was that, in order to become a man, he literally had to incorporate the male genital. At the same time, he did not want this "incorporation" from a man, because it was equally essential that his *mother* give him access to the father's penis so that *he* could then possess *her*. In his sexual game with the artificial penis, Jason was enacting a common fantasy of little children, in which they lie between the two parents; the father puts his penis into the little boy, who then develops a strong penis that can go into his mother: a concrete version of internalization fantasies in their oral, anal, and phallic aspects. These object representations eventually become the foci for stable, if deviant, identifications to the parental couple in the fantasized primal scene, thereby laying the groundwork for a highly conditioned and compulsive form of sexuality in adult life. All that Jason had achieved in the way of identification to his father's phallic qualities was the pursuit of innumerable sexual adventures — a superficial, adhesive kind of identification, for which, as we have seen, he had to pay dearly. This identification was further complicated by the fact that masculinity was symbolized in the pursuit of partners whose ethnic origins were different from his own.

After much painstaking work, we were able to conclude that

Jason had introjected what he came to think of as a "crazy" part of his mother. This introject had given rise to two conflicting paternal images: On one hand, his father was imagined as possessing an idealized, uncastratable penis, constantly erect, with no real man behind it; on the other hand, he was a dangerous and denigrated role model, uncaring and lacking in any real substance, and thus equally detached from a truly masculine image. These paternal representations supposedly had left the mother incomplete, empty, and deranged. Jason felt as deprived of phallic enrichment as he believed his mother to have been. His basic erotic scenario, like many neosexual creations, was constructed somewhat in the manner of a dream. As evidenced in the session above, the women who excited Jason sexually were those who, in his fantasy, had incorporated a powerful penis, which he in turn absorbed anally, thus rendering his own penis *phallic* and capable of penetration.

Jason's highly invested sexual game with the dildo played the same role in his psychic economy as the compulsive seeking of addictive substances. In the latter case, the aim of the act is to absorb a substitute for the soothing maternal functions of the primitive "breast mother." Jason's compulsive sexual pursuits carried this meaning as well. Although the literal incorporation of part-object substitutes is based on an unconscious wish to obtain or repair what is missing or damaged in the internal world, it is evident that these acts are not the equivalent of the *psychological* processes of incorporation and introjection. On the contrary, *the felt need for external objects in the form of compulsive sexuality or substance abuse is evidence of the breakdown of the internalization processes.* The addictive acts are unable to repair the damaged representation of either penis or breast with regard to their symbolic significance. They relieve anxiety only temporarily and therefore acquire an addictive quality in that they must be continually pursued.

In the following three years, Jason created a stable relationship with a professional woman colleague and they became the proud parents of two children. Although Jason still needed the solitude of his own apartment from time to time, when he felt unable to face the demands of conjugal life, he became increasingly attached to his partner and a most loving and concerned father to his children. He still had recourse to masturbation when disquieting events arose in his life, but he claimed to have lost all interest in his earlier sadomasochistic practices and no longer sought to have his lover penetrate him with a dildo. He did retain erotic interest in anal intercourse as a variant, but this desire was devoid of compulsive elements. His endless questioning prior to intercourse had lessened considerably. He reported that his friends and colleagues hardly recognized him because he was "so much less crazy." Jason himself stated that he was learning how to differentiate *his* reality from other people's. He reiterated that during the past two years he had experienced true happiness for the first time in his life.

We had reached the point in Jason's psychoanalytic voyage in which the addictive dimension of his sexual life had completely disappeared. However, the narcissistic terror of losing his ego boundaries and sense of individual identity, which had contributed a powerful dimension to his neosexual compulsions, was still in evidence in other aspects of his life and deserves a chapter to itself.

CHAPTER 12

Sexual Deviation and Psychic Survival

> *For me, most psychoanalytic theories of sadism and masochism are boiled water masquerading as gourmet's delight. . . . We must be careful, especially those of us who pride ourselves on our empathy, not to think we understand certain experiences that are well beyond our own; we must be especially careful when our convictions are buttressed by consensual validation.*
> — Robert Stoller

AMONG THE MANY erotic techniques employed to bestow narcissistic reassurance about the body and self as an integrated and libidinally vital unity, masturbation plays a preeminent role. Experiencing pain, anxiety, and even the threat of death may become an essential accompaniment to the masturbatory activity. Jason's deviant masturbation ritual, in which he risked his life, deserves mention at this point. His scenario presents a vivid illustration of the double polarity of neosexual inventions: On one hand, they are an attempt to circumvent the interdictions and castration anxieties of the phallic-oedipal phase; on the other hand, they are a desperate attempt to master anxieties encountered at a much earlier phase, when separation from the mother arouses the terror of bodily disintegration, annihilation, and a sense of inner death. These anxieties are also frequently accompanied by emotions of infantile rage. In other words, the addictive act serves to ward off both *neurotic* and *psychotic* levels of anxiety.

During his childhood and adolescence Jason lived in one of those old buildings that were standard in Paris some 30 years ago, in which each person who stepped out of the elevator had to send it down again to the ground floor. In his masturbatory act, Jason would take the elevator to the top of the building in which his parents lived, then send it down, during which time he would climb up the steel cable until he reached the mechanism near the roof. Suspended over a void of some 40 meters, he would cling to the cable while masturbating with the steel cord between his legs. This practice was fraught with danger from various points of view, of which the dominant risk was that, at the moment of ejaculation, he might loosen his grip and crash to the ground floor several stories below. Indeed, his fear had become highly eroticized.

We were able to reconstruct many other hitherto unconscious meanings that lay behind his masturbatory invention. Jason had used all the infantile magic at his disposal to fill the meaningless or dead spaces where he found no reassuring reflection from his mother that confirmed his individual existence or his sexual identity. The *void* eventually came to signify the terrifying female sex itself, fantasized as a dangerous and empty genital—since Jason had no representation of his father's penis as playing any part in his mother's sexual life. There was no belief in an inner father who would prevent Jason from being absorbed to his death into the mother's body, as his infantile sexual longings dictated. This primitive form of castration anxiety, which, as we have seen, is a dynamic factor in serious psychosomatic disorders, is revealed just as frequently in those who have created neosexual acts and relationships in order to avoid terrifying or frankly psychotic fantasies. Without knowing it, Jason had carried his frightening image of the sexual act into all his adult love relations.

Added to the eroticized danger implied in his autoerotic act was the possibility that Jason's father might catch him masturbating with the steel cable and kill him. For Jason, his act was an unconscious equivalent of incest and therefore would provoke his father to murder. (I sometimes thought that the whole scenario also resembled an intrauterine fantasy, with the steel cable taking the place of the umbilical cord!)

We concluded that Jason's scenario represented a means of rendering tolerable and exciting his fear of becoming a *void* in his mother's eyes, of falling into nothingness as an individual. The empty space that had to be braved was also connected with a gap-in-knowing, a void concerning the true nature of human sexual relations. For example, as the analysis progressed, it came as a shock to Jason to recognize that his mother was not asexual but, on the contrary, intensely interested in her sexual life with her husband, and that his father felt both attraction and admiration for her. (It is possible that the parental quarrels in themselves were imbued with eroticism.) The horror of becoming the void, the nothing, which Jason believed he represented to his mother, had become attached to his genital. In turn, therefore, his penis became nothing, devoid of masculine quality, and in need of reinforcement through the magical absorption of an imaginary penis belonging to another man.

In his masturbatory scenario, Jason had managed to eroticize both his phallic castration anxieties and his primal fears of annihilation and death. Like many addicts, he was flirting with death in his sexual game in an attempt to prove that, in spite of his aggressive impulses and sexual desires, and in spite of his conviction that he didn't exist in his mother's eyes, *neither she nor he would die.* Not only would he triumph over death, but these very anxieties would be the cause of his greatest sexual pleasure. Here we find the three-fold triumph of the addictive solution: defiance of mother, of father, and of death itself. Jason's ritual, although relentlessly compulsive and addictive, had in fact been a major discovery — a triumph — in face of a horrifying experience of emptiness.

That he was attempting to create a barrier against this plunge into a world without meaning, as well as fending off the fantasy of being sucked into an endless chasm, came as a surprising revelation to Jason when it was enacted in the transference. This behavior slowly became accessible to interpretation during the period in which he experienced the phases of depersonalization. In his own words he was constantly threatened with "plunging into the void." The analysis itself became an anguishing experience in which I played a dual role: I was the mother who would lead him to his death, and I was also the father who would find words to give meaning to his profound fears, thus protecting him from dissolution.

Following is a fragment from a session in the sixth year of our work together. By then, Jason's dread of nothingness had completely disappeared, but we continued to gain further insight into the significance of these alarming voids and their links with childhood memories.

THE VOIDS CONTINUE TO FILL

JASON I watch the way you dress, each elegant detail. But the important thing is that your clothes now become *my* clothes. I feel good as I lie down. You've seen what lovely clothing I now permit myself to buy. [*Jason used to dress in a way that was inconsistent with both his profession and his means.*] But my scarf is very old and dirty—and I'm forbidden to wash it, because then it wouldn't be me any more. Like when I was a kid. I would scream when my mother insisted on buying me new clothes and throw atrocious public scenes. It was worse for me than for her! *She* was trying to destroy my fighting spirit; *I* was fighting for my life.

JM [*The fragility of Jason's childhood sense of self is evident in his need to feel that his* clothes *kept him together. He appears to have invested them rather like transitional objects; perhaps they play the role of the environmental mother of early infancy, reassuring him of his bodily integrity and psychic security.*]

JASON That makes me think of my terror of those voids—you remember—when I was staring into nothing and didn't know who I was. [*Pause*] That's exactly how I felt whenever we went out to buy new clothes. My mother wanted to rip off my clothes so I'd have no defense—and then she could just devour me. I had to hide everything from her in order to exist. I'm thinking of my masturbation rituals, hanging over that 40-meter drop.

JM Another void? [*This is the first time it has been possible for Jason to connect his states of inner deadness, which hid the foreboding of non-existence, with his childhood fears and his adolescent sexual practices. Earlier attempts to interpret his associations in this perspective, whether attached to the transference or the objects of the past, had simply led to Jason feeling confused.*]

JASON Ah, yes, but that was a void that was exciting! It was the real danger of the situation that was so erotic and made me ejaculate. And, of course, the risk of getting caught!

JM [*At last Jason understands how he had managed to render tolerable, through eroticization, the psychic factors that were the cause of his greatest anxieties. The parents' communications about sexuality appeared senseless to the small boy's mind. Thus Jason was obliged to invent a new primal scene, which he subsequently integrated into his neosexual creations, thereby giving meaning to his subjectivity, existence to his penis, and access to sexual pleasure.*] So you refused to feel the fear of nothingness and the fearful fantasies of your mother's body?

JASON Yes, and I refused to comply with what she wanted me to be — sexless.

JM Refused to be a void for her?

JASON *Eh, voila*! As you once said, I was never anything but an adjective. I was sure that I was nothing more than that for my parents: "You're a brilliant boy," "You're a dirty boy," "You're a crazy boy!" But no one, you understand, *no one* ever told me I was a *boy*! [*There is a long pause and Jason begins to cry. After mastering his emotion, he continues.*]

How could I know I was a boy? Or even what it was to be a boy? And that it was *good* just to be a boy? I became a man by accident. I wasn't, really. I just looked like one, acted like one. Had to be better than the Arabs, the Jews, and the Africans! Had to lay more girls than they could. Always the adjective! The *big* fucker. I still was not a male. Just a phony. But now I've become one. Out of the void I've created a real cock! The work we're doing here, it's like a birth process. Do you remember my very first session on the couch? I said that I was coming out from between your thighs. It's as if I were watching my own birth as a baby. Like a wish that I'd never admitted to myself. Why did I not exist as a boy for my mother? [*Suddenly shouting*] JOYCE! ARE YOU LISTENING? *NOM DE DIEU, SAY* SOMETHING!

JM Afraid that you do not exist as a boy for me?

JASON It's worse than that. It's as though you don't exist either.

JM So you've turned me into a void? As though you are condemned to empty me — your mother — out? [*This refers to material from the previous session, in which Jason expressed the fear that he might use up all my ideas and become too heavy a load for me to bear.*]

JASON Yes, I see it now. I devoured my mother! The big danger was to empty *her* out, turn *her* into a void. She was always telling me what a voracious baby I was, how she had to pinch my nose to make me give up the nipple . . . and how much she always did for me throughout childhood — tore her guts out for me, she did! See, even as a baby, I was only an adjective — *bad* baby! [*He laughs in a somewhat discordant way.*]

JM [*I feel his anxiety acutely and search for the underlying incorporative fantasies that are seeking expression.*] As though your mother also was afraid of being devoured by you?

JASON She *was*! And she made *me* feel dangerous. Why was she so afraid? I know, that's called *projection*. I was afraid of devouring her and she was afraid of wanting to eat me! I'm thinking of my grandfather's missing leg. For hours on end, I used to ask questions about where it was. Another void!

JM You imagined she had eaten it?

JASON Yes! But that was a void I had to admire, whereas my father, who had two legs, wasn't worth a damn. [*Beginning to shout*] I COULD HOBBLE ABOUT ON ONE LEG, BUT FROM MY FATHER I WASN'T ALLOWED TO TAKE ANYTHING! NOTHING AT ALL!

JM [*He begins to shout louder as his feeling of panic mounts and he relives his childhood anguish of disappearing as an individual for his mother. It seems important to remind him that we have already discovered that his father's existence was a precious element in his dilemma as well as giving him the possibility of accepting that he, in turn, could exist as a sexual being.*] Except for the "constant seducer." Even if it were an adjective, it was something you took over from your father.

JASON *Tiens*! I sure did! Without that, I'd have been psychotic. I was crazy, you know, just like that boy Sammy you wrote about. We were very alike. When I first came here, I was a closet psychotic!

JM But the adjectives helped you to survive.

JASON Yes . . . they sure did. And my father was proud of my intelligence. He used to say I was going to become a world-famous professor. Oh, yes! I became a surgeon for all of them—to repair my mother, to replace my grandfather's leg, to fulfill my father's ambition. For years I repaired the whole world, while I stayed empty and damaged. Like you once said: a psychic hemorrhage.

At this point in our work, Jason's compulsive masturbation had notably diminished, although it tended to return whenever he was in the throes of narcissistic pain or anxiety. He was still subject to sudden phobic terror of crowds, of specific sights, of buying flowers or food, or of eating certain foods—but he continually tried to reach the underlying significance of these anxieties.

THE SURVIVAL OF THE SELF

After eight years all the above symptoms had disappeared. "Why did I have to go through 45 years of pain in order to know real happiness?" Jason asked with astonishment. Although Jason had overcome all his compulsive sexual behavior, and now felt totally secure in his sexual identity, he was still wrestling with the problem of psychic survival and the need to reassure himself of his subjective identity. Following is a summary of my session notes illustrating these remaining issues.

JASON [*Instead of lying down, Jason sits on the couch for a while, as he often did when he was anxious.*] I'm doing very well, my work is better than ever, and I've been invited to another foreign country to give lectures on my surgical specialty. [*He then talks about his two children and how important it is for children "to have a father who knows how to lay down the law, to make firm rules, especially when the children grizzle all the time."*]

JM [*Sensing a certain tension in his words and manner, I remark that he seems to want to tell me what a fine man, surgeon, and father he is, but is he not also like a grizzly child who doesn't want to follow the analytic rule — to lie down on the couch and say what comes into his mind?*]

JASON [*Lying down*] You don't like working face to face? Is that it?

JM I'm more interested in what you're trying to control by sitting up and not letting your mind wander freely. Is there something on your mind that makes you want to avoid the moment of separation when you lose sight of me . . . and run the risk of plunging into the void again? [*No doubt Jason's wish to sit up coincided with the hope of confirming his existence in* my *eyes, as the associations that follow indicate.*]

JASON Sure, that's always a problem! But it's also to avoid telling you what's on my mind: I met a clochard (beggar) on the way here today. I hate them! Can't tell you how much!

JM What does a beggar mean to you?

JASON Oh, I know very well: People who can't care for themselves, always dependent on others. Me — I went to school alone from the age of three and it was a very long walk. I was afraid, of course, but my mother insisted. "You're got to learn to cope" she would say.

JM [*I imagine myself as little Jason, begging for something to which I had no right, like maternal protection. He could not run the risk of looking like a* clochard *in his mother's eyes!*] You didn't have the right to beg for your mother's presence?

This sequence brought to mind an observation that has often moved me: that of children like Jason, who develop very early, autonomous behavior. Jason learned to read and write before going to school; as a school child he often helped his father in the pharmacy, searching for the medications prescribed, even sometimes commenting on the way in which they were to be used. In later life such children often feel destroyed by their early success, as though the small child of the past will never be recognized or cared for. The success of three-year-old Jason, going off to kindergarten on his own, was the very sign of his failure, of his feeling of helplessness, that had to be hidden. He was an unacknowledged *beggar* for his mother's concern and attention. It was Jason's father who exhorted him to be intelligent, who dreamed of a great professional future for him — a dream that he fulfilled, but at a heavy price: His professional success cost him anguish in almost every other domain of his life. In many ways, sexually and socially he was still three years old when he began his psychoanalytic voyage.

JASON Sometimes I don't even feel I have the right to buy myself a new scarf or some flowers. If I do, I'll die. *She* bought the clothes, *she* bought the flowers. If I do it, I'm terrified I'll become my mother and have to fight to be my own self once again. [*The family man, good father, successful surgeon has finally agreed to listen to the frightened child who is unsure of his self boundaries.*] I don't know why, but I'm suddenly thinking that I'm terrified of getting fat. [*In French, he had said "peur de* grossir*," a verb derived from the same root as* grossesse, *meaning pregnancy.*]

JM Afraid of *"la grossesse"*?

JASON Yes, that might be it because I'm especially afraid of getting a big belly! But what's this fear of getting fat, or getting pregnant, got to do with my hatred of beggars?

JM Perhaps a part of you is a beggar there, too; that part of you we have often talked about, that would like to be a woman and be able to bear children? [*I had the thought, but did not say it, that perhaps he himself wanted to be the mother to that little Jason through identifying with a helpful maternal introject. There is a long pause, during which I recall the different ways in which we have explored his profound envy of women and his wish to take their place.*]

JASON Yes! I'm thinking about my excellent professional work, which is my way of creating children, I guess. It occurs to me that the pleasure I find in my work today is now greater than my fear of dying as the price for being so successful. Finally, in spite of everything negative that my father represented for me — even if it was hateful in my mother's eyes, and even if I suffered thinking that my father was always bedding women—at least he gave me *some image* for myself. *Bof!* I could talk about Oedipus and all that. I've read the books, but it's something far further back than my being in love with my mother.

[*Jason now recalls a painting by Salvador Dali called* Virgin and Child, *in which the child is seen inside the mother's belly. He again reminisces about his first session on the couch, in which he imagined he was being born out of my womb. I had later interpreted this image as his wish to be born as an* individual, *no longer afraid of being confused with other people.*]

For a long time I invented myself without any reference to reality. [*Long pause*] But even if I were psychotic, at least that allowed me to not get completely confused with my parents and vampirized by my mother. I became the spectator, always watching *others* to discover how I was supposed to act. I've paid heavily for that, all those years, haven't I? What with those bouts of constant nausea and the terrible years of high blood pressure.

JM [*I have made no reference to the somatic aspects in Jason's analytic adventure. In summary his hypertension was psychosomatic in nature, whereas his nausea was a purely hysterical symptom. Like everybody, he maintained the possibility of using either type of regression or compromise in states of stress. He now brings up some entirely new material.*]

JASON You know, when I was little—I don't think I ever told you—I was terrified of water. My mother would exhort: "Go on, go on! Everyone loves swimming in the pool. Jump in the water!"

JM [*There is a long silence. I intervene because it seems to me that Jason has become like a child trembling on the brink of a swimming pool.*] So how did you manage?

JASON You see, if only my mother had said, "Jump in *your* water," not the water *everyone* else jumps into, I wouldn't have been afraid. But I was scared spitless that I would dissolve into everyone else, that I would no longer be *me*. I used to run away screaming.

This account of Jason's psychotic anxiety presents an interesting comparison with its parallel in many asthmatic sufferers, who also are frequently terrified of jumping into water or even of putting their heads under water, but who are unaware of the fantasy of disappearing into the other (the mother). When the asthmatic attack occurs, the frightened child is forced to stop breathing for unknown reasons. As an outcome of analytic work with many respiratory sufferers, I have discovered a similar terror of loosing their boundaries. In addition to the factors discussed in Part III, clinical observations of this nature led me to postulate a buried link between psychosis and psychosomatosis.

Here we see that Jason had to maintain a prudent distance from others in order to avoid the risk of merging with them, of no longer existing as a separate person. There were similar episodes that we had analyzed some years earlier, such as his panic reaction at the prospect of eating chicken, because he was afraid the chicken would peck him from inside and then eat him. Jason's continuing food phobias were largely based on such unrecognized psychotic anxieties. Others, plagued by the same terrifying fantasies, might have produced food allergies! In this context, Bion's (1967) theory of "bizarre objects" may be applicable to psychosomatic as well as psychotic ways of psychic functioning.

JASON This terror of water — it's that same child. He's still here in me and he still talks to me. But the difference is that now I talk to him, too. And more than that, I'm convinced that you also have a little child in you. I can hear her when you laugh or when you say certain things that awake the little child in me. Once you know that your analyst also has a small child inside, then you're no longer in danger. I needed to be like you so that I myself could come to life. But above all, I had to know that I was *different* from you and that we could never be confused with one another!

JM [*Jason has finally become a good parent to himself, using both maternal and paternal capacities to care for his frantic inner child. He no longer holds his parents responsible for all the miseries of his past. Today he allows them, too, to be separate people, with problems of their own, like everyone else.*]

JASON It's so important to me to know that your inner child and mine are not the same — that we are, and will always be, two different people.

JM [*This fear of loss of boundaries was unrecognized by Jason when he began his analysis. Such fears predispose certain individuals to psychotic decompensation, others to psychosomatic explosion. Jason has combatted his dread of losing his sense of identity with his complicated sexual accomplishments, each dealing with specific elements of his global anxiety.*]

JASON For years I confused dreams with reality. Now I use my dreams to face difficult realities. In spite of what I told you about my fear of water, nowadays I adore swimming. [*He falls silent, and I have the impression he is searching for the means of communicating a difficult idea.*] But, you know, I still have to use a little inner picture to be able to dive into the water.

JM [*Jason then refers back (as he had on many occasions) to a horrifying scene he had witnessed as a young boy during the German occupation in France. He watched four German soldiers grab a girl by her arms and legs and throw her into a swimming pool in the Seine. He claims that this scene had excited him sexually, but he has never before told me that he uses this identical image, today, in order to be able to dive into a swimming pool!*]

THE EROTICIZATION OF TERROR

Through Jason's recent disclosure, we see once again how the most frightening experiences can be rendered tolerable if they can be eroticized. In the recalled scene, Jason *becomes the girl* who is to end up in the swimming pool; he is also the sole focus of the four soldiers' interest. Thus both bisexual wishes and homosexual longings are gratified. With this constructed pseudo-virility, Jason is then able to dive into the pool without fear of being annihilated.

His invention was a triumph over his different internal persecutions: his global terror of his mother; his belief that he had no right to separate himself from her; his fear of becoming confused with her and thus losing his sense of identity. Through his pseudo-virile fantasy, four soldiers are safely stationed between him and the most frightening internal image of his mother (projected onto the water that will absorb and engulf him).

JASON You know, my mother played a very important role in the French resistance during the German occupation, so she would have been furious if she'd known how enthralled I was by the S.S. men. But I needed a container of my own in order to separate from her. I know now I used the German soldiers this way. When I saw that scene — their frightening uniforms, their big boots — it became so exciting. In my mind I *also* was wearing those big boots and could walk down the street without being afraid.

JM Tell me more about this "container" you needed so badly. [*I, too, am*

*trying to situate myself at this moment, because the end of the hour
is approaching.*]

JASON Well, I've struggled all my life against feeling confused. I tried to
use words to keep me in place . . . like when I asked those questions
all day long when I was a child . . . and when I first came to analysis.
You remember? I got confused about us, too. I confused our names.

JM Yes. Perhaps it was another way of trying to find yourself?

JASON Yes, that's it! I know now I was only trying to find out who *I* was
and what differentiated me from another . . . and trying to find out
what was the difference between a mother and a father, and the
difference between a woman and a man, and . . . and which one I
was supposed to become, so that I could just *be*. I hardly dared hope
I could also be a man! [*Long pause*]

To be or not to be . . . to have a name, not to be just an adjective
. . . to be someone, as long as I was different from everyone else.
Isn't that the real question? [*Long pause*] Well, there will always be a
hermaphrodite deep down inside me, and there'll always be a little
child too, who *wants* to confuse man and woman and *wants* to confuse one person with another. But that's my child and I know now
that I can look after him and keep him alive. *Voilà!*

It is the end of the session. As he stands up to leave, Jason
remarks, "You know, this was a very important session." I reply
that I think so, too, and that I might ask his permission one day
to quote it for a scientific meeting.

At his request, two days later I gave him a copy of what I had
captured of the session hour. He pointed out that I had omitted
his reference to Salvador Dali and the "virgin birth." (This omis-
sion may have been due to an unrecognized countertransference
reaction. Although my conscious feeling was one of immense pleasure at Jason's remarkable progress, perhaps another part of me
was sorry to realize that Jason was now "born" as a subject and
that, before long, he would no longer need me!)

The analysis continued for two more years. Toward the end of
our analytic voyage I asked Jason formally for permission to use
the session notes. This he gave graciously and also sent several
pages of personal comments concerning the material of the session, his associations to it, and to our work in general. He expressed at length his conviction that what had been particularly
helpful was his impression that I cared intensely about our work

and about understanding and identifying with his suffering. He added that I had "put much of myself" into our combined voyage. Since then, from time to time Jason has given me news about his professional and personal life and his continuing feeling of achievement and creativeness in both areas.

Perhaps some readers consider this analysand to be a psychotic, a serious hysterophobic, grave obsessional, narcissistic, or perverted character neurotic. What does it matter how we label him? Let's say he's just a human being trying to survive psychically, by every means at his disposition. And, indeed, he has survived in more ways than one. Even though certain phases in our work alarmed and terrorized him, he has succeeded in living as full a life as most humans might hope to achieve, thanks to his unflagging courage in pursuing his analytical adventure.

Jason's analysis, and that of other neosexual inventors, has helped me to experience the overwhelming anxiety that lies beneath the compulsive and addictive nature of deviant sexual acts. The intensity of the intolerable anguish arises, in part, from the relatively unmitigated oral and anal impulses that characterize incorporative infantile love. It is essential to recognize the extent to which neosexual creations are desperate attempts to come to terms with the difficulties of living as well as combatting fears of castration and annihilation. *Anxiety* is the mother of invention in the psychic theater. My analysands have taught me that their erotic inventions serve to repair rifts in the fabric of sexual and subjective identity as well as to protect the introjected objects from the subject's hatred and destructiveness. In this way confused sexual identity, infantile rage, and inner deadness can be transformed into an erotic, if inexorable, game.

Without the capacity to eroticize archaic conflicts, they could potentially give rise to more serious outcomes of a psychotic or psychopathic nature. With the miraculous discovery of the neosexual solution, in place of what was once meaningless, there is now meaning; in place of inner death, there is a feeling of vitality. In this kind of psychoanalytic voyage, being aware of the dynamic significance of neosexualities enables us to await patiently the release of their hold on the analysand's mind and life, even though such patients clamor for immediate freedom from the power their creations wield over them. In spite of the severe restrictions and compulsivity to which many sexual innovators are submitted, and in spite of the immense anguish and life-threatening factors that sometimes accompany addictive and neosexual practices, we must recognize that through such self-curative attempts and reparative aims, the destructive impulses of Thanatos are shackled as Eros triumphs over death.

PART V

Psychoanalysis on the Couch

CHAPTER 13

Deviations in the Psychoanalytic Attitude

> *I do not wish to arouse conviction; I only wish to stimulate thought and to upset prejudices . . . we do not even demand of our patients that they should bring a conviction of the truth of psychoanalysis into treatment or be adherents of it. Such an attitude often raises our suspicions. The attitude we find most desirable is a benevolent scepticism.*
>
> —Sigmund Freud

SOME YEARS AGO I was invited to participate in a symposium to discuss "the perverse and near-perverse in clinical practice" (McDougall, 1988). My first question was the following: Since our practice inevitably involves two active participants, on which side of the psychoanalytic fence are we to look for signs of these perverse or near-perverse manifestations? At our analysands? Or at *ourselves*? Ideally, of course, we attempt to look at both sides of the fence at one time. In so doing, we might ask ourselves whether there is such a thing as a *perverse psychoanalytic relationship*, or whether countertransference might be infiltrated with perverse elements, thereby creating undetected complicity with certain analysands. Pronouncements by analysts that a given individual's psychic structure is perverse usually reveal a tendency to speak of the so-called pervert as the one who is on the other side of the fence (he or she is abnormal; we are normal). These clinical considerations are less frequently addressed in psychoanalytic writings than questions concerning the theoretical aspects of what constitutes the perverse and near-perverse in our *patients*.

Having written a weighty amount of material over the years on the unconscious significance of deviant sexualities (McDougall, 1978a, 1978b, 1985a, 1986b, 1989), I have had ample occasion to question my own intellectual investment, as well as that of my colleagues, in these particular clinical issues. I am reminded of a time when a small group of Parisian analysts, including myself, decided to meet regularly to discuss our findings with regard to sexual deviations. At the time I was rather struck by the specific libidinal interest each of us displayed in certain aspects of human sexual behavior, probably aspects that had received the least attention in our personal analyses! One colleague, who did not participate in the book we eventually published (Barande et al., 1972), and who may therefore remain anonymous, recounted the many hours he spent at the local zoo carefully studying what he called "zoo perverts." This colleague provided a "candid-camera" vision of his observations with such exquisite detail, that I sometimes wondered who was the more excited—the boys who, under the guise of studying monkeys, were furtively masturbating, or he who, under the guise of scientific interest, was furtively observing them?

We might also question Freud's fascination with human sexuality and his ceaseless explorations of its myriad complications and aberrations. Perhaps we owe his momentous discoveries of the unconscious and the erotic childhood secrets that are concealed in dreams to the fact that he himself suffered from sexual problems—but was curious enough, and honest enough, to want to understand their origins.

This reflection raises the complex question of the relationship between symptom formation and creativity. I have remarked that Freud's definition of perversion was essentially the same as his definition of sublimation. Was my zoo-attracted colleague, so agreeably absorbed in his observation of the boys and the monkeys, engaged in a perverse or a sublimatory activity? While we are all quick to recognize the link between the voyeur and the graphic artist, the sadist and the surgeon, the exhibitionist and the actor, or the fetishist and the philosopher, we are less inclined to dissect the libidinal roots behind our own choice of profession. Have we replaced our voyeuristic wish to usurp the secrets of the primal scene with the admirable desire to know? Have we replaced the wish to possess both the male and female fertile capacities of our parents with the desire to understand and create explicative theories about our analysands? Have we replaced our guilt about having perpetrated fantasized attacks against the significant objects in our inner world by the need to heal and repair the psychic world of others? To what extent are we constantly dealing with unacknowledged parts of ourselves through our analytic work? What of our often totally unconscious (or at least disavowed) homosexual, narcissistic, criminal, and megalomaniac tendencies? To what extent do we use theoretical beliefs as a defense against too close an identification with our patients?

With regard to the subject matter of the above-mentioned symposium, perhaps it could be said that perversion, like beauty, is in the eye of the beholder. There is little doubt that humankind's leading "erotogenic zone" is located in the mind. This holds as true for analysts as for analysands. It is the analyst's eye that observes and then creates the labels that define what is and is not perverse in human sexuality and in everyday life! We must remind ourselves that, from the viewpoint of our analysands, their deviant or near-deviant behavior—whether expressed in the choice of sexual acts or objects, in addictive sexual pursuits, or in the perversity of their character traits—is almost invariably experienced by them as an integral part of their personality and identity, even though they may suffer from the awareness of public censure regarding their predilections. When we—the observing specialists, the "sexperts"—proclaim this or that behavior, relationship, act, or fantasy to be perverse, upon what grounds do we make these determinations? According to *whose* norms and value judgments: our own, those of Freud, those of the psychoanalytic institutes, those of society?

In recent years much has been written about the ethics of psychoanalytic practice. However, we have failed to examine the extent to which our theory and practice are affected by the value judgments of our theoreticians and practitioners. Moreover, the value system intrinsic to our discipline as a whole is, with few exceptions, an infrequent topic of investigation—as if the goals and values of our metapsychology and its implied treatment aims were self-evident. Like any other art or science, psychoanalysis incorporates the fundamental values of Western culture, as Ethel Person (1983) remarked in a thought-provoking paper on value judgments and sexism in psychoanalysis.

Freud claimed that the value most essential to psychoanalytic thought and practice was the search for truth. But this value is certainly not unique to psychoanalysis; dedication to truth is the basic ethic of all scientific research.* One value is certain: psycho-analysis, whether considered to be an anthropological science or a therapeutic art, has been acknowledged from its inception as a discipline whose goal is to question the obvious, to challenge es-tablished beliefs, and to reveal the unconscious elements that lend passion and distortion to social, political, cultural, and religious options. Therefore psychoanalysts, and psychoanalysis itself, would surely not refuse to submit to the same rigorous examina-tion that, ideally speaking, we expect from scientists in other fields (Person, 1983).

Person's article on Freud's value judgments and their effect on his theories of female sexuality demonstrates the extent to which Freud himself was influenced by the mores and value judgments of the Victorian era. Person suggests that he mistook the Victorian woman of his epoch as representing an enduring model of feminin-ity. Although he believed himself to be an objective observer, Freud's two renowned articles on female sexuality reveal, in limpid fashion, the extent to which he was imbued with the conventional, moralistic attitudes of his day. As already recalled, toward the end of his life, Freud admitted that he had lived long enough to discover that he understood nothing about women and their sexuality!

Furthermore, Freud believed that psychoanalysts, once ana-lyzed, would be completely free of moral judgments toward their analysands. Was this not a naive hope? Despite our respect for the Freudian ideal, is it even possible to conceive of such freedom from personal value judgments?

The Analyst's Goals and Values: A Field for Reflection

Coming now to the concept of psychoanalytic values in relation to the perverse or near-perverse in clinical practice, let us consider

---

*In this respect we might recall the position of Karl Popper (1959) who claimed that, while theories must make predictions that can be tested, tests can never verify a theory—they can only falsify it.

the following questions regarding the analyst's vulnerability to deviating from or perverting the psychoanalytic ideal of non judgmental neutrality:

- How do our value judgments affect the construction of our psychoanalytic theories regarding sexually deviant or near-perverse behavior?
- What is the effect (explicit or implicit) of these value judgments upon our clinical work?
- Taking into account the considerable divergence that exists among the many schools of psychoanalytic thought, to what extent is our thought and practice subtly perverted through the idealization of theories and theoreticians?
- Over and beyond our dedication to truth, over and beyond the different psychoanalytic schools of thought, is it possible to discern an ideal, in terms of stated goals and implicit value judgments, that is specifically psychoanalytic? That is, do we have a fundamental system of values, over and beyond the inevitable sociocultural values, that distinguishes psychoanalysis from other scientific and artistic disciplines?
- If this unique value system could be discerned, to what extent would our personal (acknowledged *and* unacknowledged) value judgments deflect us from upholding it, thus permitting a measure of perversion to affect our clinical work?
- To what extent does our ideal value system coincide with, or deviate from, society's value judgments? Are we to judge ourselves as perverse, if we find we are in opposition to society's judgment of what is and is not perverse?

As practicing analysts, we presumably have a goal in mind when we offer potential patients, perverse or otherwise, the possibility of engaging in the psychoanalytic adventure with us. Most analysts would agree that the overall aim of psychoanalysis and psychoanalytic therapy is directed toward the acquisition of self-knowledge. And, no doubt, we would add the hope that our analysands would use this knowledge to good account, so that as a result, their lives would be experienced as a worthwhile venture, despite the suffering and disappointments that are part and parcel of human existence.

If we examine Freud's topical and structural models of mental organization in order to detect the specifically analytic goals concealed within them, we might identify the following: first, the aim of making that which is unconscious conscious; and second, that of gaining insight into the ego-superego structures and oedipal organizations to which they have given rise. The implied goals might be stated as those of permitting individuals to discover the truth about their infantile incestuous wishes and their attendant fears as well as the truth concerning their megalomaniac narcissism and destructive impulses. Hopefully, insight into these fundamental truths would better equip individuals to make judgments about themselves, their relationships to significant others, and their roles in the societies in which they are citizens. The implicit value of these goals presumably would be that self-knowledge, thus gained, is not only an intrinsically worthwhile possession but also a useful acquisition in the service of living.

However, the estimation of self-knowledge, like the dedication to truth, is in no way unique to psychoanalysis. Clearly we need to look beyond these goals if we wish to find a more fundamental value unique to the psychoanalytic way of thinking and working — a dimension that might be considered an original contribution to the value judgments of our culture. Hopefully, this clarification would also open a deeper perspective on our clinical work with patients described as having perverse characteristics.

"To Love and to Work"?

Freud was the first to broach the subject of psychoanalytic goals and values. In his paper, "Types of Onset of Neurosis" (1912), he proposed as a definition of mental health "the capacity for achievement and enjoyment, which is on the whole unrestricted." Toward the end of his life, in the *New Introductory Lectures* (1933b), Freud concluded that psychoanalysis would be incapable of producing a *Weltanschauung* of its own and, in any case, had no need of one; being a science, it would simply adopt the scientific *Weltanschauung*. He nevertheless proposed that the aim of psychoanalytic treatment was to enable the individual "to love and to work" (with pleasure).

At first glimpse, such goals appear to be founded on unassailable values. Who would challenge them? But further reflection gives rise to difficult questions. How do these goals apply to those who can only achieve a love relationship if it is submitted to rigid conditions, such as are present in sadomasochistic or fetishistic behaviors? Would it be our goal to enable patients to discover their fetishistic and sadomasochistic potentials? And what of those whose work and earning power are based on activities that are illegal? (I recall the distress of one of my colleagues when he discovered that his patient, a young medical doctor, was paying for his analysis by practicing illegal abortions.) As for the capacity to love, years of psychoanalytic experience have taught us that there are analysands who need to become aware of their *hatred* and learn how to manage and use wisely the aggression that then becomes available to the ego. Beyond the hatred for life's inevitable frustrations, which lies deeply buried in every person's heart, there are also external circumstances that require an honest appraisal of their hateful aspects (as Freud certainly would have admitted).

With regard to Freud's definition of mental health as "the capacity for achievement and enjoyment which is on the whole unrestricted" and the ability to work, there are patients who need to learn how to *stop* working, or to discover that their pleasure in their work conceals a compulsive, perhaps even a perverse, dimension—those, for example, who use their work as others use drugs: to escape mental pain and avoid reflecting on the factors that have caused it. Individuals who are continually preoccupied with "doing" rather than "being" leave no space in their lives for imagination and dreaming. In the course of analytic treatment these psychic activities are revealed to be experienced as unconsciously forbidden (leading to thoughts that are considered to be sexually taboo), dangerous (a potential path to madness), or terrifying (in that they may cast open a total void).*

A careful reading of Freud reveals an ambiguous attitude toward imaginative life, whether expressed in perverse or in sublimatory ways. When imaginative pursuits are indulged as a personal pleasure and are not destined to be expressed in the form of creative acts, Freud tends to treat these pursuits as a symptomatic avoidance of external reality. Even his own pleasure in creative works carries a note of sanction, for example, when he talks of having "succumbed" to the charm of Leonardo da Vinci's genius,

---

*In defense of the "imaginary," a film of Woody Allen's, *The Purple Rose of Cairo*, comes to mind. It tells the story of a young married woman, devoid of any gratification in her life, who falls passionately in love with a cinematographic *image*. This image detaches "himself" from the screen, even while retaining all of his imaginary characteristics. There comes a moment when the young woman must choose between the reality of the actor and her screen-image lover. She chooses reality—and loses everything!

as though it were a weakness. In a remarkable book on Freud and fantasy, Monique Schneider (1980) notes that "the struggle between the powers of deduction and those of the seductive charm of creative work appear to be likened to a transgression, an avowal for which he [Freud] must excuse himself" (my translation). Thus a closer look at Freud's ideal of enabling individuals to love and to work without hindrance reveals that his underlying values, like those underlying his concepts of femininity, were covered with a thin veneer of Victorian duplicity that reflects hidden moral judgments about any pleasure that is derived from the world of fantasy. (The same duplicity can also be detected in Freud's ambiguous attitude toward masturbation, on the one hand recognized as an integral part of human sexuality, and on the other, as a pathological manifestation.)

In attempting to understand those analysands who constantly flee imaginative life, consuming every second in action, I created the term "normopaths" to connote how their appearance of normality often concealed a pathological defense against psychotic forms of anxiety (McDougall, 1978a, 1985b). Moreover, in many cases, certain such patients, through constant criticism, brutally impose their symptom on others, with the aim of making the less normopathic among us feel guilty! Using Robert Stoller's (1988) definition of perverse behavior as that which seeks to harm and "dehumanize," might not such individuals be considered as displaying "near-perverse" behavior? Borrowing Stoller's metaphor regarding the ambiguous nature of the near-perverse, we might say that the normopath, like the near-perverse in Stoller's presentation, "does everything in the missionary position." It could be added that these interminable toilers, who may be included in the category of "work addicts," display a form of psychic functioning that frequently increases psychosomatic vulnerability. (Perhaps this is merely a perverse attempt on my part to explain why I do not wish to resemble them!)

THE WIDENING SCOPE OF PSYCHOANALYTIC VALUES

Since Freud's time many other analysts, influenced by the theories of the period and the charismatic quality of certain theoreticians, have attempted to formulate additional analytic goals with their attendant value judgments. These include "the attainment of genitality," "adaptation to reality," "the acquisition of autonomous ego functioning," "the capacity for stable object relations," "the desire to become a parent" (especially for girls!), "the enjoyment of healthy narcissism," and so on. While there is no reason to take exception to the "attainment of genitality" as a possible aim in psychoanalysis, there is a need to know according to which model this genital sexuality is to be judged. The normative approach of Freud (1905), as defined in the *Three Essays*? "Confrontation with reality" has an equally acceptable ring to it, but as a goal it presupposes a concept of what constitutes "reality." Reality, as recognized by any given individual's ego, is a *construct*, slowly created by the discourse of parents and society from childhood onward; it is not an immutable given. Therefore, whose definition of reality, and whose subsequent reality sense, is to serve as our standard? The same criticism might apply to standards of narcissistic health. As for the goal of achieving "stable relationships" or the wish for parenthood, while an individual analyst may personally value these, it is not for psychoanalysts to wish for, or implicitly impose upon, their analysands, either partners or offspring! If we unwittingly promulgate these normative standards as part of our analytic aim, are we not more than a little perverse? Are we not behaving in a self-idealizing and omnipotent manner?

Clearly we need to look beyond surface values, such as those of genitality, adaptation, and narcissistic gratification, if we wish to define a more specifically psychoanalytic goal. Of the different values enumerated, the most valid and uncontaminated value judgment remains the search for truth—provided we could define it! Bion (1965, 1970) is the analytic thinker who has most consistently elaborated Freud's conception in this respect. Bion proposes that the psyche has the capacity to recognize truth, since it is the impact of emotion that gives the ring of truth. For Bion, affect is the heart of meaning and thus is the most precise indicator of true experience and judgment; it therefore becomes an essential goal of analysis to reveal "psychic reality" in these terms. Bion also develops the idea that the psyche is capable of attacking and deforming true thoughts and, consequently, may generate *lies*, which are then used in the service of the destructive and death-dealing impulses.

In spite of my profound interest in Bion's conceptions, I still find it necessary to look beyond the pursuit of "truth" and "reality," even if these achieve validity by being qualified as "psychic." To the extent that these goals are all basically normative, they do not qualify as essential components of a *psychoanalytic attitude.* On the contrary, they may pervert it. To hold such aims as fundamental psychoanalytic values leaves us vulnerable to the danger of imposing values of a moral, religious, esthetic, or political nature. Such impositions would hinder our functioning as analysts and put pressure on our patients to conform to *our* system of values, instead of discovering their own systems and assuming or modifying their values in consequence.

This latter contingency could well constitute an outstanding perversion of the psychoanalytic ideal of neutrality! And yet, insofar as societal values are concerned, it is an unavoidable one. Psychoanalysts are not usually in opposition to the fundamental sociocultural values of the community to which they (and their patients) belong. Any society that seeks coherence and continuity will make laws to maintain a set of ethical values, considered— rightly or wrongly—to be essential to the survival of that particular society. Yet given the nature of their work, psychoanalysts can scarcely avoid questioning the place of deviancy and its near-perverse qualities in their given society.

DEVIANCY AND PSYCHOANALYSIS

When is deviant social behavior considered acceptable and when might it be judged pathological? To censure all deviant behavior, in any or all social institutions, would be equivalent to putting an end to any progress in the domain in question, because deviancy contains the seeds of the new. If, on the other hand, any deviation is openly acknowledged and approved (particularly if it threatens to harm the individual or other members of the society), the survival of the institution or the society could be threatened by anarchical eruptions. As analysts we cannot elude the problem of social values as they relate to our exploration of deviancy in the human psyche.

Indeed, psychoanalysis runs the risk of being judged subversive (if not perverse), in that its practitioners profess neutrality. We do not seek to judge our patients — either to commend or to condemn them. Our only avowed aim is to understand their psychic experience and to communicate that understanding, with the hope that they, in consequence, will assume full responsibility for their choices and their acts. Our practice (as well as our basic ethic) is focused on helping each analysand become conscious of his or her repressed fantasies and conflicts, with the result that hitherto unacknowledged sets of values, formerly accepted as basic truths, are also brought into conscious awareness. Seeing these values clearly for the first time often leads patients to question their religious, political, ethical, and esthetic beliefs as well as their sexual choices and practices.

The continuation of psychoanalysis itself, as a doctrine or a practice, might be endangered if our stated goals of rendering people more aware of their formerly unconscious conflicts (and therefore more apt to question standard social beliefs) were considered deviant and threatening to the existing order. (As everyone knows, there are countries in which it is forbidden to practice psychoanalysis!) At the same time, if as analysts we implicitly agree to compromise values that threaten our essential neutrality toward our analysands, or to adopt values that impede the elaboration of our theoretical reflection, then we ourselves run the risk of losing our identity and becoming assimilated into a religious or a political group rather than a scientific one. I will return to this question in the following chapter, when considering quasi-religious attitudes toward psychoanalytic concepts and schools of thought that may infiltrate and perhaps distort our psychoanalytic goals.

Sexual Deviancy and the Law

In matters of sexual deviation, societies have definite opinions. In their inevitable concern for safeguarding the ethical structure that maintains their stability, societies tend to treat as illegal any sexual act that is thought to threaten the welfare of their children or infringe upon the rights and liberties of their adult citizens. It is understandable, for example, that sexual abuse of minors or sexual behavior that is forced upon a non-consenting individual (such as occurs with exhibitionism or rape) are acts that are usually punishable by law. Other sexual deviations, such as fetishistic or sadomasochistic practices between consenting adults, which affect no one but those who wish to engage in them, do not come within the scope of the law in most Occidental societies.

In this respect homosexuality arouses further reflection. In societies where homosexuality is illegal, even being judged as a crime that warrants the death sentence in some cases, a homosexual orientation is apparently considered to be a serious social threat with contagious qualities. The belief appears to be that if homosexuality is not circumscribed, it may spread throughout the community and endanger the survival of the species. However, less than cursory observation confirms that heterosexuals do not become homosexual merely by interacting with homosexuals — nor vice versa! Although as analysts we are well placed to observe these facts, in the discussions that take place in symposia and psychoanalytic congresses, there are always a few members of our profession who appear to treat all homosexual orientations as pathological. Presumably these opinions reflect unconscious projections of the supposed dangers of homosexual relationships on the part of the analysts concerned.

We are all liable to discover that one of our patients is participating in those sexual activities (child abuse, exhibitionism, rape) that are condemned by law. For example, an analysand may reveal in the course of analysis that he is a pedophile or a voyeur capable of sadistic attack upon the objects of his observation. Even though we may listen with apparent equanimity to the analysand's associations around these themes, concentrating on their unconscious significance, at the same time we tend to identify strongly with society's protective aims toward its citizens.

When this subject was broached among a group of venerable analysts in the Paris Psychoanalytic Society who were discussing ethical questions, two members protested that "one should refuse to take such patients into treatment." But others responded that we are rarely informed in advance of a patient's sexual predilections especially when these are not the reason for seeking psychoanalytic help. The protesting colleagues then suggested that such analysands should immediately be dismissed from treatment. Others (including myself) contended that this way of solving the problem did not display an analytic attitude, supposedly dedicated to comprehension, not condemnation.

When we find pedophiliac, exhibitionistic, or sexually sadistic patients on the couch, we are obliged to study our own countertransference attitudes closely if we wish to interpret with equanimity the lawless dimension in such patients (often linked to a history of a missing or abusive father or mother, and sometimes to a sexually arousing-and-rejecting father or mother). Elaboration of our countertransference affects should enable us to maintain the analytic frame, which, though particularly resented by such patients, is also deeply reassuring as a paternal presence. We can then interpret with empathy the fragmented pregenital impulses and link them to the incoherent erotic relationship with the mother or father of early childhood. We may also find ourselves having to analyze unconscious incestuous wishes toward our own children, or be led to explore our own unacknowledged sadistic, voyeuristic, or exhibitionistic tendencies. The fact that these may be successfully repressed or sublimated should not prevent us from probing more deeply into our unconscious psychosexual dimensions, and indeed, such ongoing introspection is essential if we hope to advance our self-understanding as well as that of our patients.

With regard to homosexuality, the issues are somewhat different, since in most Western societies this sexual variation is no longer regarded as illegal as long as it occurs between consenting adults. Even though homosexuality is not punishable by law, as already mentioned, a number of analysts take the stance that all homosexualities are symptomatic. These analysts harbor a secret desire to transform their homosexual patients into heterosexual ones and, indeed, some openly proclaim that this is their avowed treatment aim. Positions of this kind raise inevitable questions regarding the analyst's countertransference to homosexual analysands. Such a desire in the analyst would be comprehensible and appropriate, if the wish to live a fully heterosexual life were consciously sought and were a specifically stated goal of the analysand. Equally understandable would be circumstances in which homosexual relationships constitute a defensive structure against the fantasized dangers of heterosexual attraction; however, this is not the case with the majority of homosexual men and women. Richard Isay (1985, 1989) has published relevant papers on this countertransference experience, which he equates with homophobia. Limentani (1977) and Leavy (1985) have also made notable contributions in this area.

In the absence of an acknowledged or a discovered wish for

sexual reorientation, we need to ask ourselves what justification can be found for an analyst imposing his or her sexual preferences on patients with other predilections. Even when analysts believe that homosexuality invariably indicates a symptomatic solution to internal conflict, it should be remembered that such "solutions" frequently reflect the best adjustment that the child-within-the-analysand was able to make in the face of circumstances unfavorable to heterosexual development. As a result of the parents' unconscious problems and their effect upon the family discourse, these "adjustments" often involve difficulties in understanding sexual roles or in facing the inevitable renouncements and narcissistic wounds of sexual realities. Taking this standpoint into consideration, it seems likely that undermining homosexual solutions could give rise to depressive symptoms or to a serious disturbance in identity-feeling.

Some prominent analysts even maintain that homosexuals cannot be treated psychoanalytically. Two experienced colleagues, one from Europe and one from the United States, related almost identical incidents. Both had prepared papers dealing with aspects of homosexuality, which they illustrated with clinical cases. Both were asked publicly by indignant colleagues how they justified accepting "such people" into treatment and why they referred to their work as "analysis," since "homosexuals are unanalyzable." (Of course, some homosexuals *are* unanalyzable — as are some heterosexuals!) Espousing such prejudices may indicate a certain idealization of heterosexuality. Yet we are well placed to know that heterosexuality is no protection against psychological disorders!

When analysts maintain heterosexual goals for homosexual patients, which the patients do not hold for themselves, or maintain that analysis is not appropriate for homosexuals, it is probable that the underlying countertransference positions are linked to unconscious homosexual fears and wishes. These in turn give rise to values of a normative and (in terms of the analytic ideal) near-perverse kind. The analytic couch should not become a Procrustean bed!

In attempting to articulate a genuinely psychoanalytic attitude toward the analyst-analysand relationship, it seems justifiable to state that analysts should never wittingly impose upon their patients their system of values, their sexual preferences, their political opinions — or the theoretical convictions of their particular school of psychoanalytic thought. Any other attitude is *a perversion of our analytic role*. I cannot claim that all analysts respect this particular ethic; I am merely stating that ideal (much as it was promulgated by Freud).

Deviancy or Delinquency?

It is surprising to discover that analysts sometimes fail to distinguish between behavior that is *deviant* and that which is *delinquent*. This lack of distinction is particularly apparent when sexual deviations are revealed in the course of an analysis. For example, recently I (along with 200 other analysts throughout the world) received an invitation to collaborate with a small group of analysts and lay supporters, whose mission was to combat "perversion." The leaders of this group had secured both the funds and the interest of highly-placed political figures toward the goal of banning all pornographic and erotic expressions in the media, particularly in film. I protested that watching pornographic or erotic films was not necessarily a perversion, nor was it the role of psychoanalysts to decide which films adults should or should not watch; that the project might be better pursued individually by those who felt personally concerned, rather than collectively, under the aegis of psychoanalysis.

In response, it was explained to me that erotic films were causing the dissolution of happy marriages. To support this contention I was sent a "case history," in which a woman in her mid-fifties, who described herself as "highly religious," complained that an entirely harmonious marriage had been cast asunder because her husband began watching pornographic movies in which the sexual act was exhibited "in all its crudity." These movies had "disgusted" the wife and were considered by her to be the cause of her husband's love affair with another woman.

When I challenged the theory that an "entirely harmonious marriage" of 30 years' standing could be demolished by one member watching erotic films, and suggested that perhaps the marriage had not been as harmonious as the lady proclaimed, I was furnished with a second reason to support the movement: namely, that young children were being employed to play roles in pornographic films. I was shocked to learn this (and equally disturbed to realize that such employment would also require the complicity of parents), but again protested that this was a problem beyond the scope of psychoanalysis—and, indeed, constituted a scandal requiring the intervention of the law and the provision of legal protection for these children. The first argument concerned the realm of deviancy, which was idiosyncratically diagnosed as delinquent behavior; whereas the second argument was not concerned with deviancy, but came into the entirely different category of illegal practices.

It seems to me that confusions of this kind stem as much from unconscious fears and wishes as they do from psychological or legal concerns. When an analyst (or any individual) proclaims that this or that theory, practice, or person is "perverse," he or she may be saying, in effect: "Don't look at me, the very model of normality, but cast your eyes over *there*." The pervert is always someone else! If in our analytic stances, we fail to interpret our own splits and projections with the same assiduity required for analyzing the splits and projections of our patients, we risk becoming a sententious, moralistic, and hypocritical community.

CHAPTER 14

Beyond Psychoanalytic Sects in Search of a New Paradigm

> *I will moderate my zeal and admit the possibility that I, too, am chasing an illusion. Perhaps the effect of the religious prohibition of thought may not be as bad as I suppose.*
> —Sigmund Freud

IN ADDITION TO examining the degree of respect we hold for our patients' personal value systems, let us look at the respect that we display—or do not display—toward one another, within our own field. While we preach impartiality as a value to uphold in regard to other people's ideals and options, we do not necessarily apply this to our colleagues when their theoretical and clinical beliefs happen to run counter to our own! Even though we may recognize that their theoretical convictions, like our own, are usually the fruit of serious clinical research and long years of experience, we tend to dismiss them as heretical. At the same time, we endow the leaders of *our* schools of analytic thought with quasi-religious fervor. Concepts and findings are treated as articles of faith rather than as scientific theories; leaders are idealized as though they were priests and prophets. Freud (1927, 1930), in his own way, led a crusade against what he called "religious illusions" (although he tended to replace religious faith with faith in psychoanalysis!). Psychoanalytic theory and practice is infinitely more complex today: Today we have sects rather than schools, doctrines rather than theories. We frequently fail to remind ourselves that a theory is no more than a set of postulates *that has never been proved* (and which may remain forever incapable of proof). If it were otherwise, our conceptual models would no longer be theories but laws. *Is not our leading perversion, then, the belief that we hold the key to the truth?*

Although theory is essential to any science, one does not find in other professions the same passionate defense of theories as in our own, where venerable societies split into two, in a spirit of unusual violence that can continue for decades, and lead to total refusal even to discuss theoretical and clinical differences of opinion. How might we explain this phenomenon?

Psychoanalysis differs from other sciences in that very few of its theoretical concepts are demonstrable. (In this respect, our concepts do bear a certain resemblance to religious beliefs — there is not much hard data to support either.) But over and beyond that obvious explanation, perhaps we are also witnessing a *transference phenomenon*. The experience of personal analysis and case supervision, as well as the close teacher-pupil relationship that characterizes the transmission of psychoanalytic knowledge, are all marked by strong positive and negative transference affects. These, if not recognized, may readily be used in near-perverse ways. They certainly contribute to the violence that usually accompanies our theoretical and clinical divergences. The sanctification of concepts and the worship (or denigration) of their authors appear to me to be sequels to unresolved transference ties. Adherents then become "disciples" who no longer question their theoretical models or continue with their own creative research. The unquestioning dedication of such disciples to their analytic schools of thought may dissuade them from truly *hearing* their patients and thus prevent them from searching for further insight when their patients do not fit their theories. In certain respects, these disciples appear to have incorporated their leader's theoretical stance without any true introjection of, and identification to, the psychoanalytic goal: a constant search for the truth — one's own and that of one's analysands.

One further disquieting aspect of psychoanalytic sects is the fact that their theoretical beliefs frequently prevent the converts — whether of Hartmanian, Kleinian, Lacanian, Winnicottian, Sullivanian, Kohutian, or Bionian persuasion — from benefiting from each other's discoveries. Instead they divert their energies to trying to convert others! "Free thinkers" in these communities run the risk of excommunication; intellectual terrorism takes on the aspect of religious persecution of the "Infidel," the unfaithful who dare to question the holy doctrine. In this respect a comparison might be made with those who have constructed deviant sexual scenarios, which they protect with force, claiming that theirs is the true sexuality and that "the others" are unwilling to admit it.

THEORY AND OBSERVATION

In spite of the danger of perverting the psychoanalytic attitude through the idealization of analytic theories and thinkers, we must face the paradoxical relationship of theory to practice. For it is evident that theoretical convictions play a fundamental role in all fields of science and art. No one can practice psychoanalysis without a solid theoretical foundation; indeed, without the background of the Freudian metapsychology, it would be impossible to think psychoanalytically. Observation, in whatever domain, is never free of theory; it is always directed toward proving or disproving some existing theoretical standpoint. There is no such thing as "pure" observation (Roos, 1982, 1986). This point of view has been consolidated over the years in the writings of Popper (1959), Kuhn (1962), and Feyerabend (1975). Nevertheless, it is *observation* that first motivates new hypotheses; the problem arises only when the attachment to theory precludes further observation.

Although the confirmation of existing theory is an integral part of any scientific discipline, it is a remarkable fact that dedicated researchers in every field tend to find what they are seeking in order to confirm their theories. In psychoanalysis (as in any other science), until changing clinical problems force us to question our existing concepts, we discover only what our theories permit us to find. Perhaps the saying, "I'll believe it when I see it" should read, "I'll see it when I believe it," where research is concerned. Our cherished concepts appear to be continually self-confirming. At the same time, the desire to confirm existing concepts must be accepted as an inevitable "given" when such research is undertaken; it does not *necessarily* pervert or invalidate the value of the findings in question. (There are many roads to clinical truth and, in this respect, we resemble the blind men around the elephant.)

Thus, in confirmation of their preexisting theories, analysts explain that psychic change and symptom cures are due to the fact that some part of what was unconscious has become conscious . . . that "where Id was, there shall Ego be" . . . that "autonomous ego-functioning has increased" . . . that the patient has "worked through the depressive position" . . . that the "basic signifiers of desire" have been revealed . . . that "beta elements have developed into alpha functioning" . . . that a "transitional space" has been created where none existed before . . . that the self has been liberated from its "grandiosity and self-objects" . . . (or that the "internal theater" has been reconstituted to the satisfaction of both analyst and analysand!) And so on. Irrespective of the analytical explanation that is proffered, each explanation reveals that *the account of an analysis is always a narrative written by two people.*

Thus we are not astonished to observe that patients in treatment with psychoanalysts who hold widely divergent theoretical concepts and clinical approaches effect important psychic change in their way of functioning. It would be presumptuous to imagine that it is our theories that bring about psychic change and symptomatic cure! Nevertheless, we need our theories to make order out of the chaos of mental functioning and to attempt to understand why psychic change should occur at all as a result of "the talking cure." In addition, our theories help us to face the uncertainties that besiege us daily in our clinical work as well as provide some protection against the inevitable feeling of solitude that the clinical situation creates. In belonging to a particular school of psychoanalytic thought, we are members of a family and, therefore, less alone with everything that defies our understanding — for there will always be elements that bypass our comprehension in any given psychoanalytic session. Thus even though we cannot work without our theories, at the same time we must be ready to challenge them when observations so indicate.

I am neither denigrating the value of theory nor regretting the diversity and apparent contradictions that are evident in the different schools of analytic research. We all belong to the same family to the extent that we are interested in the psyche and its ways of functioning or failing to function. Let us now attempt to discern a more global psychoanalytic position that, hopefully, overrides theoretical differences.

VALUE SYSTEMS AND
PSYCHOANALYTIC PARADIGMS

Thomas Kuhn's (1962) seminal book, *The Structure of Scientific Revolutions*, formulates the important concept of the "paradigm," which he defines as a constellation of beliefs, techniques, and values that are shared by all members of a given scientific community. The question of a paradigm shift with regard to our metapsychology merits a fuller exploration than I am able to give at the present stage of my reflection. Psychoanalytic research may well be in a period of transition, out of which new paradigms will emerge. Although the creators of the major schools of psychoanalytic thought have brought many important modifications to Freud's basic concepts — sometimes extending his thought, sometimes reducing it in scope — in my opinion there has been no true paradigm shift (as defined by Kuhn) in psychoanalytic theory since the publication of Freud's life work.

However, if we consider diagnostic categories as forming part of a psychoanalytic paradigm, then there has been a "shift," in that psychoanalysis was originally designed to study and treat the so-called classical neuroses, not borderline, psychotic, addictive, or psychosomatic states. Yet today, these conditions constitute a considerable portion of many an analyst's caseload. I shall leave aside the challenge as to whether neurotic states, as classically defined, ever existed in a pure form (except, perhaps, in the mind of the psychoanalyst) as well as the inadequate nature of their conceptualization when limited to the phallic-oedipal level of psychic structure. The complex unity that represents a human personality cannot be comprised within this one dimension. This said, it is evident that the continually widening scope of psychological problems that patients bring to psychoanalysis forces us to reexamine our conceptual frameworks and the theoretical and clinical modifications that these entail.

Before leaving this topic I would like to emphasize one point. There has been a tendency to refer to analysands suffering from psychosomatic, narcissistic, borderline, psychotic, or so-called sexually perverse symptomatology as "difficult patients" (it would probably be more appropriate to refer to difficult *encounters* between analyst and analysand). We must remember that the psychic organizations that give rise to neurotic symptoms also hold many mysteries and present just as many difficulties in the course of analysis as do the more primitive systems of defense. In my opinion, there is no such thing as an "easy psychoanalytic patient"! The fact that an analysand's unconscious conflicts and fantasies may be simple to understand does not mean that they are simple to analyze. Many a psychotic delusion is also relatively simple to decode, but the analytic process is not rendered any easier for this reason.

WHAT ENSURES PSYCHIC SURVIVAL?

It is time to return to the exploration of a fundamental value underlying our theories of psychic functioning and clinical practice. A summary syllogism comes to mind: If societies seek to safeguard social survival, and if medicine seeks to safeguard biological survival, might psychoanalysis not claim as its ethic the goal of safeguarding the factors that contribute to the *psychic survival* of human beings?

But what exactly *is* psychic survival? Perhaps it could be conceptualized as the ability to sustain a sense of one's identity, in both its subjective and sexual dimensions, as well as maintaining a feeling of narcissistic stability, even though levels of self-esteem are constantly affected by fluctuating circumstances. In such a definition we still risk falling into the trap of our own unconscious and its perverting influence on our judgments. What is and is not considered to be essential to psychic survival in human beings? How do we judge the psychic organization of an individual whose survival techniques differ widely from our own or from those of the majority of citizens? Setting aside the problem of unconscious collusion in making these value judgments, the mere definition of what constitutes "normal psychic health" is no easy matter. As with physical health, it is always simpler to point to what is "abnormal" than to define the "normal," yet we cannot elude this question.

The concept of "symptom" is in itself a normative one—it is "normal" to be free of neurotic or psychotic symptoms. Perverse and near-perverse manifestations, by the very use of these terms, are included in the category of symptoms. At the same time, all symptoms are childlike attempts at self-cure in the face of un-avoidable mental pain.* There is a paradoxical demand in the mind of the future patient who comes for treatment in order to get rid of his or her suffering. Even if certain philosophies and religions hold to the idea that life on earth is a vale of tears and that suffering is the normal lot of humankind, the social values of the last two centuries suggest the opposite: We are not "supposed" to suffer. Not only does the suffering of the future analysand therefore make no sense, since its source is unconscious, it is also judged socially "normal" to be free of suffering! The fact that symptoms are the result of strenuous efforts to survive psychically and, at the same time, to be able to function in an adult world, compromises much of the psychic energy available for combatting them. The analysand's expressed desire to lose his or her symp-toms is the product of conscious aims only. The reasons that originally rendered symptomatic construction necessary, perhaps vitally so, are unknown to the analysand. Their discovery will become one of the goals of treatment—and, hopefully, will bring about psychic change and a modification in the patient's mental suffering.

Although the elements that contribute to the psychic survival of a given individual and to the survival of humankind as a whole do not necessarily coincide, certain generalities can be discerned. My own perspective—that psychological symptoms, inhibitions, as well as sexual deviations, are all attempts at self-cure in the face of conflict and the obligation to find solutions to the difficulties of being human—applies equally to object choices and activities that are not judged symptomatic because they are acceptable to society. Our sublimatory activities, for example, are also attempts at healing ourselves psychologically. The universal traumata to which humankind's young are exposed are composed of unpalat-able realities: the existence of otherness, the discovery of the

---

*I am not claiming that all analysts would give this conception a dominant position in their own scheme of psychoanalytic values, and I must make allowances for its potentially deviating effect on my own thinking and practice!

difference between the sexes and the generations, and the inevitability of death. Admittedly, some solutions to these conflictive situations are more acceptable than others. Those who seek the help of psychoanalysis bring with them the sequels of failure in their attempts to deal with the universal traumata of human life, particularly when this struggle has been riddled by the unconscious conflicts of parents, along with the parents' problematic solutions to these same realities (McDougall, 1982b).

In some cases the incoherences and perversions within societies themselves (internal clashes, warfare, genocide horrors) have had a traumatic impact on individuals, forcing solutions to overwhelming anxiety and depression from which the parents could not shield their children. Eroticization is one attempt to deal with traumatic suffering. For whatever reasons, events leading to shock or strain traumata have obliged the children of yesteryear to make sense of what appeared unacceptable or senseless, in order to preserve their own right to exist and to invest their self-image and personal life with meaning. That the meaning thus created is deemed by others to be pathological, symptomatic, or perverse does not invalidate its positive purpose: the drive to survive. This inexorable search for the means of psychological survival seems to be as profoundly and ineluctably rooted in the human being as is the instinctual thrust toward biological survival. Furthermore, when techniques of psychic survival are debilitated or extinguished, biological survival itself might be endangered: The sudden failure of symptomatic defenses can lead to death that was not programmed by the individual's biological clock — such as suicide or a fatal psychosomatic "solution."

The perspective of self-cure as the purpose of all psychological symptoms is no mere metapsychological position. As with any other value explicitly or implicitly attributed to psychoanalysis, this concept also leaves its mark on both the development of theory and the way of conducting analytic treatments. In turn, diagnosis and prognosis will be affected as well as the nature of interpretations and the choice of what to interpret and what to pass over in silence. Thus this theoretical approach to clinical work should be subjected to the criticisms already formulated regarding other theoretical perspectives.

Most analysts would agree that patients tend to *protect* their past solutions to mental conflict and psychic trauma, in spite of the suffering they entail, in spite of the conscious wish to find other less destructive solutions, and in spite of the hope of finding creative satisfactions, gratifying relationships, and greater pleasure in living. The analyst, whose aim is *not* to "socialize" or to "normalize" his analysands, will consciously strive to treat with deep respect the precarious symptomatic equilibrium constructed by the distressed and anxious child that is hidden within every adult. Such an approach requires us as analysts to probe thoroughly through our own neurotic bastions, social facades, perverse dimensions, and psychotic cores. If we take psychic survival to be a fundamental psychoanalytic value, then we are also obliged to ponder deeply several theoretical relationships: the distinction between deviancy and delinquency; the similarities and differences between perversion, creativity, and criminality; and the role that narcissistic and psychotic organizations play in the different "solutions" enumerated here.

Current research is increasingly involved in exploring the complexities of the narcissistic economy and the nature of psychotic thought. Interwoven with the inevitable problems of our psychosexual organization, and the desires and frustrations that form an ineluctable part of normal adult life, is the intricate challenge of preserving, above all, our sense of identity. Here the struggle is no longer centered on conflict concerning "the right to love and to work" but on "the right to exist."

Addressing the problems that arise from the difference between the sexes and generations, from castration anxiety and the nature of the oedipal organization, Freud (1937a) proclaimed that the "bedrock" with which we had to contend was anatomy. Perhaps our bedrock today also includes the drama of otherness that gives rise to annihilation anxieties of a narcissistic or psychotic order. Annihilation anxieties could be considered as a prototypic form of castration anxiety, linked to the inherently traumatic discovery of the existence of one's enduring dependence upon, and inevitable submission to, the existence and wishes of others.

LOVE, HATE, AND DISAFFECTATION

When there is a failure in meeting these universal traumata by the self-healing attempts contained in the construction of neurotic or deviant sexual symptoms, humankind's psyche has recourse to more primitive defense mechanisms: splitting, pathological projective and introjective identifications, disavowal, and the extreme form of psychic defense that Freud designated as *foreclosure*. These must now replace, and try to accomplish, the work of repression. Whether the solutions tend toward neurotic, perverse, or psychotic organizations, in each case the struggle between love and hate predominates. Neurotic and perverse organizations generally restrict the effect of this struggle to perturbation in the adult's sexual and narcissistic wishes, whereas the psychotic outcome is globally concerned with the protection of individual existence and the sense of personal identity. The psychotic sectors of the individual are more vividly marked by the forces of hate and destructivity; these also run the risk of being turned back upon the individual.

Beyond the neurotic/perverse and the psychotic solutions, there is a third possible outcome in the exhausting fight against affective flooding and mental pain that occur when difficulties in significant relationships and achieving narcissistic satisfactions are encountered: namely, the solution of total *disaffectation*. The passions of love and hate, although in opposition one to the other, are nevertheless both on the side of life. The true opposite of love is not hate but indifference. Love and hate, in all their myriad forms, and the innumerable transformations to which they give rise—creative and sublimatory activities, neurotic, psychotic, perverse, and characterological solutions—are all protective barriers against the danger of the final defense: *the destruction of affect*, and with it, the loss of all meaning in relationships.

Disinvestment of one's own psychic reality, as well as that of others, leads to the disturbing symptom that I have called "disaffectation" (McDougall, 1984). The disaffected state that follows this disinvestment makes the world, and one's relationship to it, feel meaningless. Neosexual, neurotic, and psychotic constructions are all desperate attempts to give meaning to life. Indifference and disaffectation render the individual concerned invulnerable to psychic suffering. Such individuals may fall prey to the call of what Freud (1920) named the "Nirvana Principle" and consequently cease to deal with mental conflict by cutting psychic links—by destroying the messages and their meaning—and thus gliding towards psychological and, potentially, biological extinction.*

Although at this point the curtain of the psychic theater may rise upon acts of a psychotic or a suicidal nature, we more commonly observe that the "empty fortress" of psychosis, behind which the secret self attempts to survive, is transformed into a false battlement, hiding the true emptiness that results from the annihilation of meaning and destruction of desire. Psychotic compromises, extreme though they may appear, are nonetheless attempts to find a solution to mental pain through dislocating language and meaning. In contrast, the solution of disaffectation results in the psychic ejection of any mental presentation capable of mobilizing affect; hence the destruction of the very awareness of suffering. Since affects are the principal messengers between body and mind, the destruction of many, perhaps of all, psychic presentations accompanying affective arousal tends to result in a radical split between psyche and soma (McDougall, 1982b). In regressing to the preverbal world of the infant, the psyche, deprived of word-presentations, has no protection against the violently dynamic effects of what Freud named "thing-presentations." This unconsciously contrived organization against mental pain requires neither a cautious retreat from the world, as in the schizophrenias, nor recourse to paranoid or depressive shields against relationships with others, nor recourse to deviant modes and manipulations as a way of maintaining some form of relationship to outer and inner objects.

When, on the contrary, human relationships are disinvested of their libidinal and narcissistic significance, the individuals thus affected can go about their lives with only "false-self" adjustments, through which they seek to discover the clues to living by watching others and, thereafter, reacting in the way they believe the external world demands. In all probability such individuals will be neither perverse nor psychotic. These are the "supernormal" (i.e., pseudo-normal) personalities who are more vulnerable than others to addictive solutions, fatal accidents, and psychosomatic deaths.

We all harbor within ourselves a "normopathic" potentiality of

---

*This theme is developed more fully in *Theaters of the Body* (McDougall, 1989).

this kind; provided that other psychological survival techniques exist, the danger to biological survival is lessened. As analysts we must be equally aware of our own normopathic aspects and those of our analysands. If these aspects are not detected and rendered analyzable, interminable analyses, or the outcomes noted above, may be the consequence. We may even be (somewhat perversely) reassured to discover the existence of deviant sexual or character-ological creations as a childlike attempt to combat the forces of castration and death, rather than the danger of psychotic or psychosomatic solutions.

As mentioned in previous chapters, severe psychosomatic pathology, while it can lead to death, presents a paradox in relation to the life impulses. The capacity of the psyche to capitulate before the forces of anti-life, even though this capitulation may result in biological death, is constructed in the service of survival! This paradox invites a further exploration of the much-debated Freudian theory of a "death instinct." Is the psyche that appears to espouse death-like wishes imbued solely with self-aggression and self-hatred? And in that case does such a patient have no other outcome than to deflect the hatred and aggression to other people, as Freud proposed? Is the death drive to be understood as a profound *longing* for a state of non-desire and nothingness? Could it not also be conceived of as a desperate will to *live*? After all, Freud claimed that the destructive death drive was in itself derived from the *libidinal* drives, and that it was only when these drives became estranged from the life impulses that severe pathology followed. (Perhaps here we catch a glimpse of a paradigm shift to come.)

Adopting the need to ensure psychic survival as our fundamental value will oblige us not only to confront our own neurotic, perverse, psychotic, and normopathic aspects, but also will alert us to the danger of allowing feelings of futility, of psychic death, to install themselves within us when faced with the disaffected world of some of our patients. Avoiding this psychic pitfall requires repeated (and sometimes even violent) incursions into our own countertransference attitudes, if we wish to maintain respect for each personal equilibrium — however symptomatic it may appear — that has been constructed against mental pain by the creative child within. Only in this manner can we hope to liberate this child's desire to live an adult life as fully as possible — a life in which love, hate, and suffering are no longer feared and can finally fulfill their profound, life-preserving functions.

Let us remind ourselves that we are all psychic survivors, that our work as analysts allows us to confirm, every day, the compromises we ourselves have created to deal with our own past psychic traumas. Indeed, it is frequently these very traumas that gave birth to our vocation to become analysts, as well as stimulating our curiosity about the mysterious workings of the mind. (From this viewpoint it seems highly probable that intelligence itself should be regarded as a symptom!) In turn, our patients enable us to maintain and deepen our insight into our own psychological problems. Thus, with each analysis and with every analysand, we further our own analysis and rediscover psychoanalysis itself.

References

Aulagnier, P. (1975). *La violence de l'interprétation*. Paris: Presses Universitaires de France.

Aulagnier, P. (1979). *Les destins du plaisir*. Paris: Presses Universitaires de France.

Anzieu, D. (1985). *Le Moi-peau*. Paris: Dunod.

Anzieu, D. (1986). *Une peau pour les pensées*. Paris: Clancier-Gueneau.

Barande, I., Barande, R., McDougall, J., de M'Uzan, M., David, C., Major, R., & Stewart, S. (1972). *La sexualité perverse*. Paris: Payot.

Benjamin, H. (1953). Transvestism and transsexualism. *International Journal of Sexology, 7*, 1.

Bion, W. (1956). The development of schizophrenic thought. In *Second thoughts*. London: Heinemann, 1967.

Bion, W. (1962). A theory of thinking. In *Second thoughts*. London: Heinemann, 1967.

Bion, W. (1963). *Elements of psychoanalysis*. London: Heinemann.

Bion, W. (1965). *Transformations*. London: Heinemann.

Bion, W. (1967). *Second thoughts*. London: Heinemann.

Bion, W. (1970). *Attention and interpretation*. London: Heinemann.

Bollas, C. (1989). *Forces of destiny: Psychoanalysis and the human idiom*. London: Free Association Books.

Burch, B. (1989). *Unconscious bonding in lesbian relationships: The road not taken*. Unpublished doctoral dissertation, Institute for Clinical Social Work, New York.

Federation of Feminist Women's Health Centers (1981). *A new view of a woman's body*. New York: Simon & Schuster.

Feyerabend, P. (1975). *Beyond method* (3rd impression, 1980). London: Verso.

Frame, J. (1988). *The Carpathians*. London: Bloomsbury Publishing.

Freud, S. (1905). Three essays on the theory of sexuality. In J. Strachey (Ed. & Trans.), *The standard edition of the complete psychological works of Sigmund Freud* (hereafter *SE*), vol. 7. New York: Norton, 1953.

Freud, S. (1908). Creative writers and daydreaming. *SE*, vol. 9. New York: Norton, 1959.

Freud, S. (1909). Analysis of a phobia in a five-year-old boy. *SE*, vol. 10. New York: Norton, 1958.

Freud, S. (1912). Types of onset of neurosis. *SE*, vol. 12. New York: Norton, 1958.

Freud, S. (1913). The disposition to obsessional neurosis. *SE*, vol. 12, New York: Norton, 1958.

Freud, S. (1915a). The unconscious. *SE*, vol. 14. New York: Norton, 1957.

Freud, S. (1915b). Instincts and their vicissitudes. *SE*, vol. 14. New York: Norton, 1957.

Freud, S. (1915c). Repression. *SE*, vol. 14. New York: Norton, 1957.

Freud, S. (1919). A child is being beaten. *SE*, vol. 17. New York: Norton, 1961.

Freud, S. (1922). Some neurotic mechanisms in jealousy, paranoia and homosexuality. *SE*, vol. 18. New York: Norton, 1955.

Freud, S. (1923). Remarks on the theory and practice of dream interpretation. *SE*, vol. 19, New York: Norton, 1961.

Freud, S. (1927). The future of an illusion. *SE*, vol. 21. New York: Norton, 1961.

Freud, S. (1930). Civilisation and its discontents. *SE*, vol. 21. New York: Norton, 1961.

Freud, S. (1931). Female sexuality. *SE*, vol. 2, pp. 225–243. New York: Norton, 1961.

Freud, S. (1933a). Femininity. *SE*, vol. 22. New York: Norton, 1964.

Freud, S. (1933b). The question of a Weltanschauung. *SE*, vol. 22. New York: Norton, 1961.

Freud, S. (1933). Revision of the theory of dreams in New introductory lectures on psycho-analysis. *SE*, vol. 22, pp. 7–30. New York: Norton, 1964.

Freud, S. (1937a). Analysis terminable and interminable. *SE*, vol. 23. New York: Norton, 1964.

Freud, S. (1937b). Constructions in psychoanalysis. *SE*, vol. 23. New York: Norton, 1964.

Harding, E. (1971). *Woman's mysteries: Ancient and modern*. New York: Harper & Row.

Hooker, E. (1972). *Homosexuality*. Department of Health, Education and Welfare (Pub. No. HSM) 72-9116, pp. 11–22. Washington, DC: GPO.

Horney, K. (1924). On the genesis of the castration complex in women. *Feminine psychology*. New York: Norton, 1966.

Horney, K. (1926). The flight from womanhood. *International Journal of Psychoanalysis, 7*.

Isay, R. (1985). Homosexuality in homosexual and heterosexual men. In G. Fogel, F. Lane, & R. Liebert (Eds.), *The psychology of men*. New York: Basic Books.

Isay, R. (1989). *Being homosexual*. New York: Farrar, Straus & Giroux.

Kahnert, V. (1992). *The function of the destructive instinct in painting*. Manuscript submitted for publication.

Kaplan, L. (1989). *Female perversions*. New York: Aronson.

Kavaler-Adler, S. (1993). *The compulsion to create, a psychoanalytic study of women artists*. London: Karnac Books.

Kernberg, O. (1976). *Object relations theory and clinical psychoanalysis.* New York: Aronson.

Kernberg, O. (1980). *Internal world and external reality.* New York: Aronson.

Kestenberg, J. (1968). Outside and inside, male and female. *Journal of the American Psychoanalytic Association, 16*, 457–520.

Klein, M. (1945). The Oedipus Complex in the light of early anxieties. *International Journal of Psychoanalysis, 26.*

Klein, M. (1957). Envy and gratitude. In *The Writings of Melanie Klein*, Vol. III. London: Hogarth Press & The Institute of Psychoanalysis, 1975.

Krystal, H. (1978). Self-representation and the capacity for self-care. *Annual of Psychoanalysis, 6.* New York: International Universities Press.

Kuhn, T. (1962). The structure of scientific revolutions. *International Encyclopedia of Unified Sciences, 2,* 2.

Lawrence, D. H. (1989). Posthumous poem in *The heart of man.* London: Bloomsbury Publishing Co.

Leavy, S. (1985). Male homosexuality reconsidered. *International Journal of Psychoanalytic Psychotherapy, 22,* 116–124.

Lefevre, P. (1989). The Faustian bargain. Unpublished paper given to Montreal Psychoanalytic Society, Canada.

Lichtenstein, H. (1961). Identity and sexuality. *Journal of American Psychoanalytic Association, 9,* 179–261.

Limentani, A. (1977). The differential diagnosis of homosexuality. *British Journal of Medical Psychology, 50,* 209–216.

Limentani, A. (1984). Toward a unified conception of the origins of sexual and social deviancy in young persons. *International Journal of Psycho-analytic Psychotherapy, 10,* 383–401.

Limentani, A. (1989). The significance of transsexualism in relation to some basic psychoanalytic concepts. In *Between Freud and Klein* (pp. 133–154). London: Free Association Books.

Mahler, M. (1968). *On human symbiosis and the vicissitudes of individuation.* vol. 1. New York: International Universities Press.

Mauriac, F. (1950). *La vie de Racine.* Paris: Gallimard.

McDougall, J., & Lebovici, S. (1960). *Un cas de psychose infantile.* Paris: Presses Universitaires de France.

McDougall, J., & Lebovici, S. (1969). *Dialogue with Sammy.* London: Hogarth Press. (revised edition, London: Free Association Books, 1989)

McDougall, J. (1964). Homosexuality in women. In J. Chasseguet-Smirgel (Ed.), *Female sexuality: New psychoanalytic views.* Ann Arbor: Michigan University Press, 1970.

McDougall, J. (1978a). *Plea for a measure of abnormality.* New York: International Universities Press. (revised edition, New York: Brunner/Mazel, 1992)

McDougall, J. (1978b). The homosexual dilemma. In I. Rosen (Ed.), *Sexual deviation.* Oxford: Oxford University Press.

McDougall, J. (1982). *Théâres du Je.* Paris: Gallimard.

McDougall, J. (1984). The disaffected patient: Reflections on affect pathology. *Psychoanalytic Quarterly, 53.*

McDougall, J. (1985a). *Theaters of the mind: Illusion and truth on the psychoanalytic stage.* New York: Basic Books. (revised edition, New York: Brunner/Mazel, 1990)

McDougall, J. (1985b). Parent loss. In C. Rothstein (Ed.), *Trauma and reconstruction.* New York: International Universities Press.

McDougall, J. (1986a). Eve's reflection: On the homosexual components of female sexuality. In H. Meyers (Ed.), *Between analyst and patient*. New York: Analytic Press.

McDougall, J. (1986b). Identifications, neoneeds and neosexualities. *International Journal of Psychoanalysis, 67.*

McDougall, J. (1986c). Un corps pour deux. In *Corps et histoire*. Paris: Les Belles Lettres.

McDougall, J. (1988). Perversions and deviations in the psychoanalytic attitude: Their effect on theory and practice. In *The perverse and near perverse in psychoanalytic practice*. New Haven, CT: Yale University Press.

McDougall, J. (1989). *Theaters of the body*. New York: Norton.

Morgan, C. (1991, February 7). *Dreams in the fetus and the newborn*. Paper presented to the Los Angeles Institute and Society for Psychoanalytic Studies.

Ogden, T. (1986). *The matrix of the mind: Object relations and the psychoanalytic dialogue*. Northvale, NJ: Aronson.

Ogden, T. (1989a). *The primitive edge of experience*. Northvale, NJ: Aronson.

Ogden, T. (1989b). On the concept of an autistic-contiguous position. *International Journal of Psychoanalysis, 70.*

Ogden, T. (1994). *Subjects of analysis*. Northvale, NJ: Aronson.

Ovesey, L., & Person, E. (1973). Gender identity and sexual psychopathology in men; a psychodynamic analysis of homosexuality, transsexualism and transvestism. *Journal of the American Academy of Psychoanalysis, 1*, 53–72.

Ovesey, L., & Person, E. (1974). The transsexual syndrome in males: Secondary transsexualism. *American Journal of Psychotherapy, 28*, 1.

Person, E. (1983). The influence of values in psychoanalysis: The case of female psychology. *Psychiatry Update*, 36–50.

Pontalis, J-B. (1980). *Loin*. Paris: Gallimard.

Pontalis, J-B. (1990). L'inquiétude des mots. In *La force d'attraction*. Paris: Seuil.

Popper, K. (1959). *The logic of scientific discovery*. London: Heinemann.

Richardson, D. (1984). The dilemma of essentiality in homosexual theory. *Journal of Homosexuality, 9* (2/3), 79–90.

Rodman, G. (1987). *The spontaneous gesture: Selected letters of D. W. Winnicott*. Harvard: Harvard University Press.

Roheim, G. (1950). *Psychanalyse et anthropologie*. Paris: Gallimard.

Roheim, G. (1953). *Les Portes du rêve*. Paris: Gallimard.

Roiphe, H., & Galenson, E. (1981). *Infantile origins of sexual identity*. New York: International Universities Press.

Roos, E. (1982). Psychoanalysis and the growth of knowledge. *Scandinavian Psychoanalytic Review, 5*, 183–199.

Roos, E. (1986). The part analysis plays in psychoanalysis: An historical perspective. *Scandinavian Psychoanalytic Review, 9*:31–55.

Rothstein, A. et al. (1986). *The reconstruction of trauma*. New York: International Universities Press.

Sachs, O. (1985). *Migraine: Understanding a common disorder*. Los Angeles: University of California Press.

Schneider, M. (1980). *Freud et le plaisir*. Paris: Denoël.

Seccarrelli, P. (1989). *Inquilino no proprio corpo*. Colloquium presentation in Belo Horizonte, Brazil.

Seccarrelli, P. (1994). *La formation du sentiment d'identité chez le transsexuel*. Unpublished doctoral dissertation, University of Paris.

Segal, H. (1957). Notes on symbol formation. *International Journal of Psychoanalysis, 38.*

Simon, W., & Gagnon, J. (1967). The lesbians: A preliminary overview. In W. Simon & J. Gagnon (Eds.), *Sexual deviance*. New York: Harper & Row.

Socarides, C. (1968). *The overt homosexual*. New York: Grune & Stratton.

Socarides, C. (1978). *Homosexuality*. New York: Aronson.

Stern, D. (1985). *The interpersonal world of the infant*. New York: Basic Books.

Stoller, R. (1968). *Sex and gender*. New York: Aronson.

Stoller, R. (1975). *The transsexual experiment*. London: Hogarth Press.

Stoller, R. (1976). *Perversion: The erotic form of hatred*. New York: Aronson.

Stoller, R. (1988). In: *The perverse and near perverse in psychoanalytic practice*. New Haven: Yale University Press.

Stoller, R. (1991). *Pain and passion*. New York: Plenum.

Stoller, R. (1992). *Observing the erotic imagination*. New Haven: Yale University Press.

Welldon, E. (1989). *Mother, madonna, whore*. London: Heinemann.

Winnicott, D. W. (1951). Transitional objects and transitional phenomena. In: *Playing and reality*. New York: Basic Books, 1971.

Winnicott, D. W. (1960). Ego distortion in terms of true and false self. In: *The maturational processes and the facilitating environment*. New York: International Universities Press, 1965.

Winnicott, D. W. (1971). Playing: A theoretical statement. In: *Playing and reality*. New York: Basic Books, 1971.

Winnicott, D. W. (1990). On the split-off male and female elements. In: *Psychoanalytic explorations*. Cambridge: Harvard University Press, 1989.

Wrye, H., & Welles, J. (1993). *The narration of desire: Erotic transferences and countertransferences*. New York: Analytic Press.

Index